QURRATULAIN HYDER
AND
THE RIVER OF FIRE

The Meaning, Scope and Significance of her Legacy

Edited by
Rakhshanda Jalil

AAKAR

QURRATULAIN HYDER AND THE RIVER OF FIRE
Edited by Rakhshanda Jalil

© Aakar Books

First Published, 2011

ISBN 978-93-5002-100-2

Published by
AAKAR BOOKS
28 E Pocket IV, Mayur Vihar Phase I, Delhi 110 091
Phone : 011 2279 5505 Telefax : 011 2279 5641
aakarbooks@gmail.com; www.aakarbooks.com

Printed at
Mudrak, 30 A Patparganj, Delhi 110 091

To Tabi,
my sensible and beautiful sister,
with memories of days well spent

Contents

Introduction

I shall begin this Introduction to a selection of scholarly essays in a most unscholarly manner. I shall begin on a personal note.

Jab Ahmad-e-Mursal hi na rahe to kaun rahega? ('When even the Prophet of God was mortal, who shall remain?') These were Qurratulain Hyder's words of condolence, spoken softly and addressed to no one in particular, when she came to meet my mother and me in the early weeks of 2001 shortly after I had lost my father and my mother hers—in quick succession. I suspect she said these words more to herself than to either of us. For, she knew that it was only a matter of time when the Call from *Koh-e-Nida* (the Mount of Summons) would come for her too — just as it must for everyone one day. She knew that in the words of the poet: *Maut par kis ko dastgari hai, Aaj woh kal hamari baari hai* ('Who has control over death/ Today it is his, tomorrow it shall be my turn'). And when the Call did come for her on 21 August 2007, she went quietly into the night, leaving behind a legacy as complex and multi-layered as her own persona.

With her aureole of crimson hair framing an intelligent aristocratic face shadowed by large, brooding thoughtful eyes, Qurratulain Hyder, or Aini Apa as she was fondly called, was a silent, daunting, almost haughty figure in public. In private, when she allowed the formidable persona to drop, she could be witty and inquisitive, girlishly loquacious and delightfully gossipy, warm and humane. Never much of a public speaker, she preferred to speak through her pen, her steady companion of over seven decades. A voracious and eclectic reader herself, her writing reflects not just all she learnt and absorbed from her prodigious learning but more importantly, the liberal, human, tolerant worldview that was as much the hallmark of her writing as it was of her personality.

Born with an impeccable literary lineage — her father was Sajjad Hyder Yildirim and her mother Nazar-e Sajjad Hyder, both early and vigorous proponents of Urdu fiction — Qurratulain Hyder wrote her first story at the age of 11. Her first collection of short stories, *Sitaron se Aage*, published in 1945, established two singular qualities about this rising star on the Urdu firmament: one, her steadfast refusal to write only on 'womanly' subjects; and two, her ability to consistently produce polished, lyrical prose at a time when poetry held sway. Over the years, she produced a formidable array of travelogues, translations, novels, plays, novelettes and short story collections, each more liltingly—and evocatively—titled than the other: *Mere Bhi Sanamkhanae, Safina-e-Gham-e-Dil, Agale Janam Mohe Bitiya Naa Kijo, Gardish-e-Rang-e-Chaman, Fasl-e-Gul Aaye ya Ajal Aye, Patjhar ki Awaaz, Hamin Chiragh Hamin Parwane, Kaar-e-Jahan Daraaz Hai, Akhir-e Shab ke Humsafar*, among others.

Hyder went away to Pakistan briefly but returned, disillusioned, in 1961. She worked with *Imprint* and the *Illustrated Weekly of India*, enjoyed spells of Visiting Professorship at the Aligarh Muslim University and Jamia Millia Islamia but all along reading and writing remained the mainstays of her life. Accolades and honours were bestowed upon her in ample measure; chief among them being the Bharatiya Jnanpith in 1989, the Sahitya Akademi Award in 1967, the Soviet Land Nehru Award in 1969, Ghalib Award in 1985 and the Padma Shri followed by the Padma Bhushan in 2005.

Named after a character from one of her early novels, *Mere Bhi Sanamkhane*, and having spent several pleasurable hours talking to her, I mourned her death for it marked not just the passing of a great literary figure, a champion of women's rights and a woman of remarkable convictions. I mourned, equally, the loss of one of the last of the living embodiments of our secular nationalist heritage and a vocal proponent of composite culture. Learning classical Indian music, wearing a sari or cutting her hair short, in no way, detracted from her sense of self. That she was, in no way, a 'typical' Urdu writer was, I suspect, a source of much joy to her. She could wear her erudition and her lack of affectation with equal ease. She could also be brusque and offhand with those who rubbed her the wrong way. Noted Urdu poet from Pakistan, Zehra Nigah and Ameena Ahmad Ahuja, the calligraphic artist from India—both friends of long standing —testify to Aini's humaneness. Both also vouch for the fact that Aini was never, at the best of times, one to suffer fools gladly, and she detested, above all else, affectation. Intellectual pretentiousness, in particular, horrified her, especially among the female of the species!

Imbued by an all-consuming Nehruvian idealism and steeped in a legacy of non-sectarian, multi-cultural, multi-religious 'Indian-ness', Qurratulain Hyder remained, till the very end, a profound scholar and aesthete, and the high priestess of pluralist inheritance. Despite failing health, she continued to hold small soirees at her NOIDA residence and rejoiced in inviting friends to home-cooked meals. My last telephone conversation with her was regarding an obscure French ballad which she had come across many years ago, a line of which had got stuck in her memory. She wanted me to locate the rest of the ballad with the help of the French teachers at the Jamia. Unfortunately, the ballad was either very old or not very well known; I regret that I was not able to help her or to meet her as often as I would have wanted to. In a world of falling standards, Aini Apa upheld her own rather high standards of good writing and good form. For her, it can indeed be said: *Aalam mein tujh se lakh sahi, tu magar kahan.*

While much ink was spilt on Qurratulain Hyder the novelist and social realist when she was alive, more was spilt in the days and weeks immediately after her demise on 21 August 2007 in a hospital in NOIDA as obituaries tumbled out in print — in Urdu, English and Hindi. As is usual on such occasions, they were mostly hagiographical; few dwelt on the real persona that Qurratulain hid so well behind the mask of erudition and poise. A seeker after truth, she travelled like the wandering mendicant, touching millions of hearts with her words, but always holding back a part of her real self, for it was this that she kept for her true communion with the Beloved. It was this real self that she sheltered from the world and its prying eyes but revealed to a handful who came to her, unbidden and undaunted.

Several months after her death, some of us at the Jamia Millia Islamia—where she was associated as Writer in Residence, where her books, paintings and other personal effects are housed in an archive, and where she herself lies buried in the University graveyard—began to feel the need to revisit her legacy in the company of those who knew and loved her as well as those who had read and admired her and still others, who wished to place her work, critically and objectively, in the trajectory of post-Independence writing. We had, at the Jamia, already paid her a tribute in the form of an *honoris causa* degree given posthumously at the Annual Convocation held in October 2007. And so it was decided to organize a seminar where all this could be done and hopefully a beginning could be made where, at long last, Aini Apa could get the real recognition she deserved. A two-day international seminar was duly organized from 5–6 February 2008 entitled 'Qurratulain Hyder and the River of Fire: The Meaning, Scope and Significance of Her Legacy'. Most participants, unfortunately, chose to interpret the title of the seminar in the light of her seminal novel, *Aag ka Darya*. And apart from the usual hagiographical accounts, most of the papers presented during these two days —in English, Hindi and Urdu—chose to dwell on this one novel alone.

My purpose in organizing the seminar under the aegis of the University's Outreach Programme had been to offer 'the River of Fire' as a metaphor in which the writer must sink or swim whenever he/she chooses to cross from one bank to the other, that is from the moment he/she crafts a piece of writing to the time it is read and understood by his/ her reader. I was also hoping that the participants would look at the River of Fire as the River of Time and place not just Hyder's own oeuvre but also of many of her younger and older contemporaries in the context of post-colonial constructions. It was with this objective that I had also invited presentations on other writers, such as the eminent Hindi writer Shivani. While we did not have much luck with contributions on writers other than Hyder, we did get an excellent presentation on Shivani by her daughter, Ira Pande. There was also Fatima Rizvi's long essay on 'Post-colonialism and Marginality in the Fiction of Ismat Chughtai, Khadija Mastur and Qurratulain Hyder'. Most other delegates to the two-day seminar chose to dwell exclusively on Hyder and on *Aag ka Darya* in particular.

In hindsight, perhaps it was too esoteric a title to give a seminar and despite the many explanatory letters sent along with the letters of invitation, the title was indeed misleading. The purpose of the seminar had been to get together an eclectic group of people — from across disciplines, languages and nationalities — to explore the scope and significance of Qurratulain Hyder's legacy. For while there was no denying that she was a great writer across a wide spectrum of readers, there had been virtually no attempts to 'locate' her, as it were, in the continuum of post-independence studies nor any serious effort to examine the worth and substance of her legacy. The outcome of the seminar, however, was not entirely satisfactory. For one, it placed too heavy an emphasis on *Aag ka Darya* alone — neglecting the bulk of her vast and varied oeuvre. For another, save for her niece, Huma Hyder, no one made any attempt to look at the woman behind the formidable writer. Yet, it seemed a pity to fritter away the gains of these two days of deliberations. More so, since there is virtually nothing of any value on Qurratulain Hyder available in English. What exists is usually in the form of Introductions to the volumes of short stories or the translations of some of her novels. What you have before you is a combination of some of the seminar papers as well as others that were not a part of the seminar. Some essays have been reproduced; their sources have been duly acknowledged and I express my gratitude to Prof. M.U. Memon, Editor of the *Annual of Urdu Studies* and to Oxford University Press, Delhi for giving permission to use them. I am also grateful to the late Khalid Hasan who sent his loving tribute to Aini Apa.

A great deal of water has flown down the River of Time since the seminar was organized at the Jamia. I, too, have moved on. I am on extended leave from the university and this collection of essays is in the nature of a personal initiative rather than one undertaken on behalf of the Jamia. It is being assembled in the hope that it will create interest in her among English readers. It will also be, one hopes, a fitting tribute to a writer who straddled the world of English and Urdu letters with equal ease.

December 2010   **Rakhshanda Jalil**
New Delhi

PERSONAL PORTRAITS

1

A Rainbow of Reminiscences

HUMA HYDER HASAN

I am trying to collect all the fond memories that I have of Aini Khala. These memories remind me of a rainbow as one colour after another layers the reminiscences. Like the rainbow, my memories of Aini Khala* have no dark or grey colour; they are adorned in bright, vibrant robes.

As a child, I had heard from the family elders (and later understood on my own), that when Sajjad Hyder 'Yaldrum' proposed marriage to Nazrul Baqar, one of the considerations (and I suspect the main), was his passion for female education. At that point of time, Nazrul Baqar was an author of great promise. The elders also waxed eloquent on the wedding offerings (*Bari*) sent by Sajjad Hyder to his bride— a Turkish veil (*burqua*) and a few books. The Sunni Syed family of Nehtaur, to which Yaldrum belonged, did not look askance at this alliance but on the contrary, encouraged Yaldrum and brought, with all honour and happiness, the (Shia) bride home.

---

* Young and old, most people called her Ainnie or Aini Apa. They spell it in different ways. Here, for the sake of consistency, I have chosen to retain 'Aini' throughout. – Editor

Yaldrum's first posting was at the Andaman-Nicobar Islands, under British rule at that time and used for the deported Indian prisoners (mostly freedom fighters), known as *Kaala Paani*. It was here that Aini Khala received her primary education. In her own words, '.....one day the age of illiteracy ended. Father was sitting in the verandah, going through the fresh post received from (mainland) India. I was on the floor immersed in a giant sized *Adabi Duniya* and *Naye-Rang-e-Khyal* where a fairyland *bazaar* showed an array of carpets and a beauteous courtesan being bid for. The picture had a *sher* inscribed under it. I showed the picture to father and wanted to know as to what was written. Taken aback and with some sadness he said that here I would remain a total ignoramus.....' Thus began her education at Port Blair.

The young writer couple was blessed with two children —Syed Mustafa Hyder and Qurratulain's Hyder. When the children were quite young, their mother Nazar-e Sajjad fell ill, and her battle with her ailment turned out to be quite long drawn. Qurratulain, apart from nursing her mother, used to take down notes dictated by Begum Sajjad. In this enlightened environment, Qurratulain's writing aptitude took wings.

My paternal grandfather, Syed Nisar Hyder was posted as Deputy Collector at Barabanki and Syed Sajjad Hyder (also my maternal grandfather's elder brother) lived in Faizabad, Lucknow. My grandmother recounted that during the oft-occurring Shia-Sunni disturbance, Nazar-e Sajjad with her children used to arrive at Barabanki saying, 'Bhabhi, allow these travellers within. I have fled from the Sunnis of Lucknow to seek shelter at my Sunni *sasural*.'

It is not easy to place Aini Khala strictly as a Sunni or as a Shia. People from both sects were dear to her. At the same time, however, she was critical of the dogmatic traditions prevalent in both sects.

As a child, I had heard from my mother about Aini Khala's stupendous writing achievements. All this was from afar as she was then in Pakistan and we were in India. In

1958, my mother took me along to Pakistan to visit her mother, brother and sisters, who had opted to leave India. The shadows of Partition loomed large over the family reunion. Amongst the gathering of all the cousins, I could feel Aini Khala's distinctly partial and particularly affectionate attitude towards me. I realized that my coming from India, having a keen interest in the fine arts including classical dance, music, drama, etc. put me on a slightly elevated position compared to the other children. I was simply overjoyed.

This relationship continued till 21 August, 2007, when she breathed her last in the ICU of Kailash Hospital at Noida. Taken in for treatment by her physician Dr. A.K. Shukla for congestion in the lungs, no one knew that she would never return home. The mention of Dr. Shukla brings to mind a conversation often exchanged between Aini Khala and me. My suggestions for consulting another doctor always brought a definite 'No' from her, on grounds of it offending Dr. Shukla, her long time physician.

Me: But Aini Khala, he charges a fee. His consultation is not free. So I do not see any harm....

Aini Khala: Dr. Shukla is such a sweet person. He has been treating me for years. I do not want him to feel let down.

No further arguments were brooked.

Another interesting aspect of her persona can be gauged from her attitude towards her four servants—Haldar, her driver and maids Rehana, Ameena and Mary. She thoroughly disapproved if they were referred to as servants and would insist on them being called 'domestic help'. This was usually followed by a small explanation how after 1947, with the establishment of democracy, all citizens have become equal. It was at times stressed that in England this was so, as the denizens of that country were more civilized.

When Dr. Mushirul Hasan, Vice-Chancellor, Jamia Millia Islamia, proposed to have a museum established in the memory of Aini Khala, where her books, paintings, awards, felicitations and artifacts could be maintained for posterity, we accepted his offer in all earnestness and without much ado. As I was getting all these packed, the thought did cross my mind that distributing her things amongst family members would have restricted her memory to a few. With the museum, Aini Khala would belong to the future generations too. All those who have given shape to the museum deserve our sincere thanks for the efforts that have gone into it.

The memories of Aini Khala are integral with fun-filled activities that she was so fond of and frequently initiated—fancy dress parties, informal *bait-baazi*, picnics, visits to lesser known historical sites, circuses, concerts, etc.

Whenever, I visited her she used to call out for tea and Rehana, her maid, would be prompt in serving it with various accompaniments. If ever I asked her to join, she would invariably say in good humour that she was not foolish like me to have tea during warm days. If in consideration of a warm day, she was not asked for tea then too it was an invitation for a light-hearted rebuke. On both such occasions there was laughter all around.

The arrival of old and dear friends prompted her to repeat Zauq:

> *Ae Zauq kisi hamdam-e-dairina ka milna*
> *Behtar hai mulaqat Masiha-o-Khizr se*

The passing away of a friend or a relative saddened her for days. The demise of my father, Syed Jarrar Hyder, marked the end of an era. Aini Khala was no doubt affected by his death, but she was wary of a bigger tragedy. Her heart was heavy with the fear of us three sisters deciding to dispose of the over-a-century-old house and other inheritance at Nehtaur. She used to say that the disposal of the property would result in erasing the family history and traditions. This establishment was the last remaining milestone of the family — the others being sacrificed at the altar of Partition. Then with a sigh, she would leave the final decision with us, but with a cautionary note that selling the property may result in our becoming unknown millionaires, lost in some big town, losing out on our identity.

On a visit to Nehtaur she asked the local people the distance at which Mandawa was located. 'Maalan' the twin river of 'Gaagan' (passing through Nehtaur) flowed there. It was Aini Khala who had concluded that Mandawa was the background of Kalidas' play 'Shakuntala'. She would often lament the lack of cultural interest on getting no answers. When she saw several village women taking cane-laden bullock carts, she used to celebrate this as the gain of freedom and democracy which accorded equal rights to women, so much so that they were in the driver's seat.

Some memories are from Bombay. It is said that when her novel *Aag ka Darya* was published, a leading author derisively commented in public that Aini's father had a very large library and the novel was the result of reference to this library. Another well known Urdu poet, who was present, countered this saying that Sajjad Hyder's library however large would not be comparable to the Bombay Municipal Library. He suggested that the author should refer to this library and produce a better book.

Speaking of Bombay, she always placed the city notches higher than other cities. Had she seen the Mumbai of today, maybe she would have had a slightly different opinion. She admired the freedom with which women worked shoulder-to-shoulder with their male colleagues in all fields. She often remembered the time she spent in Bombay with her wide circle of friends

Her indifference to worldly matters is well brought out in the manner she acquired a flat, paying the full amount, in Sukhdev Vihar when she shifted to Delhi from Bombay, without even having a look at it. Later she realized that the flat did not suit her and she rented another flat in Zakir Bagh. She did not even get the papers for the Sukhdev Vihar flat registered in her name. It was a different matter that the original owner cooperated fully in transferring the Sukhdev Vihar flat in her name. Several such anecdotes abound in her life.

Her departure from this world has left a big void in the family and has particularly left us bereft of a very loving aunt. She has left with us such wonderful memories and recounting a few of them in the form of a colourful rainbow is my personal tribute to her.

Translated from the Urdu by Rafiul Hasan

2

Talking to Aini Khala

NOOR ZAHEER

She has moved from the first floor flat of Sector 25 to a ground floor flat in Sector 21 of NOIDA. In Sector 25, she was just a block away and I would often drop in for a cup of lemon tea. She moved to Sector 21 after a stroke that affected one of her legs.

'But I am still not so far that you have to let a month pass before you come for gobhi gosht.'

I swallow this with a big gulp of the golden liquid, thanking my luck for her obviously increasing forgetfulness. I have turned up after four months!

'Bhai, make gobhi gosht for Noor. After all she has come after four months!'

She looks at me impishly as I choke over the tea in surprise. 'Yes, my memory is still good. It is only that I don't want people to be embarrassed and apologetic. It is all right; everyone has a right to be busy.'

I try to figure out where to begin. It is going to be a long talk and she has recently started falling asleep in the midst of a discussion. I don't want to waste time. She doesn't let me.

AK (Aini Khala): You wanted to talk.

NZ: Yes, about you.

AK: Autobiographies are an invitation to lie. *[The twinkle flashes for a split second before her eyes become solemn. She is over eighty and beautiful.]* So, what do you want to know?

NZ: *Are you unhappy with the way you have always stood alone?*

AK: *[She does not pretend to misunderstand. She knows that it is not her physical solitude I am talking about.]* When literature undergoes a churning, as it must from time to time, there are often people—writers — who make a major contribution to this churning. They are the people who break the old moulds, the established formats and strike out for something new. Then there are the conformists or the conventional thinkers who in all their creativity and effort to produce something new, never think beyond the already thought. It is natural for a confrontation to take place between the two.

For my own part, I have always respected the conventional or the established but have tried consistently to strike out on an untrodden path.

NZ: *Did it hurt that your first major contribution to literature was initially condemned and* Aag ka Dariya *was rejected as the blasphemous blathering of a non-writer?*

AK: Yes, it did. I did not expect such a violent reaction. Though I did think that what I had written was bound to create some ripples, but I never imagined it to be such a storm. In a way, it was a blessing in disguise. It brought my writing into the limelight and with time, I learnt to accept the brickbats with the bouquets. What did hurt and still hurts is the way my book was criticized for being unIslamic. Literature cannot be segmented or compartmentalized into religions. There is only good literature and bad literature. Or maybe there could be a mediocre one to cover the grey area between the two. *[Pauses]* The highly populated grey area! *[Laughs]* Let's have more tea.

NZ: *Yes, one could take the positive view of all the negative criticism, but what I am not able to understand is the way the Progressive writers maintained a very diplomatic silence on the entire episode.*

AK: It was painful but not entirely uncharacteristic;

especially now when I look back, I find their attitude very expected. Look, the period of giving the shock treatment to society to shake it out of its lethargy was over. *Angare*[1] , the early stories of Dr. Rashid Jahan, Saadat Hasan Manto and Ismat Chughtai had already become works of the past. You must also remember that things were moving at a tremendous pace. More events crowded a month in that period than happened in several years just a couple of decades ago. With so many issues at hand, it is but natural that the main thrust of any organization would be to survive as an establishment. With that, it must be expected that with the untimely death of Premchand and the removal of Sajjad Zaheer from the literary scenario, the punch had gone out of the Progressive Writers' Association (PWA). It was now merely an organization, like so many others and no longer a movement that nurtured creative experiments.

NZ: *But the entire concept of PWA was to turn the flow of the Indian literary stream in a new direction. One of the important definitions of this new direction was supposedly a search for the new and the unexplored, something that* Aag ka Darya *did.*

AK: There is a difference between a movement and an organization. A movement has a flow that should be forwards. An organization is the gelling of that movement. It is like the stream flowing into the lake. The focus then becomes the lake, which is considered the life source. Dams are built, banks fortified, *ghats* constructed to make it accessible, desilting planned. The lake lies there, clean, clear, cool and deep—but stagnant. In the process, the stream that is feeding the lake is neglected. That is why new movements, new streams have to continue to be born, to keep the flow, the life alive.

Once PWA became a concrete organization, it was only natural that all that was conventional would seep into it. The infighting, the politics, the hierarchy and most importantly the dominance of the office bearers, who were more often than not non-writers, might have kept the organization alive but it killed the movement. Unfortunately, nothing else

replaced it. But one must admit that at one time it did nurture
the cream of Indian literature. In Urdu, the PWA was a major
force, giving to literature, writers who transcended the
language barriers and became universal litterateurs like
Saadat Hasan Manto, Krishan Chander, Khwaja Ahmad
Abbas, Rajinder Singh Bedi, Ismat...

*NZ: You talk so warmly of Ismat Chughtai in spite of 'Pom
Pom Darling'?*

[She keeps quiet for a long while. Have I over-stepped
decorum? If I have done so then I would be politely shown
the door. I know she is quite capable of it. I wait with baited
breath, trying to decide whether I should repeat the question
or ask another one. When our eyes meet, hers are strangely
clear and hold my gaze with the look of one who has nothing
to hide.]

A K: We all have our shortcomings. I must have seemed
very different.

*NZ: But wasn't it 'the different' that had attracted Ismat
Chughtai to Dr. Rashid Jahan? She is on record about stating the
great influence that Rashid Jahan had on her, mainly because she
was so different from anyone else that Ismat Chughtai had been
exposed to.*

AK: Sometimes, what we accept from our elders, we are
not able to take from our juniors. In a society that largely
survives on conventions, it is difficult to keep them at an
arm's distance. They do creep into our life, often without
our knowledge. Over the years I have understood her reasons
for having that kind of an attitude.

*NZ: I have not, Aini Khala. Maybe I like to find ideals in the
seniors all the time. It would have been a matter of personal pride
for people like me if she had bonded with you and stood up in your
defence. I would like to know your analysis of her not forming that
kind of sisterhood.*

AK: My concerns were very different from those of the
Progressives. They were involved in changing and analysing
the present life, the span from one's birth to one's death. My
concerns were different. I was interested in life as a whole.

Life that is a process of finding a reason to live and struggle, to survive in different eras and epochs... It was a difference of philosophies.

The Leftists have always and still do their reviewing and analysing through Marxist spectacles. For them there is no before or beyond of life. But for me, I would feel like a person with no roots if I didn't think of the past and the future as being me. If you adhere to one, you can't appreciate the other. I think that is what it was.

NZ: I remember a discussion taking place in our house some time in 1971. Abba[2] wanted to invite you to chair a session of a seminar being planned by the PWA, while all the other members of the planning committee were opposing it. From what I remember of the outcome, you did come to the seminar and not only chaired a session, you also spoke at length about the shortcomings of the Progressive Writers' Movement.

AK: Well, I don't know about the opposition to my being invited to this particular seminar, but one could not refuse Banne Bhai [Sajjad Zaheer]. He had that persuasive manner and, of course, the close links of our two families could not be denied. When he asked me to chair a session I had to accept. But I had made my position clear to him and he had told me to speak my mind freely. So I did just that. But then not everyone is as broad minded as he was.

NZ: I have heard this from other writers too. Since you knew him so well, do you think that this was the reason for being a successful organizer?

AK: There is never one reason for success of that kind. Banne Bhai was warm, loving, soft spoken, caring and of course broad minded. With that you must also remember that he had no ambitions of his own. He did not want to project himself as a great writer, a capable organizer, a fine leader. He only wanted to do more and more work for the cause of the writers. That is why he went on beyond the PWA in the 1960s and first founded the Asian Writers' Organization and later expanded it to the Afro-Asian Writers' Organization. Such a man was sent to Pakistan by the Communist leaders to organize a revolution. Can one ever have faith in a party that has such a misguided leadership?

NZ: You were in Pakistan while he was there. Did you ever meet him?

AK: I must tell you one incident. This is hilarious. I had gone to the Lahore Gymkhana with some friends. Over coffee, I looked around and saw a Pathan, in the traditional dress of *salwar kameez*, flowing turban, long unruly beard covering his face sitting alone at a table, a short distance away from ours. I remarked to a friend, 'If one was to shave off that Pathan's beard and moustaches he would look almost like Banne Bhai'.

My companion smiled and said 'That he would... because he is Banne Bhai!'

I became so excited that I jumped up and ran to his table and said 'Adaab, Banne Bhai, do you recognize me, I am Aini'. He did not answer and turned to look the other way.

Just then, my friends grabbed me and pushed me out of the door urgently whispering in my ear, 'Are you mad? He is in disguise. Do you want to expose him and get him arrested?'

I met him almost ten years after this incident and the first thing he did was apologise for having had to ignore me that day at the Lahore Gymkhana. How can anyone not obey such a man? I knew he had been opposed every time he had wanted to give me a platform in PWA but in spite of that, whenever he asked me to come, I could never refuse.

NZ: You just said that both your families were very close...

AK: Oh yes. So close that the first sweets from your mother's side to your father's house were taken by my parents. Khan Bahadur Raza Hussain, your maternal grandfather was my mother's godbrother. In those days a relationship formed was a relationship lived. My first sewing set was presented to me by your Nana. I was eleven when your parents were married and I remember your father as the shyest of bridegrooms. He looked almost like a *gudda*[3], shyly smiling at all the rituals. Impossible to think of him as a leader addressing mass rallies, as I saw him doing later. Your mother I knew well. I even have her photograph when she did her High School. It is in my latest book that has been published by the Urdu Academy, Delhi. Those were good days when everyone seemed to care for everyone else, the very atmosphere was warm and full of regard for one's fellow beings. Not that this era does not have its positive side and I am always one to look more at the future than at the past.

[She keeps quiet for a while, giving me time to ruminate this one. When I am through, I look up and find her asleep. Her rhythmic breathing brings in her full-time help, Rihana, who comes in with a silk *dulai* to cover her. I get up quietly and follow her out.

'How long has this been happening?' I ask Rihana.

'A few months,' the answer is indifferent, the expression is not. She looks worried.

'How long does she usually sleep?' I ask.

'Usually 15 minutes, sometimes half an hour, never more than forty-five minutes. You can leave or wait, as you wish,' Rihana says.

I decide to wait and thumb through her books ignoring the terse warning, 'She doesn't like her books to be touched.' Aini Khala wakes up after about 20 minutes and calls Rihana to come with a comb. Her hair has been recently tinted in a double shade of henna and burgundy. It is thick and crisp and its tangles have her scolding the girl for being rough. Hair done, clip in place, she asks for lipstick and is offered a tray full. She selects one, applies it with finesse and turns to me.]

AK: So, where were we?

NZ: *We were talking about the PWA.*

AK: Oh yes! The formation of PWA with its thrust on Left-committed writing washed away the contribution of a number of earlier writers, who should have been rewritten and re-evaluated, for having been there before the arrival of the Progressives. These writers were trying in their own way to reform society and religions. Hence their works should not have been consigned to the dustbin. If nothing else, they did form the staircase for the PWA.

NZ: One cannot help feeling that the concept of reformation has been pushed into the background by the more fiery and exciting beliefs of total revolution. Do you think this has had a negative effect on society as a whole?

AK: While revolution is a single event, reformation is a continuous process. Stopping it is in a sense curbing the process of change. As a child, I remember the concern shown by my mother Nazar-e Sajjad Hyder and Lady Wazir Hasan, your grandmother for the education of Muslim girls. Though they were themselves not very educated, your grandmother even less so, but they would regularly visit the Karamat Hussain Muslim Girls' College.[4] They would talk to the girls living in the hostel, check the food being cooked for them, visit their rooms. In a way they would try to make the girls feel comfortable and not give up studies because they were not being well looked after. These women did this entirely on their own and out of concern for the community. This feeling is missing today; perhaps that is why the community is not moving in the direction of progress.

NZ: The outright rejection of the reformist writers and the projection of the Leftist writers as the central pen wielders must have come about because of the literary critics of the period. Do you think that these writers, the critics...?

AK: Don't mix up the two. A critic is no writer.

NZ: But Aini Khala everyone divides writing into these three major groups: Fiction, Poetry and Criticism.

AK: So why don't we include the munshis and the stenographers and typists under the heading of Writers? We did till a century before. English literature is full of characters whose profession is writing and it turns out that they are clerks. Look, writing is a creative business and no critic can be said to be that. True, some good writing is neither fiction nor poetry. It might be long essays, analysis of a situation, articles highlighting and focusing attention on a certain problem, travelogues. These should be termed non-fiction.

Criticism, on the other hand, is an analysis of a creative work, hence it is an offshoot of the main work. How can it have an individual identity of its own?

NZ: *A number of these writers, the reformists you are talking about, were women including your own mother. Most of them took a male pen-name. Do you think that the coming of PWA and the openness it brought to Indian literature helped women writers evolve as individuals?*

AK: Initially, yes, perhaps because of the presence of Dr. Rashid Jahan in the core group of the founders. Her very personality was such that it did not need any support. But it has remained a man's world as I suppose it would, seeing that we live in a patriarchal society. For a female writer, it is important to have a male godfather.

NZ: *Has it, to some extent, been the reason why a section of intellectuals have not accepted you as a writer and a thinker?*

AK: Acceptability comes with its own baggage of positive and negative. While initial rejection or criticism makes the struggle tougher, it gives one time to think, imagine, philosophize and write. On the other hand, acceptability brings with it ties, commitments, packaging, showcasing, etc. In the case of any artistic exercise, time saved is time created.

As far as my own individual case is concerned, I never really found anyone, man or woman to look up to. Maybe because I have always been a non-conformist and the people whom I met were all rigid and moulded in some way or the other. When one has set out on the untrodden path, as I did right at the onset of the journey, it is impossible to come back and walk tamely on the known and accepted roads. True, the journey is a constant struggle but it is also one of adventure, of surprises and discoveries. One has to make a choice and having made it, one has to live that choice.

NZ: *Has this adventure always to be undertaken alone?*

AK: Creation, for me, has always been a single-handed exercise. There might be some who can work together.

NZ: *You are right. Even my father created his most important books* Roshnai *and* Zikr-e-Hafiz *in jail. In fact, Ammi would*

often threaten to get him jailed so that he would focus on writing
another book!

AK: [*She gazes out of the window then looks at the bookshelf*
crowded with books. Is it a shake of the head that I see, a sigh that I
hear?] In the time that your father was in jail in Pakistan,
your mother blossomed into a short story writer. True ,your
father wrote those books in jail and accepting the fact that he
should have written some more, the fact remains that your
mother's output also declined when he returned. Her life, in
which writing short stories had becomes a process of
channelizing her pent up emotions, became a satellite around
the important work that your father was doing in reviving
the PWA. It is funny that you who talk of sisterhood between
two strangers, fail to see things from a different angle. Did
your mother only want your father to be confined away from
his other commitments so that he could write a book? Or
was it a yearning for some space, some time, to reach out to
her own springs of creativity before they finally dried up?

Most of us do not express our solidarity to our nearest.
We perceive only the obvious. If a person is surrounded by
friends, family, admirers, she is not lonely. If she lives away
from the so-called society, thinks, believes and creates
differently, then she is weird and must be lonely. We judge
without knowing, without understanding because we do not
take the trouble to move to a different position and view
things from that angle.

> God, she is candid! And forthright! I come away with a feeling
> that all my beliefs, focal points, formats, knowledge has been
> given a vigorous shake. Some of them have even fallen out of
> me, leaving me the choice to pick them up and put them in
> place or let the vacancies be and wait for them to fill up if I
> have the guts to walk the unknown path.
>
> I promise myself that I shall come back and do some more
> sorting with her help. But I waste too much time preparing for
> another upheaval that would definitely be the fate of the
> meeting. She has left. I ask myself the question that she never
> really answered. Was she lonely? The woman in me laughs at

the writer wanting to clear the facts. The woman knows. Aini Khala was alone. A state reached early because one is trudging for the peak. Having reached it, one is still alone, because there is too little room. But lonely? Never! How could she be? For one who keeps the exploration alive, that so important of human activity, the little space discovered is the whole universe.

Editor's Notes

1. *Angare* (meaning 'live embers') was a collection of nine short stories and a play by four young writers, namely Sajjad Zaheer, Ahmed Ali, Rashid Jahan and Mahmuduzzafar. It was published in December 1932 from Lucknow and proscribed by the imperial government on 15 March 1933. The overtly sexual references and the attacks on religion caused a furore and drew away from the purpose of the book which was, namely, to introduce another sort of writing, one that was filled with graphic word pictures of a sick, ailing society. It caused a furore and changed.
2. Noor Zaheer's father, Sajjad Zaheer, the noted Progressive writer and founder-member of the Progressive Writers' Association.
3. A boy doll.
4. The girls' school at Lucknow was started by Karamat Hussain in 1912. It was, however, a school, and not a college as quoted here.

3

Qurratulain Hyder: The First Lady of Urdu Literature

KHALID HASAN

'Let me explain Time to you,' Qurratulain Hyder once said to me. This was in the 1980s. How comfortable, she asked, was I with the 1960s? How distant did they appear in terms of years lapsing? 'The 1960s feel like yesterday,' I had replied. 'Well,' she said, 'That was a quarter century ago. So let's us go back, taking the same unit of time you are comfortable with, another 25 years.' To my surprise, if not horror, it struck me that we were in 1935. 'And another leap into the past by the same measure,' she said, 'and we are in 1910, with the First World War still four years into the future. That is what time is. That is how time goes,' she had said.

She should have known, having written one of the greatest novels of the twentieth century in any language on the same theme: Time. I refer of course to *Aag ka Darya*. I always found it ironic that while since the late 1970s, no week has passed without some rubbishy and forgettable novel by an Indian writer, writing in English, finding publication in Britain or the US, the work of a writer like Qurratulain Hyder, including her own superb translation of *Aag ka Darya*, has never been able to make the list.

In June 1982, she wrote to me from Bombay, 'Tell me, how does one get published in Vilayat? How did this boy get such a massive novel published from London/NY? (I forget which novel by a *desi* it was that I had sent her.) This is the sort of thing that has always baffled me about the Indo-Anglicans — do you call them Pak-Anglicans? This cousin of mine Khalid Hussain Shah and his American wife Linda wrote a huge novel (*Refugee*) about our family's migration to Pakistan. It was published from NY and also got rave reviews in the US press — 'Mesmerising', etc.' In another letter later that year, she wrote in that delightful Urdu that was alone hers to write, 'Having watched books by *'unt-shunt'* types finding publication in the West, I had handed over to you a collection of my stories (in her beautiful English translation). Well, it is apparent that nothing came of it at your end. I am two-thirds done with my translation of *Aakhir-e-Shab ke Hamsafar*. How can it get published in the West? (It wasn't). You try.'

The first time I saw Aini, which is what I always called her, was in 1960 or 1961 in Karachi, but I could not muster the courage to speak to her. There used to be a street that linked Victoria Road and Elphinstone Street (I prefer to use the old names that nobody had any business to change). On that road, there used to stand the Capital Cinema, which had a wonderful restaurant on its first floor called Flamingo, which was always dimly lit and which had black steel furniture with colourful cushions. There in that cool, calm place I saw Qurratulain Hyder sipping tea with a woman friend. She was wearing a yellow sari and a spring green blouse. That I have never forgotten. Another 21 years were to pass before I could meet her. Why? Because there is a preordained place and time for everything. The year was 1980 and I was in Bombay and determined to meet, not the movie stars of my dreams, but Qurratulain Hyder. And I did. That day on, our contact did not flag and we kept a correspondence going till May 1997. Thereafter, she did not write with her right hand because of a stroke, but she learnt to write with her left. She sent me a copy of one of her books with the inscription written with her left hand that said '*Bain haath ka khel*' whose literal meaning may be 'a trick with the left hand' but which means 'executed with the least effort.' Another book, her translations of some of her stories published in India — *Street Singers of Lucknow* — she inscribed to me in English in childlike lettering with her left hand. Can destiny come up with a greater irony than to divest a magical writer like her of the ability to write with her own hand?

People were always in awe of her because she refused to suffer fools and made it quite clear on the spot the reason why she did not. Some of my friends remain surprised to this day as to how I could even think of taking liberties with her. Everyone who was younger called her Aini Apa but I called her Aini. And she let me call her Aini. When she asked me what I thought of her novel *Gardish-e-Rang-e-Chaman*, I told her I did not like it and mentioned why. I was forgiven but also told that it was not necessary that I could understand everything. She also told me that few Pakistanis would have the ear for a certain kind of spoken Urdu in UP now.

She bore with me to the point of indulgence. Over a period of years, in three instances at least she let me go with life and limb — and friendship — intact. I know of people she sent to Coventry for lesser trespasses, never to speak to them again. Now that I look back on it, I did not deserve such forbearance, which I can only attribute to some stellar influence that placed me in a house that was exempt from Aini's ire and her celebrated temper, when annoyed. Let me narrate the three incidents. In early 1981, she wrote to me (and I translate):

> Famous poet F.R. (*dareeda badan*) has arrived here, complete with husband and offspring. It is being said that she has no return plans and is looking for work. All kinds of stories are in the air. In order to earn local goodwill, she is making all kinds of rhymeless statements against that country. For instance, that the reference to Dajjal the One-Eyed has been censored out of the Quran (a professor of Islamiyat in Delhi has said there is no mention of Dajjal the One-Eyed in the Quran). One has also

heard that the sister who has accompanied her is loud mouthed and rude. Two years ago, when the lady came here and called on this humble being, her political passion was something to be seen, just like ours when we were in college. The inhabitants of the land of Confucius have been particularly welcoming to her.

Some days later, in a letter to my old friend and classmate, the late Kalim Akhtar (who must have written hundreds of thousands of words on Kashmir and why it must be free without any effect on the governments of India and Pakistan, I should add), I made mention of what Aini had written to me about Fahmida Riaz. Kalim, who used to write regularly for *Nawai Waqt*, without naming me, reproduced in the newspaper what Aini had written about Fahmida and her sister. This was exactly the sort of thing that *Nawai Waqt* has always loved. For them, here was another example of the vile anti-Muslim and anti-Pakistan Indo-Soviet lobby at work, etc. I had no idea Kalim had put into print Aini's delightful and caustic comments, which I had only conveyed to him for his amusement. Then I heard from Aini on 23 December 1981 from Aligarh. She wrote (in English this time), 'Last month Fahmida R. came to see me in Allahabad. She was almost in tears as she told me that *Nawai Waqt* had published a news item headlined '*Qurratulain Hyder ka ek Khat*', which said, '... is here with one sister and to win local goodwill.... is issuing statements (etc. etc.). This letter has been sent by Q.H. to a friend of hers who lives in the West and from whom this letter has been obtained.' Khalid, needless to say this is utterly disgusting. Can you throw some light on this shameful act? Kindly respond by return of post. (the last three sentences in Urdu). And then this in English, 'I don't feel like writing anything else.'

My response was an abject apology rendered while prostrate on the ground at her feet. Sackcloth and ashes was my defence. I also sent her an Yves Saint Laurent perfume called Opium as a 'peace offering'. On 10 February, she wrote (in Urdu):

ory, which is a great shame. But since the newspaper referredis possible that I may have written to Muhammad Umar
Memon. After writing to you in December, I inquired from him
if I had written anything to him about the lady and if it was
possible that my letter had been hijacked by someone and
delivered to Lahore. I enclose Muhammad Umar Memon's
reply. I am not one of the world's great letter writers. For years,
I do not answer letters; [it] feels like an ordeal. Except for
extremely important correspondence, I only write to relatives
and friends to whom I feel like writing. You are included in
that second category.

The last sentence was the forgiveness she had graciously
conferred on me. The matter was never mentioned again.

Another of my trespasses that Aini forgave related to an
introduction I had written to a collection of Pakistani Urdu
short stories that Faruq Hassan and I had put together (it
was eventually published by Vikas, Delhi — *Nothing but the*

Truth. I had included in it my translation of Aini's story *Photographer* and also written an introduction (I had consulted Faiz Ahmad Faiz on certain points relating to the formation of the Progressive Writers' Association). I sent the introduction to Aini for her approval. She took exception to two of its passages. They were: 'Although Qurratulain Hyder left Pakistan in the 1960s to settle down once again in India and thus, technically, may not be regarded as a Pakistani writer any longer, her stories are, in many cases, first published in Pakistan, where she enjoys a wide, appreciative readership. In any case, most of her great work was produced while she lived in Pakistan and was its citizen.' The second passage to which she took exception was: 'Her story *Photographer* is more universal. Tinged with nostalgia, it is in some ways perhaps autobiographical. Qurratulain Hyder returned to India in her early youth only to find that time is remorseless and that people grow old and change. Even culture undergoes modifications with the politics of a society. Nothing can be recaptured; only memories remain.'

Aini took me to task for writing that 'most of her great work was produced while she lived in Pakistan and was its citizen.' She wrote (in Urdu),

> Obviously, your patriotism is on the boil. While I won't say that I have ever or anywhere produced great work, have I merely 'dug up grass' (*ghas khodi hai*) since I came here, or written nothing of note? I beg of you, kindly do not drag me into this Pakistani-Indian rigmarole. I shall be grateful. If you have included just Pakistani storywriters in this collection and by including my stories, some controversy might arise, then please do not include my stories. You have been living abroad for some time and you do not know the official Pakistani standpoint on Krishan Chander and Premchand. All this is very unpleasant and (in Bombayese) I do not wish to be part of this *lafra*. Please let me off. Enough is enough. It has become quite sickening (this last line in English). Some writers thrive on such controversies so that they can get talked about more and more. I am allergic to that sort of thing. Am terrified of it. Therefore, I request you to delete the stories along with the Intro. If you

write something other than what you wrote, I would like to
take a look at it. You will be irritated and this would all become
rather boring.

She also rapped me across the knuckles, but gently, for
suggesting that *Photographer* might be autobiographical. She
wrote:

> By the way, the backdrop of *Photographer* is Sri Lanka, not India.
> In a Kandy guesthouse, there lived an Indian dancer along with
> her musicians. That was my basis for this story. I think I should
> also pen an article on the anatomy of each of my stories and
> novels.

At the end of this long letter, in which she had some agreeable
words to say about a Faiz memoir I had written (which she
translated into Urdu, an honour that will outmatch what little
I have accomplished or will ever accomplish), she wrote:

> 'My dear, if anything that I have said has caused offence in
> this epistle (her word), then forgive me, including the intro.
> '*Ant-shunt*' (all sorts of dubious kinds) people get published in
> the West, which was what made me give you a handful of my
> stories. It is obvious that nothing came of it. I have translated
> two-thirds of *Aakhir-e-Shab ke Hamsafar*, but how will it be
> published in the West? You try.

Whenever I went to Delhi, which sadly was only three or
four times, I always spent an evening with her. She would
insist that I eat and eat gluttonously. She had moved to
NOIDA, which is a relatively new settlement across the
Jamuna in UP. She suffered one bout of ill health after another
but her sense of humour, her magnanimity, her zest for life
never diminished. Her eyes gave her much trouble and in
the end she used to read, what little she did, with a magnify-
ing glass. One letter she wrote to me in May 1996 says,

> My number is minus 18-19. All the best. The address on the
> letterhead (I had had some letterheads with her name and
> address printed and sent to her) is so fine that all I can read is
> my name. This letter I have written with the help of a
> magnifying glass.

I was shattered when I read that.

The last time I spent an evening with her in Delhi, she said to me, 'I have to hear now with the help of an outlandish, outsize hearing aid, but for God's sake don't go advertising that with the slogan: *'Aini behri ho gai'* [Aini has gone deaf].' 'You know me,' I said. Among her good friends in Pakistan, I would count Raja Tajummul Hussain, Dr. Javid Iqbal, the late Ijaz Batalvi and Zia Mohyeddin. But she knew everyone and always followed what was going on in Pakistan, on the literary scene, no less than on the political front. She was very sad when Z.A. Bhutto was executed. She told me that a poor woman had come up to her and said, *'Bibi, ye Pakistani kaiasy log hain? Apnay Raja ko maar diya.'* (Bibi, what kind of people are these Pakistanis? They have killed their Raja).

Aini was a great friend of Nargis. After her death, she wrote to me:

> Yes, Nargis has left us all devastated. She was part of the times in which we were growing up – times now in the realm of mythology – (like Pankaj Malik's songs). Now when we watch those old movies on TV, they seen primitive, but how magical they were in those days! But she – Nargis – died with great dignity and very gracefully. When she died she was a grand public figure. Extremely dignified she had become, but she never stopped swearing. This was a strange paradox of her personality. Once she told me that some exceedingly old people come up to her and say, 'I have been watching your movies since childhood.' (In the same way that some white-bearded elders inform me that they have been reading my stories since they were children). But in her we had a fascinating lady.

In 1998, when I was living in Islamabad where I had been lured into coming, having been offered the director-generalship of the Associated Press of Pakistan (which I was determined to transform into a proper news agency rather than a sycophantic His Master's Voice and a purveyor of badly written government handouts) but was told to become the head honcho of the Shalimar Television Company (which was a misnomer since it did not produce any television programmes), Aini came to Islamabad. She stayed with her cousin Humaira Syed, the late Jari Ahmed Syed's wife (and Mushahid Hussain's mother-in-law). I was thrilled. I had known the Syeds since the early 1960s when as a probationary officer in the income tax service, I used to live in the now-demolished Kashmir Hotel, next to which lived Jari Ahmed Syed, Controller of Military Accounts. Kishwar Naheed and I decided to do something grand for Aini and one evening at Kishwar's flat in Park Towers, Sector F-10 (it survived the October 2005 earthquake, while the high-rise next to it fell down), we gathered many of our friends and Aini's admirers. Muhammad Mansha Yad, Raja Anwar, Begum Sarfraz Iqbal, Aftab Iqbal Shamim and so many others were part of that memorable evening (I have pictures which I have not looked at since Aini died as they would make me very sad), where everyone practically sat at her feet. She was happy and she listened to everyone, said pleasant things to many, praised some of their work and kept smiling. There she was: every inch the perfect lady and a writer without peer whom many have tried to imitate but no one has been able to match her élan, her brilliance, her wit and sense of humour, her compassion, her sense of history, her wide sympathies and her modesty about her own formidable achievement and place in Urdu, indeed in world literature. When she was leaving, I saw her into her car and said, 'Aini, I love you.'

She called Nargis a fascinating lady but far more fascinating was Aini, whom the world will forever remember (in the words of my friend Sayyed Faizi of Vienna), as 'Qurratulain Hyder the Hazir Imam of Urdu fiction'.

Rest in peace dear lady, for your like we shall never see again.

Credit: Annual of Urdu Studies, No. 23 (2008).

CRITICAL NARRATIVES

4

Qurratulain Hyder:
An Author Par Excellence

GOPICHAND NARANG

If anyone can be called a phenomenon in modern Urdu
fiction, it is Qurratulain Hyder, the author of the famous Urdu
novel, *Aag ka Darya* which, in the late 1950s, rocked the literary
circles in Pakistan, and consequent upon the publication of
which the author had to migrate back to India. Later, this
novel was selected by the National Book Trust for their
prestigious *Aadaan Pradaan* series for translation into various
Indian languages. Though the novel went through many
printings in India, but since it was published outside India
(1956), it could not be considered for the Sahitya Akademi's
award. It was her collection of short stories, *Patjhar ki Awaz*
(The Voice of Autumn), first published from New Delhi in
1965, which won the Sahitya Akademi Award in 1967.
Following this, her novel *Akhir-e-Shab ke Hamsafar* (1973), won
for her the Jnanpith Award.

Qurratulain Hyder was born in 1927 in Aligarh, into an
enlightened family of writers. Her father Sajjad Haider
Yaldram was a highly respected original writer in Urdu, as
was her mother Nazr Sajjad Hyder. Qurratulain passed her
high school at the age of thirteen, and her M.A. in English
from Lucknow University at the age of 19 in 1946. She

migrated to Pakistan in 1947 with her parents but returned to India after the publication of her magnum opus, *Aag ka Darya*, as mentioned before, and was given Indian nationality again. For some time she worked for the *Daily Telegraph*, London, and also for the BBC, London. She had attended arts schools in Lucknow and London and learned a good deal about music and painting, and had a sound knowledge of English literature besides being well versed in Urdu and Persian literary traditions. While in Bombay she worked as the editor of *Imprint*, and also served on the editorial staff of the *Illustrated Weekly of India* for many years. She was a member of the Film Censor Board of India, and a distinguished Visiting Professor at the Jamia Millia Islamia and the Aligarh Muslim University, Aligarh.

A number of novels, novelettes and short story collections make up Qurratulain Hyder's oeuvre. *Aag* ka *Darya* (The River of Fire), *Mere bhi Sanam-khane* (My Temples Too), *Safina-i-Gham-e-Dil* (The Boat of the Heart's Grief), *Roshni ka Safar* (The Journey of Light), *Kar-e-Jahan Daraz Hai* (The Task of the World is Endless Vol. I, 1977, and Vol. ll, 1979, a biographical novel) and *Aakhir-e-Shab* ke *Hamsafar* (The Travellers unto the Night's End) 1978, *Roshni ki Raftar* (The Speed of Light) 1982, *Gardish-e-Rang-i-Chaman* and *Chandani Begum* are novels. *Seeta Haran* (The Abduction of Sita), *Dilruba* (Beloved), *Chae ke Bagh* (Tea Gardens), *Agle Janam Mohe Bitya Na Kijo* (Don't Make Me a Girl in My Next Birth), are novelettes. *Sitaron se Aage* (Beyond the Stars), *Sheeshay ke Ghar* (Glass Houses) and *Patjhar ki Awaz* (The Voice of Autumn) are collections of short stories. She had written several articles in various journals in India and Pakistan. She had been writing fairly extensively in English on literary topics and arts, and had translated some books from Russian into Urdu. She had also translated *Portrait of a Lady* (a novel by Henry James) and *Murder in the Cathedral* (a play by T.S. Eliot) into Urdu. With Sardar Jafri, she had edited *Ghalib: Poetry and Letters*, and with Khushwant Singh, *Stories From India*.

Almost all of Qurratulain Hyder's fiction reflects her

preoccupation with India's cultural past, the pastness of the past, as well as its relation with the present. There is a sense of urgency about her work in that what the Indian people have now become is closely linked with what they have been, and a reflection upon their present identity has to take into account the formative processes that have shaped this cultural identity. Qurratulain Hyder is Indian and her ethos oriental but the human nature she probes is to be found anywhere, and the suffering she depicts is universal. Her work is marked by a quality of vastness and magnitude both in time and space, and undoubtedly she has produced some of the unique fiction of our times. Let me briefly dwell on her important books that have placed her firmly in the world of Urdu fiction.

Aag ka Darya, a novel, spanning Indian history from the 1950s back to the hoary past of Indian civilization, definitely to the times of the Buddha, is a witness to Qurratulain's uncanny vision that gives a unique depth and meaning to the concepts of Time and Space. In this novel, her perspective is universal and her concern, humanity at large.

The story is spellbinding and fast-paced; the short, episodic narrative mode, keeps the attention of the reader always on a high. Gautam, the protagonist, a student in ancient times begins his peregrinations in the forest and eventually reaches the horrid times of Partition. Many of the scenes she portrays remain vivid in the reader's memory long after first reading it.

Qurratulain pulls off a double effect through writing in Urdu: the implications of the theme, which appeals to all humanity and expresses the anguish of any sensitive mind, found avid readers wherever the language was read and spoken, and yet it remained a thoroughly Indian book. It also explores with the colonial past, especially looking at the advent of the English with the kind of critical sternness, seeking to give a balanced assessment of the Indian ethos down the millennia.

Patjhar ki Awaz (The Voice of Autumn) is an outstanding

collection of short and long stories and a novelette, 'Housing Society'. Handling with remarkable skill a wide range of subjects and themes, and recreating history, Qurratulain Hyder is at her best in this collection. Her sensitivity to mood and situation and her considerable powers of characterization have no parallel in contemporary Urdu fiction. Most of the writings included in this volume are marked by the basic question of the predicament of human beings, the complexity of relations, and the unavoidability of time with a backdrop of the cultural cohesion and the cultural personality of the Indo-Gangetic people.

In 'Jila-Watan' (The Exiles), one of her best long stories, while underlining the humanistic aspects of the integrated Hindu-Muslim culture, or composite culture of the great cities of Northern India, she reflects on human suffering through the portrayal of vital experiences of the generation of those times in India and Pakistan, a generation which had passed through a profound historical change and turmoil, caused by Partition, Independence and exile. In another story, 'Dalan Wala' (That Winter) typical of her impressionistic style, she effectively employs past recollections and experiences capturing the dark and bright areas of human nature, and the underlying cultural unity of the Indian people.

'Patjhar ki Awaz,' the title story, perhaps the only story of its kind by Qurratulain Hyder, depicts the predicament of a nymphomaniac, who, thirsting for love, in spite of the purity of her soul, passes from one man to another, and yet another by the sheer force of circumstances over which she has no control, and eventually in her grey days, feels like a fallen leaf drifted listlessly by the autumn winds.

Kar-e-Jahan Daraz Hai, the title of the next book, is taken from a verse by Iqbal which means 'The task of the world is endless'. The author calls it a biographical novel. It is a breathtaking book because of its scope, diversity of narrative voices, and layers of references. From the first page it snares the reader in its web of history and memory, fact and fiction, and does not let one go till the end. It is the history of a family of Nahtor, Bijnaur, which begins in the twelfth century and continues to the present. In the flowering of that particular family, however, there is also revealed to our riveted gaze the formation of that more general cultural identity, the Indian Muslim and his composite patterns of sociological behaviour.

Akhir-e-Shab ke Hamsafar (Travellers unto the Night's End), is another remarkable novel published from Bombay in 1978. It deals with one of the most fateful periods of the history of the subcontinent, i.e. from the pre-Second World War terrorist activity in Bengal and the Quit India Movement to the Partition of the country, and then to the events of 1970 and the eventual emergence of Bangladesh. The author's main concerns are psychological and existential in that, the once revolutionary characters who, inspired by high ideals, give up everything for their ideology, but with the change of time, and driven by primitive impulses and desires, stoop to the level of ordinary beings given to greed and lust; and disillusioned, they seek careers of ordinary comforts and base pleasures. Qurratulain Hyder raises some basic questions about the nature of existence and human freedom, how people rise to heights pressed by challenges, but in fact, the dark areas always persist and the scope of choices is rather limited. It is a vibrant story of different families — Hindu, Muslim, Christian and English — interwoven with each other during these three decades of revolutionary fervour. The changes wrought by the impact of these eventual years on the mentalities, aims, moral values, ideals, and outlook of the characters are depicted with profound psychological insight, and the characters of the hero Raihan, the heroine Deepali, and the younger female protagonist Yasmeen are hauntingly drawn. The atmosphere of East Bengal, now Bangladesh, its cities, rivers and jungles are also portrayed very vividly.

Qurratulain Hyder has an intense feeling for the immensity of pain, and for that cruel force called Time which overshadows all activity on earth. Time, in her fiction, is that faceless force that transforms all faces, which is linear as well as spiral, which one can ignore only at one's own peril, and which is so easily accessible, and is still as boundless as the universe itself. She urges us to recognize that the inevitability of change is the only reality, and that fact has one face of hope as well as another of sorrow. A linearly progressing Time brings changes, and change can be a harbinger of grief or joy. Should one then take sides? That would be too easy, she confides to us, too simplistic, for these issues cannot be settled by referring to the material world alone. What counts for Qurratulain Hyder is the human spirit and the relationships through which it blossoms forth. And that is where the linearity of Time turns into a spiral, bringing recognizable moments back to us if we have the necessary sensibility.

5

The Enigma of Dual Belonging: Qurratulain Hyder's Enduring Popularity in Pakistan

RAZA RUMI

Writing about Qurratulain Hyder is a daunting task, to say the least. The breadth and range of themes and subjects that her works traverse can overwhelm any reader. More often than not, her writings can remind the readers of the inadequacies of their creative response given the boundless ideas, energy and themes they are confronted with.

It is with much trepidation that I venture to discuss the huge popularity of Hyder's works in Pakistan. Her works especially her *magnum opus Aag ka Darya* (AKD) was published countless times in Pakistan and remains perhaps the most popular novel in the Urdu language. The paradox is noteworthy here: this novel is strictly not in line with the version of history that Pakistanis are familiar with; and yet it is so popular.

There is no definitive hypothesis that I wish to articulate through the succeeding pages; nor would I make any claims of original research here. My standpoint is that of a devoted reader, a handful of secondary sources and limited interviews.[1]

Briefly, this paper will focus on three major aspects of Hyder's writings that interestingly are also the highlights of her rich, complex and sadly little known legacy in the subcontinent. These three elements, in my opinion, also provide some explanation for her enduring popularity among Pakistani readers despite her decision to migrate to India in the 1960s. Notwithstanding the views of the mainstream Pakistani literary establishment, the officialdom and tragic turbulences in Indo-Pakistan relations since the 1960s, Hyder's works have continued to attract a wide readership in Pakistan.

At the outset, it should be reiterated that the sheer quality and innovation of her major and minor works place Urdu fiction at par with global contemporary literary currents. Some, including me, also argue that her works in many instances transcend several typologies of 'great' international literature.[2] Javed Akhtar's impromptu tribute at her death is instructive:

> When I say that it is a great loss, it's not only to Urdu literature, not only to Indian literature, but to world literature. I am not exaggerating at all. In the years to come, Hyder's novels will reach everywhere...The kind of work she has done... it's only because she was born in a third world country and wrote in a language that is not of the imperialistic powers, her novels have not reached everywhere. I am sure the time will come when they will reach. everywhere.[3]

Therefore, it is apparent that the intrinsic and universal quality of her works has been the primary reason for her appeal among Urdu readers. A leading Pakistani newspaper in its editorial summed it up:

> Perhaps she was to Urdu fiction what Iqbal was to Urdu poetry; as towering a presence for the second half of the twentieth century as Iqbal had been for the first half. She was a great writer who brilliantly captured an entire civilization in transit.[4]

But then there are many other celebrated and popular writers in Pakistan. What differentiates Hyder's work from theirs?

The purpose here is not to draw comparisons, as Hyder would not have approved of this. Her classic view on this has always been the same: Do people in the West compare Hardy and James? So why are we, in the world of Urdu, so keen to harp on *mawazna-e-Anees-o Dabir*[5] ?

Therefore, I shall identify three major issues or elements of Hyder's works that point towards her immense legacy as well as provide some clues to her popularity among the readers of Urdu language, especially in Pakistan. In short, these elements can be summed up as:

(a) Hyder's mastery over the genre of social history and its creative use in fiction thereby laying formidable groundwork for future historians and writers. In employing this genre, Hyder explores the concept and contours of a civilization that is, in great measure, free of borders, religions and national identities; narratives that suggest that history and eras are concurrent and non-exclusive. Therefore, the parochial national identities might determine citizenship; the past looms large over the lives of individuals and is neither separate nor irrelevant to the lives of humans. Therefore, Hyder presents the histories of people as opposed to rulers and of individuals, groups and characters that would otherwise be invisible or at best exist on the margins of what we know as history.

(b) In her articulation of post-colonial traumas, not restricted to migration, Hyder takes the literary approach to partition of India to a different level. This 'level' is beyond the brutality of riots and the blame-games. Hyder's narratives place the 1947 watershed within the framework of South Asian history and the continuous process of travel and migrations. Furthermore, the tragedy of 1947 in Hyder's vision is also located in the death of the old order and creation of a new world where new values such as wealth and consumerism define the civilizational value-system. By doing so, Hyder, in a foretelling manner, links the role of literature in the contemporary milieu of market-obsessed globalization.

(c) In her endeavours as a chronicler of the Indo-Muslim

civilization, Hyder dug deep into the complexities and contradictions of the history of Muslims in India. The ethos and construction of Indo-Muslim identity therefore has to be composite and not communal for it would negate history with anarchic results. Thus Hyder subverts the communal discourses and thereby de-legitimizes them while providing alternative sources of popular historical notions such as the Bhakti movement in *AKD* and twentieth century Sufi practices in *Gardish-i-Rang-i-Chaman*.

Social History Narratives versus the Official Histories

> What is India all about, what is the problem, why are we so full of problems, why are we like no other country? It's because there's too much history, we have too much of everything, and some of it is excellent but too much of excellence in one country, one period over so many centuries creates problems, it's not a simple story, it becomes a very complicated story.[6]

History as compiled, documented and distilled has entailed histories of rulers and the state. This tradition was also appropriated by the new states of India and Pakistan. The Indian nationalist discourse had its counterpoint in the Two Nation Theory that is supposed to have led to Pakistan's creation. Other narratives, perhaps best typified by Seervai's frank interpretation[7], were by and large sidelined. In a contested terrain such as this one, Hyder took no sides and came up with what was later to become a major discipline of historical studies: examining the concurrent eras of Indo-Pak history from 'below' and from the point of view of the people rather than rulers, nobles and court-historians.

Social history, often described as 'history from below', concerns itself with the ordinary people, the 'ruled' and how they define and steer history rather than the rulers.[8] It ventures to view itself as an inclusive form of history not limited to the statement of so-called historical fact but which can probe historical data from a people's perspective. This perspective also examines whether the masses follow the leaders or whether it is the other way around.[9]

Not that there was no tradition of popular social history versions in the subcontinent. Oral tradition, the folk lore and folk literature and several other modes of social history have existed since pre-historic times. But Hyder's modern and creative use of such a technique, often supplemented by original research, in Urdu fiction was novel.

Aag ka Darya was written and published in the highly contested milieu of the post-partition Indian subcontinent when the new nation states were rewriting their historical discourses. In Pakistan, *AKD* was a sensation right from its start when it was published in 1959. The controversy it created became its hallmark too. Hyder was allergic to this topic as it had been beaten to death in the course of innumerable interviews, profiles, essays *et al*. It is ironic that such a discussion continues to inform debates on her legacy years after her death.

AKD, for its canvas, historical consciousness and characterization, surpasses most novels written in any language. This novel dealt with the plight of the human condition in the Indo-Pakistani setting from the fourth century BC to the 1950s. Starting with the Mauryan Empire under Chandragupta, it traced the multiple eras with characters disappearing and reappearing in different guises pitted against the broad strokes of History and Time.

The innovative structure of *AKD* is truly unprecedented at least in the languages of the subcontinent. It covered four historical periods: first, the expansion of the Mauryan empire under Chandragupta in the fourth century BC; second, the end of the Lodi dynasty and the beginning of Mughal rule in the late fifteenth and early sixteenth centuries; third, the late-eighteenth-century beginnings of East India Company rule till its consolidation in the 1870s; and fourth, the two decades leading up to the 1950s that encompassed nationalist struggle, Partition, and Independence. These constitute four sequential yet discrete experiential moments that also show a grand, individual attempt to understand a civilization. We take the case of a major character, Kamal from *AKD* that would inform the argument below.

A key character, Abul Mansur Kamaluddin of Nishapur, son of a Persian mother and an Arab father, arrives in Hindustan in the fifteenth century. Mansur is a fortune hunter and passes through various stages in his Indianization, romancing with Ruqqaiya Bano Begum, a kinswoman of Sultan Husain Shah, falling in love with Champavati with whom he is never united as the war separates them. By the time Sikandar Lodi emerges as a successful power-wielder, he quits the world defined by power. By this time he has imbibed the message of the Chistiya Sufis, the Buddhist thought and Kabir's *baani*, and ends up in Bengal as a land tiller. His tragic end is caused by the rise of another fortune hunter, Sher Shah, whose soldiers kill him for being a traitor.

However, it is Kamaluddin's life and the India that he describes that sets the contours of modern Indo-Muslim consciousness. Hyder's lyrical prose describes his India in these words:

> Leaving the world of kings, rajas and commanders, Kamal saw the other world. This other world was inhabited by labourers, barbers, shoesmiths, peasants and poor artisans. This was the democratic Hindustan ruled by saints who patronized artisans and their guilds. The egalitarianism of Islam was profoundly influencing these Hindu Bhakats. Islam was being spread by peace-loving Sufis — here the sword was irrelevant. Tormented over the centuries, the untouchables were chanting Ram with these Sankats without the intercession of upper caste Brahmins. This was a unique world that was beyond the Hindu and Muslim identities. Here Love reigned — and Kamal was in search of Insaan.[10]

Kamal reappears in the third phase of *AKD* as well. He is the poor Bengali boatman Abul Mansur, as well as Kamal, a landowner in Oudh. In this phase he is again a witness to the events of 1857 and the harbinger and embodiment of the civilizational ethos that became the hallmark of Oudh.

In the modern narrative of *AKD*, Kamal is now the left-leaning, nationalist Kamal Reza who is educated at Cambridge, returns to a ruined Lucknow, and fails to find a job; the land reforms take away family wealth, his family's ancestral property is confiscated in an unfair manner and labelled as evacuee property. Thus a dispossessed family migrates to Pakistan while Kamal's alter-ego, the Switzerland-returned Amir Raza, has already migrated to Pakistan and entered the elite service of the new state. Amir Raza has already rejected Champa — another recurrent character who represents the more nationalist brand of Muslim consciousness in the novel.

However, at the time of its publication the novel represented what the middle classes (obviously the ones who comprised the readership in Pakistan) experienced. The migrants empathized with much that was said. However, Hyder's narratives were not limited to the migrant syndrome alone. It was an anguish that several Pakistanis felt and found a voice in the master chronicler of history and present that in any case had seamless boundaries:

> The black marketer is frustrated because he cannot put any more stuff on the black market. The left-wing intellectual bewails the fact that there appears to be no possibility any longer of a revolution. The Jamaat-e-Islami follower is screaming because he sees Muslim women going about unveiled and dancing in the ballroom. The middle class has a million things to worry about. Employment without a recommendation is not to be had, nor can children find admission in school or college without a word from someone in authority. Then there are those Bengali and Punjabi refugees who are tense because of their conflict with the locals. This struggle is as intense as the one between Hindu and Muslim in undivided India. Some people say that the last hope lies in a military revolution. There is one party, that is, the party of the refugees. This by far is the strangest of creatures in this country. It has come from India and is to be found in every city, town and village of the country, with Karachi serving as its headquarters. The special racket of this class is called culture.[11]

The succeeding novel *Aakhire Shab Ke Hamsafar* (ASKH), equally acclaimed, was about a group of highly charged idealists who struggle in the pre-Independence era. They are the victims of the vagaries of time, get disillusioned with life only to compromise their principles in India, Pakistan and Bangladesh, respectively. However, within the subtext ran a fascinating account of the contemporary historical consciousness, one that was not based on what the major schools of historiography could recount. As Asaduddin[12] writes:

> In describing the lives of Deepali, Raihan, Jahan Ara, Rosy and others, Hyder makes implicit comments on social mores and educational attainments of different communities at that point of time. While the girls in Hindu and Christian families have been shown as actively participating in different spheres of life, Muslim girls have been depicted as yet struggling between restrictive social norms and their half-articulated desire to achieve selfhood.

This is where the young Pakistanis in the Western part were introduced to the magic of Bengal, its rivers, culture and poetry in a well-crafted format. *ASKH* also proved to be hugely popular in Pakistan with many readers terming it as a more immediate novel as it was less complex than *AKD* in bringing together the strands of Indo-Pak history.

In *Gardish-e Rang-i-Chaman,* she explores an impressive range of subcultures, dying and flourishing, such as Anglo-Indians, Sufi *khanqahs*, street performers, prostitutes and the nouveau riche classes of the post-1947 subcontinent. Storytelling, therefore, is a statement on the concurrent eras of history and reminds the readers of what for instance, a Mughal princess would have gone through the post-1857 tribulations or how the farce of history twice repeated plays out in ordinary, everyday lives.

Agle Janam Mohay Bitya Na Kijo, a novella, ostensibly a work of fiction, can also be read as a sociological treatise of sorts, as it closely studied class exploitation. *AJMBNK* also presents an anthropological record of the dialects, music, vanishing crafts and groups of performers. Unlike several accounts of the fall of civilizations, this dealt with the death of a civilization, 'from below' to liberally apply this subaltern term. *AJMBNK* will prove to be a crucial text for historians and students of history in the future decades. The novella has already inspired a range of theatrical performances and feature films.

Hyder's popularity in Pakistan has been termed a 'back-handed compliment'[13] as her books were and perhaps remain bestsellers in Pakistan. It is a separate matter that most of them were pirated editions; and an unregulated publishing industry profiteered from their appeal. However, it is also metaphoric as to how history and a search for personal truths can remain an unstated activity in Pakistan.

By exploring the pain of partition; and reiterating that 'civilization' was a larger domain than a nation, Hyder made a point in Pakistan; and, in many ways to the limited Urdu readership in India as well. It was through her English translations and Hindi versions of the novels that this point was also made in India. As Sangari observes:

> Civilizations were not divisible into nations, national boundaries came and went; civilizations endured. Civilizational unity was perceived as made up of long-term and contemporary bonds, the textures of lives and memories and friendships.[14]

In the next section, we explore the emergence of separate identities, however problematic they might be and the inherent dilemmas and conflicts that were faced by the new citizens of Pakistan, especially those who migrated from the Punjab and United Provinces of British India.

Migration, History, the Shifting Sands of Identity

Pakistan's eminent historian K.K. Aziz is said to have remarked that Hyder displayed a firm grasp on history and *Kar-i-Jahan Daraz Hai* (KJDH) is a testament to that. Hyder's most experimental work was this autobiographical novel, which traced her genealogy from Central Asia and recounted her family and personal stories in a complex mosaic of style, technique and ever-changing ambience. Its third volume was published in 2000. As is the case of her novels, *KDJH* remains the best in its genre and the ability to expand the 'potential of experiencing life.'[15] Navigating through its interconnected stories, social commentary and ambience, the reader, slowly, becomes a part of the narrative; and starts viewing the world in a grand historical perspective and travels with its real characters.

We have to revert to *AKD* here, yet again. Kamal Raza, the archetypal Muslim refugee from Lucknow, after his migration to Karachi, wonders:

> This one has learnt only after Partition. The Hindu says when your culture and your beliefs are different, then you should go to Pakistan. What are you doing here? So these people came to Pakistan as 'mohajirs', but once here they learnt that while they had got rid of the Hindus, there was a different problem facing them. The mohajir felt frustrated both at Lahore, where there was the Punjabi, and Dhaka where there was the Bengali. Therefore, the mohajir made a beeline for Karachi. So Karachi is the mohajir centre.

To date, Hyder's words are true for what followed decades later, a movement of Mohajir identity and political struggle that is now a part of the mainstream political process of Pakistan with Karachi as its hub.

But the existential question of identity became a recurrent theme of Hyder's works. Her early novels treated these thorny issues in a romantic and idealistic manner. But her later works starting with the *magnum opus AKD* went deeper. In her later writings, with her subsequent return to India the themes of migration, identity and emergence of a new order echoed in most of the writings. Having been a migrant twice, and having lived on both sides, she had the unique experiential insight into the process of migration and what it entailed.

Housing Society explored the lives and tribulations of three migrant families and how their world is turned upside down in post-Partition Karachi. In this novel, two affluent families of yore become homeless, while the poor country cousin, through an alliance with the new political and economic classes, becomes a powerful business magnate (this aspect of Hyder's writing is explored in detail in the succeeding section). Another gem, *Patjhar ki Awaz* (The Sound of Falling Leaves) has a protagonist who meets an old acquaintance in a Lahore bazaar, bringing back memories of her teenage years in Delhi. The migrant has a new home, a new identity but there is existential angst as well the bitter turn of history.

In later works such as *Chandni Begum*, Hyder incisively traces the 'love-hate relationship between the emigré Muslims of Pakistan and their relatives left behind in India.'[16]; and needless to mention this is another theme that has not been delved into by most writers. For instance, the clichés on the plight of Indian Muslims was also treated by Hyder in *Chandni Begum* among others.

We conclude once again with what Kamal has to say in Karachi on the shifting sands of historical reality:

> Here's Karachi, the God-given state of Pakistan, the world's largest Islamic country and the capital of the world's fifth largest country, whose slums and refugee shelters can be counted among the world's marvels, especially those horrifying and filthy makeshift refuges that lie all around the resting place of the Quaid i Azam....In the Housing Society, some extremely beautiful bungalows have been built, which leads one to the conclusion that the Muslim middle class has never had it so good in its entire history. Here the new rich rule, with their new social order and their new principles.[17]

...And the New States, Classes and Sensibilities

Much like India where the initial reformism gave way to the politics of caste, elites and bureaucratic stronghold, the new state of Pakistan underwent quick transformations. A whole new set of classes emerged and fuelled by the bounties of evacuee property, a culture of consumerism became the norm. Our eternal Kamal therefore cries in *AKD*:

> Karachi is an ultra modern city. Every night its swank hotels and clubs bring to life a world of resplendent lights. Sociologists ought to investigate the quite fascinating birth, in just nine years, of this new class and its culture. The basis of this class is money: how to make it, how to get rich. While the river flows, leap in and swim because who knows, tomorrow it may run dry or it may start flowing in another direction.[18]

Raihan, the fiery revolutionary in *Aakhir-e Shab Ke Hamsafar* ends up as an industrial tycoon and tainted politician in the new Bangladesh; and the erstwhile idealists of this epic novel embrace the new realities. How ironic that we are also witnessing how the Communists in India are now attracting foreign investment while the ones in Pakistan are allies of the right wing parties. For instance, in *AKD* her statement rang true: the 'anti-British leftists' who made 'a beeline for England, deserting the toiling masses for whom their hearts used to bleed.'

More significantly, Hyder commented on what was happening in India as well. In *Gardish-e Rang-i-Chaman*, there is a legendary satire concerning Nigar Khanam, a prolific writer and more of a plagiarist and her sister, Shahwar Khanam. Through the two sisters who are stupidity incarnate, Hyder lambasts the colossal vulgarity of the *nouveau riche* for whom money is the magic which can buy everything — even culture, decency and grace. In their interaction with other people, the sisters always flaunt money, exult in their malfeasance and unregenerate wilfulness.

The archetypal characters of Nigar Khanum and her sister were not unusual, exaggerated as they might appear. In Pakistan, the *nouveau riche* had established themselves as new role models for many. However, the average middle class reader in Pakistan considered this to be a pertinent comment. Not that others were not writing about it but the fact that it came as a part of the composite panoramic whole of Hyder's novels was the unique feature.

A Chronicler of Our Times

Hyder was a grand chronicler—'a kind of Tolstoy in Urdu that our critics have ignored. When someone asked her in Bombay to write about the Iran-Iraq war she naturally began with the Arab conquest at Qadissiya.'[19]

KJDH is a testament to her status as an original chronicler whose style is original and connects with lay readers. We have noted *AKD*'s attempt to explore history in voices of everyday characters, invaders, scholars, lovers and common men and women of ancient and medieval India. Similarly, in *Gardish-e Rang-i-Chaman*, labelled as a semi-documentary novel by Hyder herself, there are chronicles of three kinds. At the broader level, it traces and records the post-1857 tragic lives of the Mughal descendants. But that is not what the novel is about. There are records of the Anglo-Indian contact and hybridization, something that William Dalrymple has painstakingly researched in *The White Mughals*.[20] Hyder had already explored this sub-set of the complex Indian universe, decades before Dalrymple's book was published. And then there is documentation of the Khanqahi system, its evolution and manifestations in the twentieth century.

Not content with fiction, Hyder's creativity in later years found an outlet in rediscovering the essentials of Indo-Muslim civilization. She dug out the first subcontinental novel, entitled *Nashtar*, authored by a late eighteenth century East India Company official, Hasan Shah. This invaluable script and its 1890 translation were lying neglected and Hyder translated and published it under the title *The Nautch Girl*, with overwhelming excitement that the modern novel was not the preserve of the English-speaking world. This discovery is lesser-known and (like many others) underrated. There were critics and sceptics, but she held her ground and had no patience for the self-flagellation which a post-colonial South Asian mind often indulges in. This is her outstanding contribution to the corpus of South Asian and world literature. Posterity will treat it as a major landmark in the evolution of subcontinental literature.[21]

This is also where Hyder stood head and shoulders above her contemporaries and successors as she explored the complexities and contradictions of the history of Muslims in India. The ethos and construction of Indo-Muslim identity therefore has to be composite and not communal.

As pointed out, Hyder's vision has been validated by several views on history. For instance, Irfan Habib's view, 'that the 'idea' of India as a cultural unity was not a modern secular invention but a much older one, that it was a product of conquest (Mauryan emperor Asoka's inscriptions in 250 BC) and travellers' visions or a view from outside (Alberuni's *Kitab al-Hind* in the eleventh century), while the affect-laden idea of India as a distinctive composite culture or a common heritage emerged from immigrants and converts (such as Amir Khusrau's *Nuh Sipihr* in 1318).'[22]

Thus Hyder's emphasis on the fact that the history of the Indo-Pak subcontinent is a narrative of travellers where eras overlap, merge and are generally concurrent. Hence *AKD* shows a repetitive sequence of characters over two dozen centuries. And her autobiographical novel, *KJDH* invokes this view as a personal and civilizational account. The ancient and the medieval 'culture', 'whether Arab, European, or Indian was a cross-national traffic, always conflict-riven, yet always familiar with, affected or influenced by, and aware of 'other' cultures, and at times almost cosmopolitan.'[23]

In such a context, her vision therefore is multi-religious directed by an unending process of change, with the old influencing the new and the new invoking the old. Therefore, there it does not subscribe to an 'insider's hegemonic assimilation' or to an 'outsider's imperious hegemony'.[24]

In *AKD*, the narrative starts with the convergence of Greek, Vedic, Buddhist, Persian, Bhakta and later 'the hybridization both of the British — from innkeeper to nabob — and the Indian — from feudal aristocracy to the colonial middle class. In each period, there is an interplay of different epistemologies, languages, and literatures.'

In this process of recounting history, Hyder demolishes

the stereotypes that emerge from the particularism of religious identities. Neither is this a propaganda tool that invokes the *One India* stereotype. There is immense complexity that confronts the communal versions of history and the Partition saga. The nationalism of Pakistani or the Indian state becomes a secondary issue. The religious or communal narrative also becomes a constructed reality. And the reader can see through it, feel with the author and flow with her grand sweep.

Kamal therefore echoes the popular sentiment of educated Pakistanis in the 1950s and perhaps 58 years later too:

> Islam! Islam has had a rough ride here. If the Pakistani team begins to lose at cricket, Islam falls into danger. Every problem in the world is ultimately reduced to this word, Islam. Other Muslim countries resent the fact that the sole contractors of Islam are these people from Pakistan. Everything is being upholstered with narrow-mindedness. Music, art, civilization, learning and literature, they are all being viewed from the perspective of the Mullah. Islam, which was like a rising river whose majestic flow had been augmented by so many tributaries to turn it into a cascading force, has been reduced to a muddy stream which is being enclosed from all four sides with high walls.[25]

In fact, the current dangers of extremism were not missed by Hyder in 1959 when Kamal articulates this common sentiment:

> The joke is that those who raise the slogan of Islam in the loudest voices have nothing to do with the philosophy of this religion. The only thing they know is that the Muslims ruled Spain for 800 years, that they ruled Bharat for a thousand years, while the Ottomans kept East Europe subjugated for centuries. Apart from imperialism, no mention is ever made of Islam's great humanism, nor is it considered necessary to speak about the open-heartedness of Arab seers, Iranian poets and Indian Sufis. There is no interest in the philosophy of Ali and Hussain. Islam is being presented as a violent religion and a violent way of life.[26]

AKD has also been termed as a means of 'reclaiming the subcontinent from the violence that had torn it apart, bulling it into a consoling civilizational *lounge duree* in which the repeated destructions of the composite culture of Awadh (in 1846, 1857, 1947) could be accommodated to the recurrent rise and fall of kingdoms' (Hasan, ibid). In doing so, Hyder also unwittingly follows Ibn Khaldun's philosophy of history by mourning for the past that is gone and articulating a vision for the future. Therefore for the Indo-Pakistan readers, *AKD* brings forth the 'civilizational' consciousness that asks for a 'loyalty that was different from older loyalties of region, religion, or language; a loyalty to the idea of civilization that was wider, deeper, and more compelling than its division into separate nations' (Hasan, ibid).

Even in her last Urdu novel, *Gardish-e Rang-i-Chaman*, the depiction of faith and conversion of a colourful card sharper is a fascinating study. It joins the narrative back to the Bhakti movement descriptions in *AKD*. The major sub-plot of *Gardish-e Rang-i-Chaman*, brings forth a modern Sufi and twentieth-century Khanqah practices that are not different from the popular face of Islam in Pakistan too. The vast majority of Pakistanis are not adherents to the puritan movements that exist in the annals of corporate media but in the quintessential Sufi vision and reverence for *dargahs*. But in Hyder's account, this narrative becomes another point of reference for popular history. Such an Islam is beyond the Hindu-Muslim divide and is independent of political nationalism.

Hyder's nuanced and highly sophisticated vision was not easily apparent to the officialdom or state-sponsored literary critics in Pakistan. Hyder writes in her introduction to the 1988 edition of *AKD* about one such critic who raised a storm:

> Siraj Rizvi was somebody about whom it is said (I don't know how true it is) that he tried once to gain favours in a personal matter from a Brigadier who was appointed at that time [1959] as a sort of 'Literary Overseer' under the Martial Law. Siraj

Rizvi had published a long and very improper essay against my novel, which was published in the daily *Jang*, Karachi (in which he had also revealed that the author was the real niece of the Indian Communist Dr. Rashid Jahan)...[27]

And, Hyder was aware of the permanent connection that she made with Pakistan:

Noon Meem Rashid's view that *Aag ka Darya* was published in the expired time did not come true because during the last thirty years, the most saleable book in Pakistan after Iqbal and Faiz is *Aag ka Darya*. Numerous unauthorized editions of this book have been published and the irony is that the front pages of these editions invariably bear the statement 'rights of publication are protected in favour of the author'.[28]

The sheer humanity of her vision therefore struck the Pakistani reader; as this was in sharp contrast to what the state wanted him/her to believe. For Hyder, the divisions of insider and outsider were irrelevant. She was more concerned about identifying the ceaseless cycles of greed and hate that disrupt the world's beauty. Her scrutiny was also the thinking man's vision.

Conclusion

Hyder's remarks in her acceptance speech at the Jnanpith Award function (1991) were telling:

My concern for civilizational values about which I continue writing may sound naive, woolly-headed and simplistic. But then, perhaps, I am like that little bird which foolishly puts up its claws, hoping that it will stop the sky from falling.[29]

So what is her legacy, after all? Is it just another woolly-headed, quaint vision of a secular India? Such a cliché will not do justice to her magnificent writings. It is beyond the labels of 'secular', 'Muslim', 'Indo-Muslim' and so on. Her works are arresting for their complexity and richness, of the inextricability of the Muslim and non-Muslim cultures in terms of literature, poetry and music, and the forces of history like colonization and independence of the subcontinent. But above all, they leave a legacy of humanism and the primordial human quest for love, belonging and search for enlightenment. This is what most of her characters end up doing in the vast maze of history and time.

Ironically in her long literary career she proved her early critics wrong, especially high profile critics such as Ismat Chughtai who had accused her of being bourgeois and removed from the people of India. Her continuous narrations of the subcontinent's myriad social history remain unmatched. And, her characters, victims of the vagaries of Time and rulers' history, bear eloquent testimonies on societal modes of class exploitation. But these characters are not part of an ideological or a deterministic script. They are continuations, manifestations of the history; and relate to the present-day reader.

The eminent Urdu writer Enver Sajjad, held[30] that Hyder challenged the kings' history in Pakistan and warned her compatriots of the dangerous seeds that the new bourgeois of Pakistan was planting in the new homeland. Whether this was the case with illegal raids on evacuee property, abuse of Islam, mishandling of the Bengali cultural separateness or denuding history, she unwittingly became an oracle of events to come. Her art was such that she said all this in the context of history — that was grander and larger than the post-Pakistan linear versions. Hyder therefore assumed an important position in the collective consciousness of Urdu readers.

This is why, Hyder, till her last, remained a unique bond between India and Pakistan. She was a regular visitor to Pakistan that was her second home in actual terms. Her family, friends and admirers were in a large number that never distanced her from the country. Like her characters, she travelled, migrated and re-migrated and became a chronicler of our times, not as a historian but as a fiction writer. In the process she defied the label of being anti-Pakistan.

There is nothing in her huge corpus of works that can be

remotely termed as 'anti-Pakistan'. Her move to India may have been propelled by the controversies but it remained a personal decision. Hyder's re-migration to India was an after-thought as she originally moved to the United Kingdom[31]. However, she eventually landed in India where luminaries like Nehru and Azad welcomed her with open arms. Pakistani officialdom and rival authors and critics may have wronged her; the readers in Pakistan remained loyal to her and gave her the recognition that writers cannot do without.

For years Hyder will live as the diva of Urdu fiction. Immensely respected and widely read in the country that in her view was not the 'other' but another facet of the rich, complex historical legacy of the subcontinent. In the words of Mustansar Hussain Tarar,[32] she created her own cult, a sort of a literary creed that kept all her readers fascinated and faithful throughout.

Hyder was truly a dual citizen in an age where acrimonies of Partition and officialdom have made it impossible to hold concurrent citizenships. But, Qurratulain Hyder, even defied that; and proved that like her vision, her belonging could be concurrent and beyond the accepted definitions!

References

1. The authors interviewed are Dr. Enver Sajjad and Mustansar Hussain Tarar. In addition, Mr. Afzaal Ahmad of Sang-i-Meel Publications, Lahore, Pakistan was interviewed on the telephone. Inputs from a small sample of readers were collected for the arguments developed in this paper. Thanks are also due to Sadia Dehlvi, India for anecdotes on Pakistani visitors rushing to meet Qurratulain Hyder during their visits to Delhi.

2. It is somewhat disquieting that Hyder's self-translation of *AKD* as *River of Fire* did not become according to Khushwant Singh, 'the rage in English that it is in Urdu'. Singh added that 'she'll have only herself to blame'. This is also a view held by others as the English version was abridged and could not do justice to the depth of the original in Urdu.

3. Javed Akhtar, Indian poet and lyricist's audio tribute to Hyder published by the Rediff website.
4. Asif Farrukhi, 'The Diva of Urdu Fiction', *Dawn*, 26 August, 2007.
5. Comparison between the two great elegists in Urdu poetry–Anis and Dabeer. This has been a favourite theme in early Urdu literary criticism. Hyder mocked this in several interviews published in, Syed Aamir Sohail *et al.*, *Qurratulain Haider — Khasoosi Mutal'a*, Multan Arts Forum, 2003.
6. Hyder in a 1998 interview given to NDTV's Radhika Bordia http://www.ndtv.com/convergence/ndtv/story.aspx?id=NEWEN20070023369&ch=8/21/2007%205:42:00%20PM
7. H.M. Seervai, *Partition of India: Legend and Reality*; monograph in the Constitutional History of India, 1989.
8. For some engaging discussion in the Indian context see, Partha Chatterjee, 'History and the Domain of the Popular'. Available on line at http://www.india-seminar.com/2003/522/522%20partha%20chatterjee.htm
9. While proponents of history from below and the French Annales school of historians have considered themselves part of social history, it is seen as a much broader movement among historians in the development of historiography.
10. Translated by the author from Urdu, *Aag ka Darya*. Sang-i-Meel Publications, 2007 edition, p. 128.
11. Translation found in 'The Vision of Qurratulain Hyder' by Khalid Hasan, *The Friday Times*, December 2008, Vanguard Publications, Lahore, Pakistan.
12. M. Asaduddin, 'The Exiles Return: Qurratulain Hyder's Art of Fiction', *Manushi*.
13. Editorial, *Daily Times*, Thursday, 17 January 2008.
14. Kumkum Sangari, 'Qurratulain Hyder's Aag ka Darya', *Muse India*, Issue 14, July-August 2007, p. 2.
15. C. M. Naim, *Annual of Urdu Studies*, Vol. 1, 1981 p. 107. Available on line at http://dsal.uchicago.edu/books/annualofurdustudies/pager.html?objectid=PK2151.A6152_1_113.gif
16. M. Asaduddin, 'The Exiles Return: Qurratulain Hyder's Art of Fiction', *Manushi*.
17. Translation found in *The Vision of Qurratulain Hyder* by Khalid

Hasan, op. cit.

18. Translation found in *The Vision of Qurratulain Hyder* by Khalid Hasan, op. cit.

19. Ibid.

20. William Dalrymple, *White Mughals: Love and Betrayal in Eighteenth-century India.*, Harper Perennial, New Edition (2 May 2003). Set in and around Hyderabad at the beginning of the nineteenth century, *White Mughals* tells the story of the improbably romantic love affair and marriage between James Achilles Kirkpatrick, an East India Company official, and Khair-un-Nisa, a Hyderabadi princess. The novel explores 'cultural intermingling and hybridity that defines both eastern and western cultures, and a convincing rejection of religious intolerance and ethnic essentialism'. (Jerry Brotton —This text refers to an out of print or unavailable edition of this title).

21. In my meeting with her, she elucidated how modern this novel is in terms of its characterization, mood and technique. There were traces in it of what was to be known at least a century later as the stream of consciousness technique.

22. Kumkum Sangari, 'Qurratulain Hyder's Aag ka Darya,' op. cit.

23. Ibid.

24. Ibid.

25. Translation found in *The Vision of Qurratulain Hyder* by Khalid Hasan, op. cit.

26. Translation found in *The Vision of Qurratulain Hyder* by Khalid Hasan, op. cit.

27. Foreword to *Aag ka Darya*, Qurratulain Hyder, New Delhi, 21 December 1988.

28. Foreword to *Aag ka Darya*, op. cit.

29. C. M. Naim, translation Outlook India Web version, 21 August 2007, Delhi.

30. Interview with the author.

31. Hyder in a conversation with the author remarked that while she loved Oxbridge and London, she decided that her sources for literary inspiration rooted in the subcontinental culture and history were missing.

32. Interview with the author.

6

Post-colonialism and Marginality in the Fiction of Ismat Chughtai, Khadija Mastur and Qurratulain Hyder

FATIMA RIZVI

Urdu fiction, dating back to approximately a little over a century, is relatively young compared with its English counterpart from whom it has been largely derived.[1] Yet, having a ready made model to draw from, it evolved quickly, thereby compelling its readers to alter their tastes and accept changes and shifts in subject, tone and technique, much sooner than the foster parent had done. Faizi's fantastic, romantic, fairy tale, *Dastan-e-Amir Hamza*[2] gave way to the sociological and didactic fiction of Pandit Ratan Nath Sarshar, Abdul Haleem Sharar and Maulvi Nazir Ahmed, whose novels were soon succeeded by the realistic fiction of the Marxist, Progressive writers. The dramatic element of the Persian *dastan* or *quissa*[3] was replaced by the indigenous 'modern' novel of the nineteenth century (Osterheld 2001:27), which eventually paved the way for the realistic and the experimental novel of the twentieth century. The political, socio-economic, cultural and military upheavals of the twentieth century wrought a rapid alteration in the depiction of life in the novel. The cataclysm of partition followed by independence was inadvertently represented in the fiction of these years.

The widely attended first Soviet Writers' Congress (1934) was a watershed that marked the role of responsible writers and intellectuals in a rapidly changing world. The proponents including Andrey Zhdanov and Maxim Gorky popularized social realism. (Ahmed, Talat 2009: 43) The writer's purpose was to serve as an instrument of change, arousing readers to react to their surroundings. In India, the *Anjuman Tarraqui Pasand Musanifeen-e-Hind* (All India Progressive Writers' Association, AIPWA), was formally inaugurated in 1936, at a widely attended conference in Lucknow; Premchand was its first president. This has been one of the most significant literary organizations of the twentieth century, created for the propagation of Communist principles. The initiators of the Progressive Writers' Movement (PWM) including Munshi Premchand, Mulk Raj Anand, Faiz Ahmad Faiz and Ali Sardar Jafri, had strong Marxist socialist leanings and sought to promote social awareness and propagate modernity. The Progressive Writers' Movement was also the watershed that marked the beginning of contemporary Urdu fiction written by women, undermining most kinds of gender distinctions (Pietrangelo 1983: 164). Though the movement gradually became increasingly politicized (Coppola 1994: 50), the art of Urdu fiction came to embody all the connotations that the word 'progressive' might carry with it. Sajjad Zaheer's manifesto of the Progressive writers (drafted in London, 1935) claimed that they would aim at an authentic and realistic portrayal of the 'turmoil and conflict of a new society' as against the spiritualism, idealism, emotional exhibitionism and the lack of rationality in the literature of the previous two centuries. (Russell 1992: 204) Urdu fiction, including that by the Progressive writers, during the crucial pre-independence years was not concerned with India's struggle for independence: it projected realistic, societal situations through linear, chronological narratives. Nevertheless, the stories were set against the backdrop of the struggle for independence which was indeed so large that it could not be ignored. (Ahmed 1992: 118) The concept of nationalism was intermingled with a sense of mourning for the barbarism and willingness of a people to give up their civilizational unity in the wake of Partition. (Ahmed 1992: 119) 'Urdu fiction in the decade after Partition was inordinately concerned with the horror stories of the rioting and the heartbreaking miseries of displacement.' (Farooqi 2008: xxx) 'Realism' as a fictional device was rather popular, but the Progressive writers were more concerned with narratives of individual loss and pain of displacement and the atrocities that attended it. (Farooqi 2008: xxx) Progressive women writers propagated modernity among the Muslim masses and pioneered an educational renaissance, especially for women. Their stories were largely concerned with the struggle of women to find an identity in a time of flux when they felt disadvantaged through various kinds of marginalization — primarily through being born as the second sex and furthermore, through economic deprivation, social and class restrictions and dogma that alienated professional groups.

Ismat Chughtai, Khadija Mastur and Qurratulain Hyder are dominant writers of modern Urdu fiction, largely responsible for its unmistakable realism. Chughtai and Mastur's concerns are in keeping with the particular creed they profess as writers of the Movement. Hyder remains politically unaligned. She stands apart from her Progressive contemporaries, both, ideologically as well as through depiction of social class and milieu, emerging as an ambassador of *l'art pour l'art* dictum of Gautier, giving priority to aesthetics and the imaginative spirit. Time and again, she has been the subject of derision of Progressive writers like Chughtai for creating upper crust protagonists who appear ensconced in their own, small, sophisticated world, rapidly being devoured by that of the teeming masses.[4] (Kumar and Sadique 2000: 123) Nevertheless, though she may not be considered Progressive in the sense of the Marxist, socialist manifesto, her works are tinged with eclecticism, humanism and modernity and reveal a deep-rooted philosophical perception of the meanderings of the river of life.

Hyder's novels are largely a bourgeois representation of economically fortunate women, who interact with the deprived. However, the larger class struggles, the transformations at the national level and personal experiences of her protagonists, in a hostile environment, lend an element of fatalism to her works. Thus, Deepali Sen's evolution is marked with determinants that help her evolve into a person who learns to accept the inevitability of change. Shamman and Aaliya, iconoclastic Progressive heroines, represent the altering visage of the new woman, who emerges more confident and adaptable in a rapidly altering social scenario. Yasmin Majid, Sita, Rashke Qamar, Motibai and Jamilun, among others, reveal the eternally struggling face of the marginalized woman. This paper attempts to analyse the foregrounded habitations of marginalized womanhood within the changing face of the emergent spirit of nationalism in select texts by Chughtai and Mastur, while drawing comparisons between these and representative texts by Hyder. The larger struggle for independence has Chughtai and Mastur emphasize the role played by the woman as a harbinger of change but Hyder emphasizes the plight of the de-centred centre. Economic and land dispossession under the Zamindari Abolition Act led to the creation, overnight, of a new marginalized group that hopelessly struggled against the unexpected.

Ismat Chughtai (1915 – 91), Urdu's pioneering feminist writer, professed allegiance with the ideals propagated by the All India Progressive Writers' Movement early in her student days. (McLain 2001: 144) Chughtai was an ardent admirer of Dr. Rashid Jahan, a gynaecologist by profession and the only woman contributor to the *Angare* collection,[5] the publication of which catalyzed the formation of the All India Progressive Writers' Association. (Russell 1992: 205) Like Rashid Jahan, Chughtai stresses the biological human self and as Priyamvada Gopal asserts, she goes a step further and claims that the woman can actually take pleasure in physical contact.(Gopal 2005: 69) Chughtai remarks that the thinking of the Progressive writers 'projected the truth of the down-to-earth realities of life.' (Kumar and Sadique 2000: 131) The works of Rashid Jahan, Ismat Chughtai, Khadija Mastur and Razia Sajjad Zaheer, among others, are largely concerned with what it is to be modern, not merely as women but as 'professionals, as middle class, as Muslims, as Indians and particularly as intellectuals with an investment in social change.'(Gopal 2005: 68) Her investment in social change is combined with a keen-eyed observation of the minutiae of daily domestic lives of women. Chughtai's oeuvre stands testimony to her unbridled spirit as it simultaneously reveals her forward thinking, modern outlook: above all, her works are fraught with the truth and virtuosity of experience and 'faith in (her) own convictions'. (Kumar and Sadique 2000: 131) Chughtai's realism revolves round the domestic lives of the ordinary people of Uttar Pradesh and Northern India. She writes with the intent of throwing light on the day-to-day lives of marginalized ordinary masses, especially women, encouraging the need for a paradigm shift in perspective and the adoption of a modern, socialist approach. Chughtai promotes freedom of cognitive, emotional and linguistic expression. While she is decidedly against the portrayal of the imperialists' lives, she is also unable to empathize with the sufferings of the peasant class and is better able to 'feel the pain of the middle and the lower middle class'. (Kumar and Sadique 2000: 131) Her liberalism, her preoccupation with Freudian psychoanalysis and human sexuality and freedom of expression led to a fallout with the Progressives who gradually narrowed down the scope of their writings to that similar to realist, Soviet, socialist literature and the portrayal of the plight of the peasant class; reconciliation came about only after several years had lapsed. (McLain 2001:145)

Varis Alvi, commenting on her art, remarks that Chughtai 'come(s) across as an insider — the young girls, women, maidservants and men she wrote about were very much a part of our households. All that she lay before us was so familiar that, like an old picture hanging on the wall at home, we hardly noticed it.' (Kumar and Sadique 2000: 209). Shamman, in *Terhi Lakeer*, (1947) or *The Crooked Line*, (2003) whose life loosely symbolizes Chughtai's own, is the product of an altering ambience in an archetypal Indian, Muslim, middle class household. Her infancy and upbringing are dotted with such emotional experiences of neglect as render a psychological imbalance in what is considered acceptable behaviour in a child. As an adolescent, she is exposed to a larger secular culture at school and college: finally, as a young woman, Shamman has learnt, like her creator, to be guided by her own sovereign spirit. Chughtai focuses on the female biological self while portraying the inner reality of various phases of psychosomatic, emotional and intellectual growth of her protagonist, from whose point of view the story has been narrated. Shamman's forced tearing apart from her wet-nurse whose love affair is discovered creates in her a longing for the warmth of the female body which in turn perpetrates an attraction for her throw-ball instructor, Miss Charan at the English Mission school. Shamman is 'rescued' from Miss Charan by the school principal, after perceptible indiscretions in their relationship are discovered. It is not till she is consciously advised by a friend that it is fashionable to indulge in heterosexual relations at the co-education college she attends, that Shamman learns of the attractions of the opposite sex. Ironically, she finds her interactions with men closer to her age nauseating and seeks solace in the companionship with the ageing Rai sahib, her friend's father. Shamman feels devastated by his death and finally marries an Irishman, Ronnie Taylor, a captain in the British army. Differences erupt between them because of their different cultures, following which, the marriage breaks up. Shamman perceives the significance of her own Indianness and realizes that a permanent marital partnership is not possible with the colonizer. In her narrative, Chughtai highlights the growing awareness of the need for Western education among Muslim masses, the sense of national pride which was fast taking root in the psyche of the people through the emergence of a hybrid national culture (a confluence of the Hindu and the Muslim cultures), and the changed society that had emerged as a product of the stratification of Western and Marxist political ideologies. A democratic and free India generated a need for freedom of personal and social spaces and freedom to make one's own choice in matters of personal requirements. Shamman's breaking away from accepted social codes of conduct is an affirmation of the free spiritedness that evolves from individual experience.

Speaking about her intent, Chughtai remarked: 'I projected a female character in my stories who refused to live by old values, that is, the false ideas of shame and honour, one who was not prepared to sacrifice her life for the sake of a mere show of so-called respectability of her family or 'khandan'.' (Kumar and Sadique 2000: 129,130) Shamman emerges as the progressive 'new woman' who assimilates the old value system of her family with the modern ideals of a new order and is guided by her own spirit. In the introduction to the novel, Tahira Naqvi compares *Terhi Lakeer* with Simone de Beauvoir's *The Second Sex* (1949), averring that there are certain portions in Chughtai's novel that seem to be 'fictionalized prefigurations of Beauvoir's description and analysis of childhood playacting and fantasy....' (Naqvi 1995: viii) The involved narrative 'reveals the fault lines in psychoanalysis, and shares contiguities with the kinds of rewritings of psychoanalysis done by feminist psychoanalysts.' (Patel 2001: 351, 352)

Khadija Mastur (1927-83), one of the youngest members of the Progressive Writers' Movement (PWM), is well known for her depiction of the economic and domestic trials of the lower middle class and the modernity she propagates as a follower of the Progressive creed. '... she is among the last of the class of writers who gave to Urdu fiction a sense of clarity of purpose and design, and in particular brought into focus the issues surrounding women's roles in the Muslim society of pre-partition India and, later, Pakistan.'(Naqvi 1998: xi) Her most popular novel *Aangan*, (1956) or *Inner Courtyard* (2001) foregrounds the psychological and emotional development of the protagonist Aaliya, and the family's stoic resistance to the rigours of poverty, against the backdrop of India's struggle for independence. Religionization of pre-Independence Indian politics and alignments of characters with different political parties become reasons for serious conflict within the family and outside. The novel also throws light on the predicament of the women of the neighbourhood in the shape of the taunts and jibes aimed at their acts of rebellion. Amma's callous remarks regarding the widowed Kusum didi's elopement and return to her father's home are a warning to Tehmina apa, her friendship with Kusum didi and her clandestine romance with Safdar bhai. 'Unbelievable shamelessness! First she runs away then she comes back to torment her parents and burn coals of fire on their breast. I ask you, could she find no other place to stay? I'll break her legs and throw them away if she so much as casts her eyes towards this house!' (Mastur 2001: 44) Haji saheb's daughter-in-law, who has eloped only three years after the death of her husband, becomes a subject of ire. 'The vengeance of God upon us, the wanton! She should be buried alive if she's ever found,' says amma, and Kariman bua responds: 'Indeed we live in the fourteenth century. There was a time when widows of thirteen or fourteen would live out their lives with nothing in view except the grave, never casting so much as a glance at any living creature. But all that is over now. Our elders spoke truly when they said that in the fourteenth century the cow would eat dung and the virgin would demand a bridegroom.' (Mastur 2001: 191)

Remarks such as these, point to the narrowness of moral codes binding on women. However, the discussion soon takes on communal overtones, since an impious reference to the cow could lead to a riot in the current time of disharmony. Najma Phuphi's and Chammi's marriages evoke the frustration encountered by women through mismatches. However, unlike Tehmina apa who suffers in silence till her suicide, both women seek divorce or separation as an assertion of their individualities in their attempt to alleviate their respective predicaments. Aaliya emerges as Mastur's new woman, confident in her capacity to support her mother financially, as a son would. Later, in Pakistan, her refusal to marry Safdar, who vows to give up his socialism in lieu of his export business, once he receives his license, can be viewed as a triumph of the 'progressive' woman who is able to cast aside her personal need for love and comfort and opt instead for the larger social cause of the ordinary, deprived citizens, in the shape of refugees from across the border. Aaliya's emancipation from the manacles of individual needs parallels India's freedom from the imperialists and the creation of Pakistan. It can also be viewed as a vindication of the disappointments of the other women in the novel. Severed from the traditional home through migrational displacement, Aaliya is faced with the dilemma of reconstructing herself socially, economically and culturally, in an alien land in the cold discomfort of the large house procured for them by her maternal uncle.

Qurratulain Hyder's *Aakhir-e shab ke Humsafar* (1979) or *Fireflies in the Mist* (1994) traces the growth and evolution of the protagonist Deepali Sarkar, foregrounding the troubled political scenario of twice-partitioned Bengal. The adolescent Deepali strikes the reader as an alter ego of both Shamman and Aaliya, but although she has strong Communist leanings and actively participates in the so-called 'terrorist' or 'revolutionary' activities of the earlier Communist leaders in the overthrow of the British, she learns, in time, that the comrades of Bengal along with her own endeavours would be crushed by both, the British as well as the Congress, which was emerging as the voice of the Indian citizen. Deepali's fiery adolescence gives way to a sober youth, also through disappointment in her brief romance with Comrade Rehan Ahmed, the dashing and enigmatic guerilla Communist leader. She finally migrates to Trinidad and marries the wealthy, uninteresting expatriate, Dr. Sen, through the efforts of her uncle.

Terhi Lakeer and *Aangan* are *bildungsromans* that encourage modernity. Chughtai and Mastur have ensured situations that focus on the social and emotional evolution of their female protagonists promulgating Marxist tendencies. It is symptomatic that both women evolve into individuals who, empowered by education, are capable of supporting themselves and their families, independent of male support. Their breaking free from long-standing, accepted codes of conduct at a time when India won freedom marks the triumph of the woman in a traditionally insular society.

The writers have left their individual imprints upon their novels. Shamman's is a story narrated through a series of tactile images that stress the biological facet in the process of growing up, in addition to the psychosomatic. 'The word 'wife' made Shamman shudder. It seemed to her that there were dozens of babies and thousands of worries sucking on Noori's body like leeches.' (Chughtai 1995: 171) On the other hand, Aaliya's story highlights the psychological-emotional aspects of her temperament in the growing up process, while accenting sensuality. 'His face was flushed and his eyes fixed on her with a painful intensity. She bowed her head at that moment, she felt that if she failed to find shelter from his gaze something unspeakable would happen.' (Mastur 2001: 115) Mastur also recreates the minutiae of environmental sights and sounds. The political goings-on form the background of both the stories but while in Mastur's *Aangan* they take the form of reported incidents, Chughtai's Shamman grows up in the midst of the reforms that are either the by-products of a larger, escalating political order or may have led to it.

Hyder's novel, distanced from the struggle for independence through the passage of time, plunges into the real politick of the struggle for independence, the people's uprisings against the British and against the zamindars and the capitalists. Rosie Bannerjee's active involvement in the bombing of the British police station, her consequent hospitalization and imprisonment and the encouragement she receives from fellow women nationalist supporters, the active involvement of comrade Rehan Ahmed earlier in the surreptitious Communist Party activities and later in the discussions with the Muslim League and the Congress, are grim reminders of the tumult of the age. Deepali Sarkar's lineage makes her an obvious choice for the comrades who are in search of daring, unsuspicious, willing candidates who will work as spies or radical activists. Deepali's reference to Ranadive and his declaration that the struggle was the people's war, to the activities abroad, of the Communist International, and to Nehru and the divide between the Communist Party and the Congress, indicate her complicity and involvement in political affairs.(Hyder 2004: 169)

Hyder's *bildungsroman* records the various experiences that shape the life of her protagonist without ensuring that the experience that the protagonist gains is measured in terms of positives. Deepali learns to cope with her particular predicament through a stoic stance inculcated by a deprived childhood. Her Bengali zamindar family that has lost its fortunes through the common tendency to live beyond its means, and her uncle, Dinesh Sarkar has been hanged by the British for involvement in a terrorist case. Aaliya is born into the family of an erstwhile jagirdar from the United Province. Both have heard of the legendary wealth of their families and strive to accept the meagre remains. Nevertheless, both derive their fortitude and stoicism from their fathers' sense of dignity and self-respect. Chughtai popularized the *begumati zuban* (i.e. the language commonly used by the women of the household) and retained her sense of humour in spite of never losing sight of her socialist intent. Mastur highlights the multiple points of view of women in her novels; her texts, like Hyder's, are enriched with inter-textual references to ghazals, folksongs and popular folklore.

Aakhir-e-shab ke Hamsafar also represents the sufferings

of several women who inhabit the margins of the class-ridden, Indian social scenario: like the many characters of a dastan, Hyder's protagonists play their different parts, evoking relevant questions as regards the larger change taking place at the national level. One of the sub-plots of the novel deals with the talented and ambitious dancer Yasmin Majid, the daughter of a poor maulvi, Maulana Majidullah. Yasmin's ambition transports her to London where she is preyed upon by a fashion designer, Gerald Belmont, who marries and then abandons her, in favour of a male partner, leaving her to fend for herself and their daughter. Yasmin's destitution leads her to relinquish custodianship of her only child who grows up with her grandmother in the Catholic faith, disliking her mother. Yasmin's abortive remarriage and her many emotional traumas and embarrassments lead her to commit suicide. The novel concludes with a concert commemorating Yasmin's skills, as part of the efforts of a young nation acknowledging its great artists. Deepali, who has travelled back to Bangladesh to be a part of the concert, reads the 'glossy brochure' circulated by the Yasmin Majid Memorial Committee which describes Yasmin as 'another celebrated daughter of Bangladesh, the splendorous dancer and poetess, the late Madame Yasmin Majid Belmont.' (Hyder 1994: 307) Deepali visualizes the futility of the grand concert, for Yasmin's diary is ample proof of the neglect incurred by the talented dancer from erstwhile East Bengal who was disowned by her family, disregarded by her country and looked down upon by the Westerner. Yasmin becomes a prototype for independent women who follow their heart's desire and meet with disappointment. Her actions are redeemed by Nasira Najmus Saher who observes: 'The maulvis did not forgive Yasmin for her waywardness. But thousands of Muslim girls were raped here during the War of Liberation. Countless had to become street-walkers. Not a single maulvi of the Islamic world protested against the horrible situation.' (Hyder 1994: 329) Deepali terms her a 'real rebel of Nazrul Islam.'[6] (Hyder 1994: 329)

Giribala's predicament bespeaks the quandary of the impoverished, young, attractive girl who is rescued from the lasciviousness of Nawab Qamrul Zaman Chowdhry of Arjumand Manzil, where she serves as a maid in his mother's establishment. Later, she is rehabilitated and converted to Christianity as Esther Giribala by the active missionaries in the land of the infidels. Her marriage to the Reverend Paul Banerjee, provides respectability to her existence but she remains always a passive recipient of the tricks of fate, unwavering in her selfless service to her husband and humanity and her stoicism against her daughter Rosie's acts of rebellion. Rosie's belligerent nationalism, her conversion to the old faith of Hinduism after her marriage with the business magnate Basant Sanyal, in an attempt to shed her poverty, raises pertinent questions on the viability of the many conversions: the imperiousness of the Biswases reveals the pompousness caused by the stratification of the Hindu caste system with a religion free of such hierarchical order.

Strife-ridden Bengal, the land of the Sundarbans of the Nawab Nazims, the Bengali babus and the Christian converts, figures as the political nexus of British India, the state that initiated politically motivated Communist activities against the British and later, witnessed blood-baths in the name of liberation. Deepali feels nauseated by the devastation the war of independence has wrought; she is filled with a sense of shame at the ease with which Rehan Ahmed has slid into his new role of master of Arjumand Manzil. She pleads with him: 'Ever since I have seen you in your new role... I have been hoping earnestly that this is also part of your play-acting. Please tell me, please, that you are still in disguise. That you have really not turned into all that you had once rebelled against.' (Hyder 1994: 321) Later, Rehan remarks: 'Look, for long years I went from pillar to post in united Bengal. Served terms in jail. Remained underground.... I grew tired. Then I got a chance to have some rest and comfort... It's as simple as that.' (Hyder 1994: 331) Perhaps, the only act that associates Rehan Ahmed with his Communist past is his marriage to the poverty-stricken Zohra, who is perhaps more of an embarrassment to him than a companion. Deepali's purchase of the exclusive woven Bootedar Balucher saris with a sense of satisfaction at their affordability stands in ironic contrast with her initial act of selling similar heirlooms from the old, prized collection that once belonged to her mother, for the cause of the comrades.

Hyder's Progressive contemporaries emphasize the positives of modernity and socialism, but she concentrates on the realistic patterns of existence, emphasizing the dichotomies and ironies that provide the various hues to humanity. She balances the plight of the capitalists and the zamindars with that of the masses, in the ensuing carnage; the message rings clear that the Nawab Nazims did not deserve their deaths any more than the others who lost their lives. The animal-like, in-cognitive cries of Mala, Jahan Ara's personal maid, bear testimony to their attachment and point at the brutal killings in the household. Rehan's rags-to-riches story leaves the reader unsympathetic towards his past affliction; perhaps only his orphaned, disinherited mother is pitiable for the quality of her life and her untimely death.

Aaliya, Deepali and Yasmin suffer alienation through their transportation from the motherland — Aaliya, through her migration to the newly established nation state of Pakistan and Deepali, through her migration to the West Indies: theirs as well as Yasmin's wilful migration are the outcome of their economic need for survival in a time of flux. While the twice uprooted Aaliya yearns for the familiar discomfort of her old home where she will perhaps never return, she tries to cope with her new identity as a mohajir by submitting herself to the emancipation of thousands of others like her herself. Aaliya forfeits personal happiness, propagating the idea that society comprises the family. Deepali's obligatory migration on the other hand, leads her to live a life of comparative comfort as Mrs. Sen — she is also able to provide for her father and aunt. Back in the newly-established Bangladesh and face to face with a new generation, she also realizes that some things will never change: Deepali feels alienated among the familiar sights and sounds of the land that she once toiled to free from the yoke of imperialism and longs to return to the comfort of her new home. Like Shamman, Yasmin realizes in the foreign land that the Eastern and the Western cultures can never be integrated but while Shamman retains the hope and will to fight on, Yasmin sacrifices herself at the altar of her abortive attempts at liberation.

Hyder took up the subject of the dispossessed Nawabs and princely states in independent Northern India, in her earliest novel, *Mere bhi Sanamkhane* (1947), or *My Temples, Too* (2004). The Kunwar Sahib of Karwaha Raj is sceptical of Dr. Salim, due to his being a self-made man. His dissipation, his self-imposed seclusion and lack of direct involvement in the goings-on around him, owing to his fear of the rapidness of change on the eve of partition and independence, bring death in the form of a reprieve. He is saved the trauma of witnessing dispossession of his ancestral land though he is aware that the new government is planning to set up a 'major refugee resettlement centre' (where) 'displaced peasants from Punjab and the NWFP were to be rehabilitated on his fertile agricultural land' (Hyder 2004: 134). Perhaps the finest indication of shifting loyalties is contained in the attitude of Lala Iqbal Narain's nephews who are impassioned workers of the Hindu Mahasabha. They advise him against giving up service at Karwaha Raj: 'Don't leave the Raj now, Uncle, this is the time to stick around. How long will these wretched Polus and Kachalus or whatever their names are, last? The government will confiscate their land and redistribute it among us. We'll look after Karwaha Raj, good and proper!' (Hyder 2004: 137) The futility of Peechu's murder and mutilation by an irate, communally-charged mob is rendered the more poignant since it comes at a time when he was in the act of saving the honour of migrant women, in the capacity of a police officer. Peechu and her father's sudden bereavements engender a mental imbalance in Rakshanda which is only augmented by her impoverishment, since, her father having left no will, according to the Talukdari law she has no share in the estate. Roshi bibi's philanthropic humanism is reduced to a cipher and she becomes an object of abject pity as she wanders semi-consciously in the dark, towards the mansion that was once her home. She strikes the reader as the suffering heroine of an inevitable tragedy. The mild, indolent Polu tries to come to terms with the rapid transformation; he visualizes a quiet life after marriage with a cousin. The conversion of Ghufran Manzil into an employment bureau (watched over by the refugee Ram Singh) for displaced men stands in stark contrast to the romance of the opulent lifestyle of the earlier Karwaha Raj residents. Trucks parked under the *moolsari* trees in the garden now, are austere configurations of the changed times.

Hyder categorically caricatures Zeenat Riaz for being several steps ahead of the other women of her age: 'Zeenat Riaz belonged to that select group of highly educated females who thought they had raised the banner of rebellion against the laws of society and the accepted standards and traditions of orthodox families. During her college days she had cooked up schemes of tremendous moral and spiritual daredevilry, but had actually ended up as a principal of a private college at a mere Rs 500 a month. She sent for more money from her well-to-do-home, lived in the YWCA and was an ardent believer in the Intellectual, Economic and Social Freedom of Women.' (Hyder 2004: 63)

Quoting Mohommad Sadiq's observation that 'in her stories it is women who are in the centre of the picture and men are there to enable her to dramatize their misfortunes', (1983, 320) Pietrangelo observes that although Hyder frequently wrote about women, female issues were not her primary concern (Pietrangelo 2004: 169). Hyder's collection of four novellas entitled *Char Novelette* (1998)[7] has her consciously take up issues of besieged womanhood. This paper focuses on two novellas from the collection — *Agle Janam Mohe Bitiya na Keejo* (1976) or *The Street Singers of*

Lucknow (2004)[8] and *Sita Haran* (1960) or *Sita Betrayed* (1999),
since they reflect Hyder's concern with conflicts of women
from diverse societal groups and communities. *Agle Janam* is
about the 'the marginal, the transgressive and the victimized
woman' (Intro. Hussein: 2004) on the one hand and on the
other, *Sita Haran* is about immigrant Sita's intrepid courage
and effort to come to terms with destiny. Hyder's female
protagonists are differentiated from her male ones by an
overwhelming desire to overcome the marginality conferred
on them by their social status or their camaraderie. The
novellas cross-examine the hypocritical social and moral
ethics that govern contemporary as well as ancient society.
Sita and Qamar's stories suggest that a woman's naïve
optimism and trust in love essentially become the prime
reason for her undoing.

Agle Janam catapults the reader into a world replete with
the low-born and the high born, a world of god men and
mafia dons, of the rich and the poor, of poets and singers, of
artistically inclined people on the one hand and brazenly
callous ones on the other. The story of Rashke Qamar, her
polio-inflicted sister, Jamilun and their friend, Motibai, a
singer from Faizabad, spans practically a lifetime and raises
pertinent questions on conventionality and modernity. These
women are subject to multiple marginalizations of fate,
poverty as well as their profession as street singers. In
addition to foregrounding the abuse of her protagonists,
Hyder draws comparisons between the situation of
Mahapara, Qamar's daughter, who leads a jet-set life among
the smugglers of Pakistan and thousands of young girls of
the Ginza locality in Tokyo. These girls have replaced the
dignified geishas of the earlier generations who were
professionally qualified artists and entertainers, often
supported by patrons like Farhad with whom they were
emotionally, sexually and economically involved, like Rashke
Qamar. The Ginza girls are looked down upon more for their
grossness of behaviour than for their profession.

Qamar writes that her embarrassment with Mahapara

stems from a 'bamboo-screen of false dignity' (Hyder 2004: 38) that she has erected before herself, like the geishas of old Japan - '— although the curtains behind which (they) lived were made of sack-cloth and the dignity was self deceptive and illusory.' (Hyder 2004: 38) The indignity of Mahapara's operations prevents Qamar from either living with her or accepting money from her, in spite of rationalizing that Mahapara is in fact doing what she and her mother have done. 'Didn't my mother, my aunt and myself do exactly what my daughter is doing now, albeit in much better style?' (Hyder 2004: 38) she writes to Jamilun.

The novella evokes India's colonial past in more ways than one: Mr Verma's companionship of Motibai is remniscent of the sexual colonization of Indian women by the British. The analogy is drawn between the Jat lass Sarwan, from Haryana, and Motibai who are both educated in the art of etiquette and culture: the former by William Fraser[9], and the latter by Mr. Verma. Farhad's folk song about General Fraser and his mistress draws parallels between colonial and post-colonial situations.

> *Choweke mien baithna chod meri Sarwan, churi kaante se khaana seekh.*
> *Lehenga pehenana chod meri Sarwan, saya pehenana seekh—*
> (Hyder 1998: 349)

> *Leave your rustic kitchen, my Sarwan, take up the forks and knives*
>
> *Shed your peasant skirt, my Sarwan, put on English gowns*
> —(Hyder 2004: 14)

Partition and Independence have been referred to only obliquely, with Pakistan continuing to gleam as the sought after land of opportunity for the poor Indian, Muslim citizen who migrated with a view to bring about an economic uplift. In Karachi, Qamar feels alienated from the motherland while she feels exiled in the country of asylum. Estrangement from Jamilun adds to her misery and isolation.

Sita Haran is a narrative about Sita Mirchandani, a

quintessential, displaced, Sindhi, Partition refugee from Karachi, Pakistan. Faced with the inevitability of reconstructing herself and her home after displacement from her homeland, Sita makes a valiant effort to resettle under altered geo-political and socio-economic conditions, with her family. The central trope in this novella is rootlessness. Once uprooted from her motherland, Sindhu Desh, Sita is unable to lead a settled life anywhere. Her forced diasporic relocation leaves her pining for the geographical boundaries of the land of belonging. Sindh becomes for her as Avtar Brah describes the birthplace, a mythic place of desire, a place to which she cannot return though she may visit the geographical territory of this place of 'origin'. (Banerjee 2007: 169) Sita's visit to Pakistan as Jamil's estranged wife, for his cousin Qamar's wedding, reveals her extensive knowledge about the land, its historical background with its many saints, its rich cultural fabric and her family's profound associations with it. During the visit, Sita undertakes a reconnaissance trip through Sindh to Lahore, but avoids visiting their old, palatial home. Wistfully she remarks to Irfan: 'Now we are a people with no land of our own. The Punjabis at least got the eastern part of Punjab.' (Hyder 1999: 65) Her globetrotting exercises make her travel full circle, leaving her confounded and heart broken. Partition, that brought in its wake mass displacement and resettlement exercises also becomes a psychological-emotional bane for both, Sita and Aaliya who struggle to recreate identities in the countries of new domicile.

Both, Sita and Qamar struggle against forces beyond their influence in order to combat annihilation. Their existentialism is largely governed by facets that dominate the female psyche. Both believe in the synergetic authority of love and continue to become emotionally involved with men who, being insensitive, persist in tormenting them. Sita's inability to find a soul mate parallels Qamar's destiny. Their search for security remains an elusive dream as the several respectable men in their lives come and go. C.M. Naim comments in his introduction to *A Season of Betrayals:* 'Sita Mirchandani in

Sita Betrayed, despite betrayals by a series of men, must remain alive to her own essentially felt need: it is as if, for her, ceasing to search for a shared and lasting experience of love would mean self-annihilation.' (Naim 1999: xi) The same is true of Qamar.

Sita Mirchandani, is educated and outgoing, with a modern perspective of life, unlike her namesake from Hindu mythology. Hyder draws analogies between Hindu mythical precedents and the modern scenario emphasizing that society has not undergone radical changes over the years. Women continue to be ostracized, tormented and treated as outcasts on the basis of social class and profession, in spite of being reservoirs of love, strength and fortitude. The treatment of the woman as a victim is not a new theme in sociological literature; Hyder's ingenuous handling of the subject in relation with a particular culture while she makes references to others, infuses it with specificity and greater variety at one and the same time.

Hyder's world view that consists of both, positives and negatives is evident in the patterns observed in the lives of her protagonists and the balanced sweep of her narratives. Nemesis is the watchword of existence, time brings with itself retribution, it is a healer and a trickster and financial comforts are in fact the bottom-line of human subsistence. Life's little ironies are continually revealed through the frustrations of man's motives. Her novels are an artiste's impression of woman in relation to the environment in which she thrives or wilts as the wheel of fortune turns. Hyder's conscious non-alignment with any political creed or her mistrust of any particular doctrine of life indicates her affirmation of the patterned imperfections of humankind's subsistence.[10] Her stories materialize as descendants of the Persian dastan, conjuring tricks of fate: as the scenes shift and the cameos unfold, Hyder captures the nuances and the spirit of the Ganga-Jamuni culture of the Indian subcontinent, thereby emphasizing the confluence of ethnicity. Like a true aesthete and a pluralist, her concern is with the creation of artifacts that are living monuments of the mythological, the literary and the cultural tradition of a land whose historical and political magnitude is largely a consequence of a convergence of cultures. Hyder's pluralism enables her to stand apart from other contemporary Urdu women writers whose texts give the impression of didactic, period doctrinaires, written with a view to engender optimistic change.

Works Cited

Ahmed, Aijaz. *In Theory.* New Delhi: Oxford University Press. 1992.

Ahmed, Talat. *Literature and Politcs in the Age of Nationalism: The Progressive Writers' Movement in South Asia, 1932-56.* New Delhi: Routledge, 2009.

Asaduddin, M. 'First Urdu Novel: Contesting Claimers and Disclaimers', *The Annual of Urdu Studies.* Vol 16. 2001.

Banerjee, Bidisha, 'No Nation Woman: The Diasporic Woman's Quest for Home'. *Interpreting Homes in South Asian Literature.* Eds. Malashri Lal and Sukrita Paul Kumar. Delhi: Pearson Longman, 2007.

Chughtai, Ismat. *The Crooked Line (Terhi Lakeer).* Intro. Naqvi, Tahira. New Delhi: Women Unlimited. 2003-06.

Coppola, Carlo. 'Ahmed Ali (1910 – 1994): Bridges and Links East and West'. *The Annual of Urdu Studies.* Vol.9. 1994.

Coppola, Carlo. ed. *Marxist Influences and South Asian Literature,* (copyright). Delhi: Chanakya Publications.1988.

Dalrymple,William. *The Last Mughal:The Fall of a Dynasty, Delhi,1857.* New Delhi: Penguin Viking. 2006.

———. *City of Djins: A Year in Delhi.* New Delhi: Penguin. 1993.

Farooqi, Meher Afshan, ed. *The Oxford India Anthology of Modern Urdu Literature.* New Delhi:Oxford University Press. 2008.

Gopal, Priyamvada. *Literary Radicalism in India: Gender, Nation and the Transition to Independence.* London: Routledge, 2005.

Hyder, Qurratulain. *The Street Singers of Lucknow and Other Stories.* Intro. Hussein, Aamer. New Delhi: Sterling Publishers Pvt. Ltd. 2004.

———. *Char Novelette.* Aligarh: Educational Book House.1998.

———. *Fireflies in the Mist - A Novel.* New Delhi: Sterling Publishers Pvt. Ltd. 2004.

————. *My Temples, Too. – A Novel.* New Delhi: Women Unlimited. 2004.

————. *A Season of Betrayals: A Short Stories and Two Novellas.* Naim, C. M. Intro & ed. New Delhi: Kali for Women. 1999.

————. 'Khadija Mastur ke Maraasle'. *Shahrah-e-Hareer. Kare Jahan Daraz Hai Vol. III.* Delhi: Educational Publishing House. 2003.

Kumar, Sukrita Paul, Sadique, eds. *Ismat: Her Life, Her Times.* Alt Series. *Approaches to Literatures in Translation.* Delhi: Katha. 2000.

McLain, Katherine. 'The Fantastic as Frontier: Realism, the Fantastic, and Transgression in the Mid-Twentieth Century Urdu Fiction'.*The Annual of Urdu Studies.* Vol. 16, 2001.

Mastur, Khadija. *Inner Courtyard (Aangan) A Novel.* Intro. Choonara, Samina. New Delhi: Kali for Women. 2001.

————. *Cool, Sweet Water, Selected Stories.* Intro. Naqvi, Tahira. New Delhi: Kali for Women. 1998.

Patel, Geeta. 'An Uncivil Woman: Ismat Chughtai (A Review and an Essay)'. *The Annual of Urdu Studies.* Vol. 16. 2001.

Pietrangelo, Valerio. 'Urdu Literature and Women' *The Annual of Urdu Studies.* Vol.19. 2004.

Osterheld, Christina. 'Nazir Ahmad and the Early Urdu Novel: Some Observations', *The Annual of Urdu Studies.*Vol.16. 2001.

Russell, Ralph. *The Pursuit of Urdu Literature: A Select History.* Delhi: Oxford University Press. 1992.

Sharar, Abdul Halim. *Lucknow: The Last Phase of an Oriental Culture.* Delhi: Oxford University Press. 1994.

Works Consulted

Akhtar, Jameel. *Andaaz-e-bayaan Aur.* New Delhi: Farid Book Depot. 2005.

Azad, Aslam. *Qurratulain Hyder: Bahaisiyat Novel Nigaar.* New Delhi:2004.

Chakrabarty,Dipesh, Majumdar, Rochona, Sartori, Andrew, eds. *From the Colonial to the Post-colonial: India and Pakistan in Transition.* New Delhi: Oxford University Press. 2007.

Kidwai, A.R., ed. *Behind the Veil: Representation of Muslim Women in Indian Writings in English 1950 – 2000.* Delhi: A P H Publishing Corporation. 2007.

Mastur, Khadija. *Aangan.Intro.* Aligarh: Educational Book House. 2004.

Zaman, Niaz. *A Divided Legacy: The Partition in Selected Novels of India, Pakistan and Bangladesh.* New Delhi: Manohar. 2001.

Notes

1. It is often supposed that the Urdu novel and the short story made their appearance in the subcontinent owing to Western or British education and administration. (Osterheld, 2001: 27). This observation is debatable.

2. *Dastan-e-Amir Hamza,* is a romantic fairy tale involving magic, charms, fairies and devils. Originally written in Persian during the Tughlaq dynasty by Amir Khusrau, it was written in its present form by Faizi in order to entertain Emperor Akbar. (Sharar 1994: 262) Several stories were written in great detail on lines of quest and adventure, similar to that of *Dastan-e-Amir Hamza,* till it began to be felt in the nineteenth century that the content of the tale should be realistic or even educational rather than magical.

3. To quote M. Asaduddin, 'In Persian 'qissa' or 'dastan' simply means a tale or a story. However, in its specific literary usage, it denotes the lengthy cycles of medieval romances which consist of heroic and adventurous tales of great courage and valour that include the deployment of supernatural machinery, magic and enchantment (tilism) and adhere to the medieval code of chivalry. (Asaduddin 2001: 78) He also avers that if the Urdu novel has indeed evolved from the tradition of the English novel, then 'it is equally true that a readership nurtured on the earlier forms of storytelling took to it quite naturally, without any sense of shock or novelty. (Asaduddin 2001: 78)

4. For more views of Chughtai on Hyder, see article entitled 'Pompom Darling' in Kumar, Sukrita Paul, Sadique, eds. *Ismat: Her Life, Her Times.* Alt Series. *Approaches to Literatures in Translation.* Delhi: Katha. 2000.

5. *Angare* (1932) is a collection of ten short stories and a drama in Urdu, co-authored by Sajjad Zaheer, Ahmed Ali, Dr. Rashid Jahan and Mahmuduzzafar. Sajjad Zaheer's works include *Neend Nahin Aati, Jannat ki Bashaarat, Garmiyon ki ek Raat, Dulaari* and *Phir yeh Hangaamah;* Ahmed Ali's include *Baadal*

Nahin Aate and *Mahaavaton ki ek Raat*. Mahmooduzzafar contributed *Jawaanmardi*—it is unlikely that he wrote his story in Urdu since his knowledge of the language was not sound enough. Mahmuduzzafar's story was written in English and translated into Urdu by Sajjad Zaheer who was also the editor of *Angare*. (Gopal 2005: 156 and Coppola) Rashid Jahan contributed a play entitled *Parde ke Peeche* and a story, *Dilli ki Sair*. All the stories in the *Angare* collection have been translated into English. The *Angare* collection initiated a tendency that aimed at an authentic, realistic representation of social and cultural life in Urdu fiction, which had hitherto remained distanced from it. The writers had strong Marxist-socialist leanings and aimed at propagating modernity.

6. Kazi Nazrul Islam (25 May 1899–29 August 1976) was a Bengali poet, musician, revolutionary, and philosopher who pioneered poetic works espousing intense spiritual rebellion against orthodoxy and oppression. His poetry and nationalist activism earned him the popular title of *Bidrohi Kobi* (Rebel Poet). Accomplishing a large body of acclaimed works through his life, Nazrul is officially recognized as the national poet of Bangladesh and commemorated in India. His poems have been quoted throughout the novel.

7. The other two novellas are *Chai ke Bagh* and *Dilruba*. A few of the novellas contained in this collection had been published in journals or collections of short stories before they were collectively brought out.

8. Also translated as *A Woman's Life*. New Delhi: Chetna Publications. 1979.

9. William Fraser was the assistant of the English Resident at Delhi, Sir David Ochterlony, years before the Mutiny of 1857. Both Ochterlony and Fraser were largely influenced by the Indian way of life and consciously adopted Indian customs, forms of dress and learnt Urdu and Persian from the ulemas or teachers. Fraser, a Scotch Highlander, had six or seven legitimate Indian wives in his opulent harem and fathered many children. (Dalrymple 2006: 64-65) Ochterlony was assassinated in 1825 and Fraser met with the same fate in 1835 while he was Resident of Delhi. He controlled the region of Haryana for several years and perhaps his liaison with Sarwan can be attributed to this time. Jacquemont records that he had

many children who were Hindus and Muslims, according to their mothers and were peasants, shepherds or mountaineers, according to their professions. (Dalrymple 1993: 109) Much is not known of what became of Fraser's wives after him.

10. On several occasions, Hyder has negated being swayed by social or political creeds. For instance, in *Shahrah-e-Hareer* she insinuates her non-alignment in the essay 'Khadija Mastur ke Maraasle', by quoting Iqbal: *'Khuda wanda yeh tere sadah dil bande kidhar jaaen'*. With regard to Leftist ideology, she remarks: *'Khwab tha jo kuch deka/ Jo suna afsana tha.'* (Hyder 2003: 318)

7

Once Upon a Time:
Cultural Legacies, Fictional Worlds of the Partition and Beyond

ASIF FARRUKHI

Once upon a time, and a very good time it was, there was a Partition. And a very important Partition it was too. All the scholars agree from Timbuktu to Trincomalee. All the good children were born appropriately at the exact stroke of midnight. Tryst with destiny and all that razzmatazz. Many were born later, mostly *bad-tameez desis*. We must refuse to even acknowledge them. Some were born earlier. As if in anticipation. So that they were ripe for the Partition when it came. There was a lot of to-do, pow-wow and much sob-sob. Everybody then lived unhappily ever after. Period. The credits roll and the story will continue in the next episode as we are promised more Partitions to come.

This is a story my father told me. He sowed the dragon's teeth and my generation reaps the harvest. We suffer the consequences. Partition is a story which makes Baby Tuckoo out of all of us. Brought up on such stories, I revisit all this frequently, much too often for comfort. It is only against such a background that I can read the Partition in Urdu literature, especially fiction, which narrates the Partition through and in multitudinous texts. All said and done about the Partition, it is those literary texts which continue to haunt me. There is no getting away from it. It turns up in unexpected places. It comes in all shapes and colours. After so many years, it still lurks in the shadows and looms around the corner, waiting to grab you unawares. I would rather confront it, face it rather than flee or beat a hasty retreat.

To begin with, the Partition is History with a capital H. For my generation it is the Great Given. No need to hark back to the time before the lines were drawn and battle out the long-drawn arguments on its validity. Now that it's there, what next? How to read it in the books that it inspired and how to read the books which flowed out of and with the tumultuous events? More often than not, the Partition is seen as either a beginning or an end. The Beginners are the historians and scholars who signpost it as the emergence of the new nation-state, the dawn of a new day. The Enders deplore and lament it as the end of a secular South Asia, where different castes and creeds had lived harmoniously for thousands of years. It is the sheer dichotomy between the two positions, which I find unsettling. Clearly it's a beginning as well as an end. In my end is my beginning and in my beginning, my end. Like a serpent swallowing its tail. You don't know where to begin and can start from anywhere.

So where do you begin? From the Partition itself. I would like to start from the actual events, rather than any fixed or inviolable ideological position. The facts are well known but let me recapitulate what for me are some of the defining features. The handing over of power to local representatives in India by British authorities was a hasty affair, for one reason or another, many of the long-term consequences were not thought out by the perpetrators. Not only much unresolved business was left behind to create a long-standing feud, the shape of the newly created dominions, as they were called, ensured the uprooting of what is described as the largest exodus in modern human history. Sheer numbers or Biblical references fail to do justice to the suffering in human terms, as the displacement was accompanied by mayhem on a scale unprecedented in a country much prone to violence. Who knows how many died, how many men subjected to brutalization and pillage, and how many women became victims of abduction and rape. But matters did not end there. A diaspora had been triggered off and the generations have continued to be indirectly affected by the announcement made at the stroke of the midnight hour. After Midnight's Children, came the Children of After the Midnight, and so on. The emotions unleashed in 1947, or the ones reaching their climax in those events, remained unabated on both sides and contributed to other partitions, most significantly to the events of 1971, a second Partition. And who knows what next? The name of Kamleshwar's Hindi novel haunts me as an unrequited but unanswered question: *Aur Kitnay Pakistan*? By all accounts, 1947 was the Mother of All Partitions.

Beyond itself, what *was* the Partition? Was it a cause or an effect? Was it the mother or a child? Certainly, it was an incision which dissected out the new inception, Pakistan, out of the parent-body of India. The analogy of a Cesarean section was used by Mumtaz Shirin in one of her short stories. This generally fine critic who studied the literature around the Partition described the large-scale violence that ensued with the events as symbolizing the loss of blood which accompanies a surgical procedure. Such symbolism seems heavy, oversimplified. It is the accompanying violence, its scope and its scale, which puts to shame the ideologically-minded scholars who would like nothing better than to describe the emergence of Pakistan as an Immaculate Conception. Not by a far cry. Shouldn't a critic as perceptive as Shirin have shown greater sensitivity to the discernable difference between hemorrhage and blood-letting? Bifurcated and dissected, Partition itself has been partitioned with different stakeholders laying claim to different parts. But who will gather the limbs of Osiris?

As we move from the topography of the events to the barest reference to a fictional artifact, we are crossing from one plane to another. The transition is swift if somewhat jerky and we do not immediately realize that we are crossing the date-line. The Partition is open to a multitude of possibilities and several readings. I would like to differentiate between two different discourses — on the one hand a socio-political analysis, and on the other, the study of the Partition as a literary phenomenon. The two are obviously related and intertwined closely so that it is not possible to artificially dissect the two, but having said that, I would also like to point out the ensuing confusion when the terms of one are admixed with those of the other. Switching one for the other is the main reason why some analysts/critics over-burden it with their pet peeves, ideological or otherwise. They read various trends and patterns in the literary texts about what they think happened or what should have/ have not taken place. Without denigrating other possibilities, I would like to focus on the Life and Times of the Partition as a literary phenomenon, particularly in the context of Urdu.

It doesn't take a literary critic to recognize the immense outpouring of fiction and poetry in Urdu focusing on the events of 1947 and the related consequences. Readers not directly conversant with Urdu can have access to representative works through a number of anthologies, out of which I would like to specially refer to *An Unwritten Epic*, the Penguin selection by Muhammad Umar Memon, and the large Urdu sampling available in Alok Bhalla's three volumes of *Stories About the Partition of India*. While these and others amply serve the non-Urdu reader at large, what about Urdu itself? There is no such collection available in the very language these works were originally written in. Here one could refer to the sadly instructive fate of *Zulmat-e-Neem Roz*, the anthology Mumtaz Shirin edited but failed to see printed in her lifetime, but let me return to it later.

The Partition rode on a high wave in the Urdu short story. The social realism accentuated by the Progressive writers had prepared the ground and the traumatic events opened up a new vein by the major short-story writers of the period:

Saadat Hasan Manto, Rajinder Singh Bedi, Krishan Chander, Ismat Chughtai as well as scores of others. In stories such as *Thanda Gosht* and *Khol Do*, Manto perfected his art to create taut, compact narratives going beyond the search for the lost ideals of humanism to a quest for what constituted the human, while *Toba Tek Singh* goes beyond political questions to what is essentially the human condition. While these stories mark an ascending point in Manto's career, for Krishan Chander, the once much-admired stories *Hum Wehshi Hain* and *Peshawar Express* now seem artistically weak, marking the beginning of this writer's decline. He retuned to the theme a few years later in his short novel *Ghaddar*, better crafted than his earlier works, but his vision remains essentially political. Bedi's powerful *Lajwanti* was written somewhat later, and remains one of the best stories from his early period. In her few stories around this theme, Ismat Chughtai did not achieve the distinction of her best work from the same period.

Following closely on their heels were other prominent writers who have at least one remarkable short story around this theme: Aziz Ahmad (*Kaali Raat*); Hayatullah Ansari (*Shukr Guzar Ankahin*), Ahmad Nadim Qasimi (*Parmeshar Singh*); Upendra Nath Ashk (*Tableland*); Jamila Hashmi (*Banbas*) and Ashfaq Ahmed who authored *Gadariya*, one of the best-known stories from the period. There are other lesser-known but distinguished writers such as the enigmatic Jawaida Jafri, who authored the unusual story, *Jagay Paak Parwardigar*, but never repeated her success.

Most of these stories focus on the riots, the brutality, the barbarism, the dehumanization and the heroics of some characters against a politically charged backdrop and the pain of being uprooted as a consequence of communal violence. No wonder the Urdu critics used the label of *Fasadat Kay Afsaney*, 'Riot Literature', to describe sch writings. This is the term used by Muhammad Hasan Askari and Mumtaz Shirin. Askari took up the interesting position that *fasadat* as such could not be the subject of literature and then went on to develop a reading of Manto's short stories, especially the vignettes in *Siah Hashiay*, which focus exclusively on these themes. In using the term *Fasadat Ka Adab*, the riots were highlighted as the main occurrence, rather than the Partition itself, which may have been seen as a cause rather than the effect, perhaps even a transient phase. History proved it to be the other way around.

While the short stories examined under each may remain the same, as a category Partition literature is broader than *Fasadat Ka Adab*. It is based on historicity and this makes it vulnerable to manipulation. In the Introduction to his anthology, Bhalla makes a distinction between the histories written by the apologists of Pakistan and its bitter opponents: 'If the first set of histories read like incantations, the second work like old demonologies.'

Consider this Introduction with Memon's Preface as a study in contrasting methods and the different purposes the Partition is put to. Bhalla begins by regarding 'The Partition of the Indian subcontinent (as) the single most traumatic experience in our recent history', and goes on to say that '(The) real sorrow of the Partition was that it brought to an abrupt end a long and communally shared history.'

Memon's Preface records his dissatisfaction with what he calls 'ideological underpinnings' working as 'as a sort of distorting filter', without going into the details of which books he is referring to and what those pronouncements are. He complains of inadequate translations but then takes an even more tantalizing position when he terms two well-known short stories of Ahmad Nadim Qasimi and Bedi as 'poorly written'. His vehement dismissal of narrow nationalistic aspirations is offered as a sharp contrast to the positions taken by other critics whom he does not name. The difference in their points of view is not so much a question of different temperaments but fundamentally in their ways of reading the Partition. Bhalla's complaint against the two sets of histories holds true for the anthologies, or at least their introductions.

The manipulation of literature in favour of a particular point of view is also borne out by the problem Shirin faced with her selection. Mumtaz Shirin had edited a special issue of her journal *Naya Daur* devoted to the riots, and she spent much time and energy writing about these fictions, making it her special area of study. Based on her critical analysis she put together a collection of what she considered the representative and important works of fiction, but as her selection was never printed, there is only anecdotal evidence and speculation as to its fate. The story goes that the anthology was submitted for publication to a quasi-governmental body but one of the bureaucrats reigning over there objected to the inclusion of a story by Krishan Chander on the grounds that it went 'against Pakistan' and the editor was asked to remove it. This was ironic as Shirin had singled out this particularly story as being weak in terms of its craftsmanship but as it was a representative story by one of the best-known writers of the day, she was not willing to delete it all together. The resulting stalemate led to the anthology being shelved and even the manuscript was lost so that years later, I had to dig out all the references from Shirin's essays to assemble a loose collection on the lines that she had worked on initially.

I have often thought about what befell Shirin's selection, wondering if it amounted to a sort of censorship, an attempt to rewrite the past. An imaginary past, ideologically correct, with its *qibla* in the right direction. Call it the riots, or the Partition, the literature around this set of events has been prone to manipulation for reasons which have less to do with literature and more with ideological positioning of the critics involved. However, this brings us to another twist in the tale. In the first instance the Partition had been written as a story, a tale which needed to be told, and then we see the Partition as the frame of stories as it provides the reference for an assessment of particular stories. This change marks a turn in the fortunes of the Partition.

* * *

So we have two Partitions then. The Partition as a story. And the Partition as the frame of stories. I want to move another step and look at another stage in the literary career of the Partition. This is the stage of Beyond the Partition, reading through the Partition in order to take a broader view, and this is best seen in the works of two powerful fiction-writers who transcend the entire category of Partition literature. These two writers are Qurratulain Hyder and Intezar Husain. Both follow on the heels of the writers mentioned above in strictly chronological terms as the former established her reputation on the eve of the Partition and the latter, just in the wake of the Partition. And the dividing line is important to both. Qurratulain Hyder does not have any single short story which could be regarded as an example of Partition literature, while Intezar Husain's long story *Bin Likhi Rizmiya* (An Unwritten Epic) was much admired by Shirin. Qurratulain Hyder's best-known novel, and undoubtedly the most widely read novel in Urdu, *Aag ka Darya* can be regarded with Husain's works as the epitome of *Fasadat Kay Afsaney* or Partition literature, as they fulfil the demands of this category and transcend/break open this category by taking it beyond Partition to a broader view of history of which Partition is one component. These two writers represent the pinnacle of achievement in Urdu fiction and we can even ask if Urdu fiction has really moved beyond these two?

Unlike the earlier *fasadat* writers, a discernable political stance is not merely a balancing act in these two writers, but it develops as their narrative technique. The Partition is a part of the story, not the entire narrative in both writers. While I am taking their names together, I do not want to set them up as a contrasting pair. There is no need for another *mawazna-e-Anis-o-Dabeer* between the two as the *Urdu-wallas* are prone to. While I consider both to be important in their individual capacity, I am also not suggesting that they are writers of equal stature.

The differences and similarities between the two pose interesting questions. *Aag ka Darya* also serves as a dividing line between Hyder's earlier and her more mature, later work. It consumes and transcends the early period mocked and savaged by Ismat Chughtai as Pom Pom Darling. The novel remains unmatched for the brightness and sparkle of its prose and the narrative technique based on her concept of time as a continuum. Qurratulain Hyder's fiction is derived from her reading of history as a narrative; it, therefore, takes a longer view of the Partition. Intezar Husain focuses on the Partition in his novel *Basti* in a manner which goes beyond the eternal present of the *fasadat* to situations which are derived from and based in history, so we have 1857 on the one hand and 1971 on the other. Intezar Husain's major novel, *Basti*, is a mid-career work, and bears an interesting relationship to the writer's other work. It draws on a number of themes from the writer's earlier and successful short stories in a manner where the author can be seen to be cannibalizing his own previous work to some extent. Although, in a number of instances portions of the novel cover the same ground, but the different components connect together to form a unified whole. Breaking out of the conventional framework of time, *Basti* contemplates historical time giving way to miraculous time.

Another point of contact between the two is the richness and multiplicity of their past, or pasts, as both seem to have access to more than one. Their techniques show the influence of the traditions of the ancient East as well as the modern European novel. Neither of them wants to give up one for the sake of the other and the ease with which they freely move from one to the other is especially difficult to grasp for Urdu critics who are inclined to be myopic and seem to resent the fact that these writers defy the straitjacketing of categories. Hence, some Urdu critics still discuss and debate whether *Aag ka Darya* is written in the stream of consciousness technique and whether *Basti* can actually be called a novel in the strict sense.

As fiction writers bracketed together by the same time-period, I would like to suggest that the experience of reading one can illuminate and enrich the reading of the other and provide us with a richer and more complex perspective. For this purpose, I would like to read together the opening scenes and the conclusions of the two novels.

Let us read the beginnings. But if we can only identify them as such. The novelist Amos Oz has pondered over this question and in his book *The Story Begins* he frames this question:

> But what ultimately is a beginning? Can there exist, in principle, a proper beginning to any story at all? Isn't there always, without exception, a latent beginning-before-the-beginning? A foreword to the introduction to the prologue? A pre-Genesis occurrence?

This is how *Basti* establishes what Oz has called 'the opening contract':

> When the world was still new, when the sky was fresh and the earth not yet soiled, when trees breathed through the centuries and ages spoke in the voices of birds, how astonished he was, looking all around, that everything was so new, and yet looked so old. Blue jays, woodpeckers, peacocks, doves, squirrels, parakeets — it seemed that they were as young as he, yet they carried the secrets of the ages.

The opening scene is rooted in the childhood of the protagonist, for whom this is a more real and intense period in his life than any other. But even before the story begins, a beginning has been made. A beginning with the world on the eve of creation.

The opening contract of *River of Fire* is invested in an insect rich in allusions:

> It was the first *beerbahauti* of the season that Gautam had seen. The prettiest of rain-insects, clothed in god's own red velvet, the *beerbahauti* was called the Bride of Indira, Lord of the Clouds.

This insect is no stranger as we encounter it in a memorable location in *Basti*, this time more symbolic than mythological, signifying the ideal of beauty that Zakir, Afzal and their friends would like to have their country achieve:

'I'm about to have some acres allotted to me. One acre will be
given over to beds of roses. One acre will be only for rain-
bugs.'

'Rain-bugs?' Irfan looked at him sarcastically.

'Fellow! Be quiet! You won't be able to understand this. In
the rainy season I roam around very anxiously. There don't
seem to be any rain-bugs here. There ought to be rain-bugs.
We have to make Pakistan beautiful' Then, changing his tone,
he addressed them both: 'Listen! You too will stay with me.
This is my command. I, and you two.'

'And the rain-bugs,' Irfan interrupted.

'Yes, and the rain-bugs. In beautiful Pakistan there will be
only beautiful people.' (Chapter 9)

You don't really have to step out of the novel to realize that
the impossibility of the situation: in the-less-than-beautiful
Pakistan, there are no beautiful people. There are no rain-
bugs either. Gautam had put the *beerbahauti* on a leaf and
sent it floating down the river. Did it get left behind at the
time of the Partition? Its disappearance is again taken up in
a later story, *Allah Mian Ki Shehzadi*, included in the collection
Scheherzade Kay Naam. A young girl and boy, on the edge of
puberty, trade *beerbahautis* for a papaya, and the exchange
turns daring as the boy touches the girl's clean tongue to see
it devoid of any spittle — the closest that any character of
Intezar Husain's has come to each other in physical proximity
— when suddenly the story is transported and the reader is
jolted into the realization that this is the realm of memory
which has just been splintered by the narrator/author's wife
watching television at high volume and commenting on the
news. The news, too, is about strained relations between India
and Pakistan, amounting to further difficulties for travellers
across the border, which in the post-Partition world have
solidified into the absolute, in spite of all the *beerbahautis*.
The shattered memory cannot be restored, except to recollect
that the *beerbahautis* have died, their death symbolizes the
loss of the childhood innocence, replaced by the politically
charged colourless present.

But the *beerbahauti* is a later interpolation. Or import. It is simply not there in the opening scene of *Aag ka Darya*, which establishes its contract through different terms. This is why I want to plead the case for considering *Aag ka Darya* and River of Fire as two separate books, parallel but distinct. The twain never did meet.

The beginning having been established, let us move towards the end. To come to the closure of *Basti*, which is intriguing in itself:

> 'Yaar,' he said to Irfan, 'I want to write her a letter.'
> 'Now?' Irfan stared into his face.
> 'Yes, now.'
> 'Now when...' he paused in the midst of his sentence, then took a different tack. 'Before...' confused, he fell silent.
> Before — he tried to get it clear in his mind — before — before the parting of her hair fills with silver, and the birds fall silent, and the keys rust, and the doors of the streets are shut — and before the silver cord is loosed, and the golden bowl is shattered, and before the pitchers broken at the well, and the sandalwood tree, and the snake in the ocean, and —
> 'Why are you silent?' Irfan was gazing steadily at him.
> 'Silence,' Afzal, placing a finger on his lips, signaled Irfan to be silent. 'I think we will see a sign.'
> 'A sign? What sign can there be now?' Irfan said with bitterness and despair.
> 'Fellow, signs always come at just these times, when all around...' he paused in the middle of his speech. Then he said in a whisper, 'This is the time for a sign...'

It reverts and connects back to the Biblical language of the opening. The weight of the scene hangs on the sign. Our expectations aroused, we are confronted by questions: What does it mean and why now? Will it really take place? Or perhaps the sign already occurred — when Zakir wants to write a letter. This is the first indication of a stirring within him, a deeper connection with relationships and feelings. Zakir who is accused by many critics as being devoid of action, is now guilty of having thought of an action. True to his character, he has not actually carried out the act — of writing the letter — but he has spoken of it to his friends. It is also significant that he discusses this intimate or almost intimate gesture with a friend He has this sense of urgency that he needs to this 'before...' But before what? This he does not articulate. As this is never specified, there is a sense of foreboding, which is reinforced by the Biblical language, going back full-circle to the opening contract. *Basti* is an open-ended novel. There is no final and firm closure of the narrative sequence, indicating multiple possibilities in the ending.

The word in the original is *basharat* with its strong religious and metaphysical reference and with it is posed the question of will there be or won't there be...'*basharat ho gi kay nahin?*' The question at the end of *Basti* is the unanswered question of Partition literature — did the miracle take place or not? By not answering the question, the novel says it all.

Now read it with the closure of *Aag ka Darya*. The mastery of the narrative form and control over technique is displayed best in the novel's conclusion as the writer brings together the various threads to weave together a final scene. It closes the long, historical narrative and its irrevocable finality contributes to the sense of tragedy it highlights. The Partition as tragedy.

As the action of the novel moves ahead, Kamal has travelled to India from Karachi after the Partition. He avoids meeting his old friends who meet again in a grotto of the Shravasti forest, in a scene which parallels their meeting in the opening scene of the novel. As they begin to talk they comment on Kamal and his visit:

'Kamal has deserted us. Betrayed his friends, gone away for good and let us down. Together, we could have challenged the galaxies.'

'We have all betrayed one another,' Gautam replied quietly. Can these Western visitors to Shravasti understand the pain in our souls? In India's, in Kamal's, in mine?'

They watched the river ripple past. Words were temporary and transitory. Languages fade away or are forced into oblivion by new tongues. Men also come and go, even the river and the jungle are not eternal. After fifty years a jungle of concrete may spring up here. The river may dry up or shrink or change course, just as human beings disappear or change the direction of their journeys.

> *Ghazalan, tum to waqif ho, kaho Majnoon ke murney ki,*
> *Diwana mar gaya, aakhir ko, veeranay pe kya guzri*

With this famous couplet, the scene tends to become a patch of purple prose. The two characters imagine Kamal in Karachi, with more than a touch of cynicism and certainly with less than approval, 'dancing with some lovely begum in the Karachi Gymkhana.'

Kamal is awkwardly placed here, but this sense of awkwardness was far more memorable in the Urdu version, specially the two lines which are placed quietly in the middle of the scene and are low-key and thus achieve a powerful effect:

> *Shaid who donon ikhattey soch rahey thay keh Abul Mansur Kamaluddin kis tarah Hindustan main dakhil hua tha aur ks tarha Hindustan say nikal gaya.*

These lines present the central theme of the novel without much fanfare. These are placed in between descriptions of the scene— two men throwing pebbles in the river and watching their reflections broken into expanding circles. The Urdu version closes with:

> *Woh mundair par say utra. Us nay aik lamba saans liya aur ahista ahista qadam rakhta basti ki taraf wapas chala gaya.*

Basti ki taraf. The road does lead towards Intezar Husain's *Basti* and perhaps it is what lies beyond, the next step, which was also the next step in history.

The end of *Aag ka Darya* too is an unanswered question: How or why did he leave? *Woh kaisay chala gaya*— This is a great walk-over. Is he abdicating from his story/history?

Henceforth history will be his absence. And the River of Fire is still a sheet of scalding wet heat. We are still undecided. The Partition likes me. The Partition likes me not. The Partition has left me. The Partition has left me not. Will there be a sign?

8

'Amma, Basant Kya Hoti Hai?':
Turns of Centuries in *Aag ka Darya*

SUKRITA PAUL KUMAR

Qurratulain Hyder's *Aag ka Darya* engages with the question
of composite culture in India in the backdrop of the Partition
of the subcontinent. In fact, it captures several turns of
centuries, both with historical linearity as well as with a sense
of history that transcends chronology. The novel deals with
the individual and goes on to present a collective identity. It
is fiction that captures the history of a single culture that
slowly encompasses many others. It engages with the totality
of existence by delineating individual lives appearing in
various ages.

> 'Time pursued me whichever way I went. I think time is very
> dangerous. Have you ever felt frightened of Time, Gautam?'
>   'Gautam, the expanse of life is very burdensome, save
> yourself from its spread.'
>   'Where does creation begin from? Where does it go? Why
> are we living? And how? Where will we go?'

A novel that opens with such daunting questions and folds
within itself the cultural history of over a thousand years of
this subcontinent as also the perennial existential dilemmas
of an individual, demands a critique that cannot be confined

to what has come to be known as the 'separate sphere' critical paradigm. The binary category of gender establishes its relevance politically and it has convincing historical determinants. However, it has been evidenced how application of the metaphor of 'separate spheres' inevitably leads to reductive and sometimes even seductive, categories such as the 'cult of domesticity', 'the cult of true womanhood', 'the female world of love and ritual'(Cathy N. Davidson's Preface to *American Literature*, Vol. 70, No. 3, September 1998). *Aag ka Darya* folds within itself both the private and public space for men and women with a dual rather than a binary vision. It is written more in freedom from the prison of gender than from within it.

'The truth is, a great mind must be androgynous', Coleridge said more than a century ago and to quote Virginia Woolf, 'Everyone is partly their ancestors; just as everyone is partly man and partly woman.' Qurratulain Hyder's creative vision in this novel interrogates many divides, of gender, of time, of religion, of race through an intense probe of the specifics themselves. The metaphor of the river emphasizes the flow of both time and human consciousness. There are continuities despite ruptures, and compassion despite conflict.

The author selects the title of her novel from the verses of the famous Urdu poet Jigar:

> *Yeh ishq nahin aasan*
> *Itna to samajh lije*
> *Ek aag ka darya hai*
> *Aur doob ko jana hai.*

Which in English is:

> *This love is not easy*
> *Do understand this much*
> *This is a river of fire*
> *And you must drown in it, to go ahead.*

Gautam Nilambar, Champa, Kamal, Hari Shankar and others

are characters from the novel, in love with life. Love that involves suffering, pain, longing and probing. The fiery river of time subsumes them, revives them and grips them into its gushing waves. They flow along with the river, century after century, birth after birth, creating in the novel a breathtakingly vast canvas of an epic scale.

But what made Qurratulain Hyder write such a novel? Ironically the stupendous journey rests on an apparently simple and innocent question asked by the author's niece in Karachi '*Amma, basant kya hota hai?*' (What is Basant, amma?) In the December 1959 issue of the well-known Urdu journal from Pakistan, *Naqoosh*, Hyder records how she ended up writing a novel of over eight hundred pages in response to that question.

Her quest needed to rest on some specific point for, after all, as she says, no one person can undertake the exploration of the whole world, the whole creation. Hyder is deeply concerned about the cultural amnesia evidenced in that simple question that comes from a girl who, ironically, reads the life of Elvis Presley so intently. She sets out to bring alive streams of collective consciousness flowing through four special phases in the history of the Indian subcontinent: (1) Fourth century BC (2) Late fifteenth and early sixteenth century (3) End of eighteenth and the whole of the nineteenth century, and the (4) Post-Partition era.

Gautam Nilambar is a student of Shravasti Gurukul in the fourth century BC; in the second phase he serves the British government; and, while he is a teacher in a Brahmo Samaj school in the third era, in our own times he is an intellectual living in London and New York with the values of his race secure in his being. In Kamal runs the vibrant stream of the history of Islamic presence in the subcontinent —the same Kamal who in the fourth century, had reached Tughlakabad through Central Asia and Kashmir. Abdul Mansur Kamaluddin comes to Jaunpur, Kashi and Ayodhya and meets a very different brand of Muslims, the Sufis. With his contact with the idol worshippers and the new land, the process of negotiation between his brand of Islam and the local culture begins. His very existence then dives into the River of Fire and when he re-emerges in later times in the seventeenth and eighteenth centuries, he comes through as a synthesis of Islamic and local culture.

After some negotiation there is mutual assimilation; and, then history witnesses in India, the progress of the unique Indo-Islamic culture. While there were several conflicts and differences, there was also a bonding and a striking of some concord. Kamal, the outsider of the fourth century BC becomes a nationalist: 'Are you a very staunch nationalist, Kamal?' asks Champa, 'Yes, every honest person should be a nationalist', is his answer. 'How is it that all the Muslim intellectuals and scholars and theologians of India are nationalists? (p.254, *River of Fire*). When his father supports the demand for Pakistan and joins the Muslim League, he is upset and says, 'You cannot discard your motherland like an old coat' (p. 254, *River of Fire*). By capturing the inner currents of the evolution of a dynamic culture, Qurratulain Hyder endeavours to clear the cobwebs on the process of, first, integration and later the disintegration of cultural harmony. The bonding that is evolved over centuries between the Hindus and the Muslims begins to crack through Partition politics generated deviously by the British rulers. While the novel is not history, it is nevertheless an imaginative reconstruction of a cultural process that has its foundations in history as perceived by the author.

Aag ka Darya was published in 1959 and was written in Pakistan where Hyder had migrated after the Partition. The personal anguish of uprooting and exile, an exile that was geographical as well as psychic, brings her into an intimate closeness and understanding of all her characters. They are the weary generations of the well-known writer Abdullah Hussain (as portrayed in his Urdu novel *Udas Naslein*) and the victims of permanent homelessness gnawing at the core of some of Intezar Husain's characters (as seen in his novel *Basti*). Both Kamal and Champa of *Aag ka Darya* require tremendous fortitude to survive the Partition. Kamal is driven, against himself, to migrate to Pakistan. As for Champa, she becomes an exile psychologically even when she stays on in India.

'Remember, how Abul Mansur Kamaluddin had entered Hindustan and how he has gone out of it'. This is not a simple statement from the novel, it carries within itself a large portion of the thematic content of *Aag ka Darya*. Once again, Kamal becomes the 'other' but not the same 'other' of the fourth century BC. Earlier he himself had perceived his presence in Hindustan as that of an alien but after a long history of negotiation, in the recent history, he is abruptly pushed into this role by political forces beyond his control. How can he detach himself from his ancestors whom he carries within himself? It is for this reason that Intezar Husain's Zakir is a professor of history in his novel *Basti*, to recapitulate and review some knots regarding Muslims in the subcontinent. The cultural heritage of the two communities, of intermingling and owning each other's customs, festivals, mythologies and languages and sharing the same geographical climate under the same sky for centuries could not simply be trashed or forgotten. This civilization had nurtured Sant Kabir or Kabir Mian and someone like Dara Shikoh who translated the Upanishads into Persian. *Mushtarika tahzeeb*, the culture of sharing got badly disrupted with the politics of extremes erupting in communal consciousness eventually. And as is well known, this was played up tactically by the British to finally lead to the Partition of the country. The River of Fire gushes forth, sweeping emotions and sensitivities, the past and the present simultaneously over rocks and crags and through inexplicable eddies.

Shifting locations, and severed from home, the post-Partition Kamal becomes a wanderer in search of his origins forever. At the same time, for many, as for him, Pakistan could be viewed as the Promised Land which may indeed have the potential to reconstruct his own identity within the

identity of his community. But as Sadaat Hasan Manto and
many other sensitive writers perceived, the common song of
the people could not be partitioned, and thus the sense of
lost-ness and desperation on both the sides. Gautam tells
Roshan Ara in *Aag ka Darya*, 'In this divided world we can
meet each other only on borders.' After all, time is not mere
blocks of historical events; and if perceived as it actually
flows, the despair of the 'disinherited mind' reduces
markedly, re-establishing the psychological connections that
cannot collapse abruptly merely through political action. The
novel asserts the need to realize continuities if only to
accommodate the new realities.

After having spent a few years in London, in 1961
Qurratulain Hyder decided to return to India. One thinks of
Champa Baji of *Aag ka Darya* who chooses to live in
Moradabad after several years of life in Europe soon after
the Partition. She comes back as 'part of the crowd, accepting
the comradeship of her fellow beings'. On his sentimental
visit to India, Kamal understands that Champa was not really
left behind and that she had chosen to be with the veiled
women and ragged urchins of her lane, and 'the under-
nourished coolies with their push-carts'. She is a wayfarer,
sadder and wiser, the serene Champa of new India — heroic
in her decision to face the insecurities and uncertainties of
her future against the backdrop of·distressing economic
problems and the impending war between India and
Pakistan. The applicability of the metaphor of the separate
spheres becomes immediately compelling in the face of the
politics of the two nations. But this is not ultimately
convincing since this metaphor does not explain the
emotional and psychological ties when cultural memories
get charted.

In the kaleidoscopic presentation of Champa Baji (of
Lucknow, Paris, London, Cambridge and Moradabad), merge
different images of Champak of Shravasti standing in the
corridor of time, Champak as the Aryani (Goddess of the
Woods), Champavati, a Sufi allegory for Kamal, as also

Champajaan, the courtesan who enchants Cyril Ashley. Enjoying her power over men, Champa comes galloping down the lanes of history demonstrating the courage of not only taking decisions but also acting upon them. She becomes the *chowdharain* of Lucknow, the head of the *tawaifs* or courtesans of Lucknow, a prestigious position and has access to the royal court. The author chooses all these Champa(s) who can operate outside the purdah and create their own space for empowerment. The cultural alienation of these characters is rooted in the patriarchal politics of constriction, exclusion and dispossession. It is within those constraints that the Champa(s) of the past determine their destinies. But then the pressures of society and politics see Champajaan as a beggar at the end of her life. And, Champa Ahmed of the post-Partition India survives amidst the poverty-stricken and backward Muslims left behind in India, while most of their relatives migrate to Pakistan in search of better prospects.

'But I saw the city chock full of Muslims,' Kamal argued. 'Only the hoi-polloi,' Bade Abba replied dismissively. 'The gentry has more or less emigrated.' (p. 400, *River of Fire*). Kamal looks at the pomegranate tree swaying in the breeze and invokes the past as he shudders with the question: 'Does Spain still haunt the Muslim mind, specially in times of crisis?' While Kamal projects the painful conflict between conviction and circumstance, Champa Ahmed's philosophic self collects and contains the anguish of Gautam, Harishankar and Kamal along with the entire crisis of Indo-Islamic culture and the crumbling of the long-cherished values.

> I am an ordinary girl. If I had been God's special person – somebody like Meera, Muktabai, Saint Sophia, one would have seen the marks of wounds on my body. My apparel would be bloody red with the murder of my purity. My hands would be pierced with nails. My head would be haloed. Bowls of poison and baskets of snakes would be sent to me. But I am merely Champa — Champa Ahmed. No one can see my wounds. Because my fellow beings too are wounded. They are weak mortals and have no vision.

Champa Ahmed is the most vibrant and living character in the novel. Self-confessedly, she points out how, like an ant, she climbs the mountain of problems in front of her. She breaks the stereotype image of a woman through her power of articulation and self-awareness. Such a woman is easily muted, invisiblized or marginalized. Not only do the readers of this novel get an insight into her personality but the delineation of this personality also offers a picture of her ancestors. A careful feminist reading of the novel could bring out all the connectives and departures of the evolution of Champa's identity as a woman in this country over centuries.

Aag ka Darya came into its English avatar in 1998, nearly 40 years after the Urdu novel. The English version is a transcreation, not a translation, by the author herself. Rewriting the novel over the turn of the century after another half a century of the fiery history of the extended Indo-Pak conflict, *Aag ka Darya* acquires greater relevance today. Its vision invokes the awareness of legacies of the Hindus and Muslims lying on the other side of the border, producing a peculiar socio-politico-cultural mosaic in the Indian subcontinent. Denial of history and heritage can in no way establish a stable identity for a constructive future. The novel is beyond giving merely sentimental or even moralistic diktats. It presents a process of creative unravelling of a past that inevitably lives in the present just as the present finds its seed in the past. But, for such a realization, an alertness about the essential flow of time rather than an amnesiac state of mind is required. A creatively selective memory animated through personal and collective consciousness explores the warp and the woof of the complex cultural weave of this region with its disruptive tears as well as knots.

The novel comes full circle when in the last chapter the reader finds herself, once again on the highway to Shravasti. Hari says, 'Kamal has deserted us — together we could have challenged the galaxies,' to which Gautam responds, 'We have all betrayed one another. Can these Western visitors to Shravasti understand the pain in our souls? In India's, in

Kamal's, in mine?' The outsider is the Westerner not the Muslim or the Hindu. Or then, really, the alienation experienced by each one is ultimately existential and from one's own self. The novel ends with the same question with which it begins: 'I...who the hell am I?' The river keeps flowing and the quest of the individual continues, the quest for identity and for the very purpose of one's existence. But then, nothing can be taken for granted, asserts the novel; for, who knows, even the river may not be eternal 'The river may dry up or change its course just as human beings disappear or change the direction of their journeys.' (p. 426, *River of Fire*)

The novel knocks at the wall of silence in the universe and searches for the meaning of human existence in specific space and time through migrations and settlements, politics and cultures, calendar years and timelessness. All this, to finally merge into some Absolute Silence. Perhaps getting ready for another Basant (spring).

> *Note*: For an exhaustive understanding of *Aag ka Darya*, the Urdu, Hindi and English texts of the novel can be used for intertextual study, for they essentially conform to the same vision despite some significant variations, specially found in the English transcreation. *River of Fire* is specially organized in chapters with titles, not given in the Hindi and Urdu texts, an attempt to perhaps simplify, for the English mind, the complex metaphor of cultural plurality evolved over centuries.

9

History and Fiction: The Depiction of 1857 in Qurratulain Hyder's Fiction

MOHAMMAD SAJJAD

E.H. Carr's conclusion that history is an unending dialogue between the past and present has become a universally acceptable fact. Memoirs and other creative writings like novels too can, therefore, be a useful source of history writing. This is not to say that fiction can be an incontrovertible source of history writing. Notwithstanding its limitations, fiction is reflective of socio-cultural realities. The fiction writer has the craft of creating character sketches and providing picturesque descriptions of situations containing details of individuals as well as collective consciousness. It is in the domain of socio-cultural details where archival documents based historiography fails to reach that the contribution of fiction writers can be best appreciated. Thus s/he mediates between past and future. Here the past is cognizable while the future is imaginable (whereas, to the historians, the past is verifiable). Through this medium s/he captures the realities. In this way a litterateur is at times a participant/observer and at times an observer of historical developments. The litterateur, therefore, is able to give at least an imaginary reality, if not actual factual realities.[1] At times a creative fiction writer uses both imaginary and factual reality along with collective memory. Thus, a fiction writer acts as a link between past, present and future. Some historians, therefore, are of the opinion that both litterateurs and historians should keep in touch with each other's domains.[2] In India, historians like Sudhir Chandra have made use of Hindi fictional writings to construct history and retrace neglected aspects of the past, particularly the evolution of nationalism in the later half of the nineteenth century.[3]

The upsurge of 1857, for various reasons, has endured in popular memory. Inevitably, it attracted the attention of Urdu writers as well. Mirza Ghalib's (1796-1869) letters and autobiographical accounts including *Dastanbu* (now Urdu translation of this Persian account is available in print) became more famous. Outside the literary domain of Urdu, other more informative and significant accounts remained less attended. Zaheeruddin Dehlvi's *Daastaan-e-Ghadar*, and *Fughan-e-Dehli* reprinted by Afghanullah Khan as *Taraz-e-Zaheeri*, Jafar Thanesri's autobiography, *Kaala Paani* hints obliquely at 1857, Munshi Enayat Husain's *Aiyaam-e-Ghadar*(1910), Khwaja Hasan Nizami's autobiography (1919), and ten (10) parts of the fiction in the series of *Ghadar-e-Dehli Ke Afsaney*, with the titles like *Ghadar Ki Maari Shahzadiyan*, *Be-chaarey Angrezon ki Bipta* (1927), *Begamaat Ke Aansu* (1928), *Roznamchas* of Ghalib and Bahadur Shah Zafar and other accounts, published in the early decades of the twentieth century are only a few such accounts waiting for the serious scrutiny of historians. However, we don't have much Urdu fiction dealing with that catastrophic event in greater detail. It is quite surprising that Pandit Ratan Nath Sarshaar and Abdul Haleem Sharar, despite their distinction for writing novels, deriving contents from India's history, have completely ignored this particular subject in their creative writings.

Nazeer Ahmad's *Ibnul Waqt* (Son of the Moment), Abdullah Faruqi's *Bahadur Shah ke Fasana-e-Gham* and Intezar Husain's *Dilli Tha Jis Ka Naam* has also given a brief narration of the catastrophes of 1857. Md. Mujeeb's drama *Aazmaish* is another literary work that depicts 1857.

It is even more surprising that a fiction writer like Qurratulain Hyder has not given as many details of the movement of 1857 as expected. Because Urdu critiques have observed that her fiction is the 'collective memory of Muslims'[4]. Another critique goes on to suggest that all her writings are in 'search of the lost ones', *unki tamam sarguzasht kho-e- huon ki justuju se ebaarat hai*[5]. Hyder is supposed to have drawn heavily on history for the content of her fiction, that in her writings, one finds the effect of the relevance (*maanwiyat*) and continuity (*tasalsul*) of history.[6] Her mastery over converting historical accounts and archival documents into creative fiction is just unparalleled in Urdu. Hyder's fiction itself says the past is intricately and inseparably linked with the present, continuity is eternal in history. Shameem Hanafi emphasizes that Hyder, with reference to real life events, creates imaginary events and then produces it with the elements of truthfulness; thus her narratives are verifiable (*qabil-e-tasdeeq*) and that her fiction are best sources to know the collective memory of the north Indian Muslim elites.[7] One of Hyder's Urdu short stories is replete with dialogues which reflect on various aspects of history and historiography. For instance, her story, 'Dareen Gard Sawaar-e-Baashad' (ahead of the dust is a man running mounted on a horse), contains at least three such dialogues: 'History is God's vision', 'God works out His plan through History', and 'History is merely propaganda for the victorious community'. Another work by Hyder, *Kaar-e-Jahan Daraaz Hai*, a family saga or auto-biographical novel, also narrates things in a similar way:

'Past is intricately linked with present, nothing happens in discontinuity. Since antiquity to eternity existence (*wajood*) is persistent (*paiham*) and continuous (*mustaqil*). Every event of the past is very close and near us. No other communities of the world than we Muslims have deeper consciousness of the comprehensiveness (*majmuiat*), continuity (*tasalsul*) and relevance (*maanwiyat*) of history (*taareekh*)'...

'The twelfth and the twentieth centuries have an interlude (*waqfah*) of not more than a moment (*barahwin aur biswin sadi ke darmeyan waqfah ek pal ek aan ka hai*)'.

On the basis of such contents in Hyder's fiction, Shameem Hanafi forms an opinion, 'Qurratulain Hyder, with reference to the realities of life, mixes the elements of actualities into imaginary events, in a way that the distinction between the historical/real and imaginary/unreal disappears. Even purely individual/personal and imaginary events are successfully woven into verifiable historical events and due to this wonderful coherence, her narrative wins the confidence of the readers and despite being individualistic, are taken as collective consciousness and experiences of the people'[8].

The fictional writings (novels) of Qurratulain Hyder such as *Gardish-e-Rang-e-Chaman, Aag ka Darya, Kaar-e-Jahaan Daraaz Hai* (family saga/autobiographical novel), have recaptured some aspects of the upsurge of 1857, in some details. More particularly, her novel, *Gardish-e-Rang-e-Chaman*, has depicted the implications of 1857 on the princesses of the *Qila e Mualla* (the Red Fort of Delhi). These princesses, Mehru and Hajjan Bi, in their attempts to escape the revengeful barbarism of the colonial regime, suffer from the oppressions of the situation and the time and for the sake of existence they end up becoming prostitutes. Critiques have not studied this novel with this perspective. Hanafi observes that this particular novel is 'relatively less burdened with history'[9]. Whereas, even this novel also derives its contents substantially from history and Hanafi himself does admit that Hyder has employed 'semi-documentation' in writing this novel and that 'her technique is Neo Historicism'.

As said earlier, these accounts or fictional representations are waiting for historians' attention and scrutiny. This paper will attempt to study these novels partly to recapture those realities and partly to explore some questions about how fiction relates to historical reality. In the process, function and truth value of fictional narratives may also be reassessed. It has been argued by authors like William Ray that 'fiction, from being a source of amusement and pleasure, has evolved as an important vehicle for representing contemporary social reality, and even shaping that reality'[10]. Acknowledgement of such utility of fiction has added new dimensions to methods and objectives of history writing. For instance, Clara Reeve, while commenting on the novel's historical referentiality said that 'the novel is a picture of real life and manners and of times in which it is written'. Collectively maintained assumptions, memories and at times 'unheard voices', are depicted more realistically through novels, as they are dependable vehicles for knowledge about society and a primary repository of cultural values. A novelist has his/her own ways of looking at the historical realities. The present paper would, therefore, study some Urdu novels of Qurratulain Hyder and compare them with existing historical accounts produced with the help of conventional sources like archival evidence. A study of this kind may help us understand and examine certain aspects of 1857 in a more informed way.

As said earlier, it is quite intriguing that a hugely catastrophic event like the Great Rebellion of 1857 has not figured as a dominant theme in Urdu fiction, unlike the Partition of 1947, which has found expression in an extremely large number of Urdu fiction and poetry. This is in contrast with English fiction, which has produced several novels on 1857 in the nineenth century, viz. Edward Money, *The Wife and the World* (1859), James Grant, *First Love and Last Love* (1868), Philip Meadow Taylor, *Seeta* (1872), J.F. Fanthorne, *Mariam* (1896). Some of these 'mutiny' novels served purposes like furthering imperial ideologies with jingoism and racism, while a few others sought to critique the cultural arrogance and restore a degree of racial harmony.[11] But all these novels remain the 'voice of the victors'.

This relative absence or inadequate treatment of the catastrophic theme of 1857 in Urdu fiction has sought to be explained by some scholars of Urdu. While Qurratulain

Hyder, in one of her Urdu short stories, has made a character of the story to express that 'History is nothing but propaganda of the victors' (*history mahaz faateh qaum ka propaganda hai*)'[12] . Ehtesham Husain, a noted Urdu critic, has made an observation that in the post-mutiny period, ruthless state repression had created an atmosphere of fear and anxiety. Moreover, people were unaware of the consequences, in this situation of uncertainties; it was difficult for the writers, hence not able to express their sensibilities and emotions/feelings[13]. He also surmises that many literary productions could not have been published, not to mention those which could not survive even after being published. Besides these reasons, Ehtesham Husain assigns another one as well, 'the agony of past, discomfitures of present, uncertainties of future, unawareness about the pulse of the age, inauguration of the new age of science and technology, defeat of new relations and emergence of hazy new relations, replacement of the administration by aliens, new print technology and information and great threat perception about the religio-cultural identity all combined to puzzle the minds of the poets and writers'.

Another reason for such limited Urdu (may be Hindi also) fiction on 1857 is because of the fact that till the early decades of the twentieth century, Urdu prose was heavily influenced by folk lore (*daastaan*) in the genre of *Alif Laila* and real events were yet to constitute the subject matter of Urdu prose[14]. This view is substantiated by the fact that there was considerable impact of the upsurge on poetry. But Hali has also written a poem in which he talks of forgetting the tribulations of 1857 and suggests the surviving victims to move on, by re-negotiating with the (invincible) British colonial state. Many nineteenth century historical accounts (in Urdu) have maintained a conspicuous silence on 1857. Shaad Azimabadi (1846-1927), in his *Naqsh-e-Paidar* and *Tarikh-e-Bihar* (1876) has made only a brief mention of the events of 1857, maintaining every precaution of avoiding value judgments[15]. Other such accounts like Ayodhya Prasad Bahaar's *Reyaz-e-Tirhut* (1868) and Bihari Lal Fitrat's *Aina-e-Tirhut* (1883) have also remained silent on the events of 1857, despite the fact that Tirhut (Muzaffarpur, Bihar) was one of the strongest storm centres of the 1857 movement.[16]

Nevertheless, the literary productions made by luminaries like Syed Ahmad (1817-98), Maulana Md. Husain Azad (1831-1910), the son of Molvi Baqar, the first martyred journalist of India, Hali (1837-1914), Nazeer Ahmad (1836-1912), Zakaullah (1832-1910) and Shibli (1857-1914) were the outcome of the treatment meted out by the colonial state to the Muslim elites[17]. They represent a formidable, enduring literary movement of Urdu. But these are more in consequence of 1857, not on the theme of 1857 *per se*. Hyder says that Raashedul Khairi (known in Urdu as *musawwir-e-gham*, i.e. depictor of tragedy) and other women novelists have depicted only victimized heroines, whereas romantic heroes have been shown weeping. The whole of India was steeped in pathos, (*saara Hindustan gham pasandi mein mubtala tha*), Hyder's family saga/autobiographical novel also says, '*colonial samaj ka adeeb aur shaair sirf rona aur rulana jaanta hai*' (the litterateurs of a colonial society don't know anything except weeping)[18]. May be, the historical consciousness of the novelist suggested that the people should forget the sense of having got subjugated and should come to terms with the colonial modernity. Probably because of this understanding, we find a clear and unambiguous expression of approval of Syed Ahmad's movement for modern education in Aligarh, in her fiction. Her most celebrated novel, *Aag ka Dariya* (River of Fire), published in 1957, though depicting vividly amazing historical cultural details of India from the sixth century BC to 1947, has written only one line on 1857. It notes, '*Hindustan, 1857 iswi ke baad, ab baa zaabta taur par Victoria ki empire mein shaamil ho chuka tha*'[19]. More than this, the novel does not focus much on the events of 1857. This sort of silence about or escape from the catastrophe of 1857 by Qurratulain Hyder is even more intriguing when one comes across such an opinion in her autobiographical account, *Kaar-e-Jahaan Daraaz*

Hai. It says that the events like the fall of Baghdad, i.e. *suqut-e-Baghdad* in 1256 AD, *Barbaadi-e- Undulus* in 1492 AD, decline of the Mughals, i.e. *zawaal-e-Mughliya* in 1857 and abolition of the Turkish caliphate, i.e. *daulat-e-Usmaniya ka khaatma* in 1919, are 'traumatic experiences' for Muslims. Yet, Hyder's creative productions fail to pay exclusive attention to the event of 1857. At one point, her auto-biographical novel/ family saga complains about the situation of helplessness that existed. It says: *yeh who badbakht zaman hai jab Hindustan 1857 ke surmaaon ka naam bhi nahin le sakta*[20] (These are the days of bad omens when one can not even commemorate the heroes of the movement of 1857). Hyder's autobiographical novel has also attempted to give references of primary and secondary sources in the form of end-notes, which is rarely a practice in fictional works. Writing about the participation of Meer Ahmad Ali Tirmizi (son of Imam Bakhsh Tirmizi, who was posted in the Meerut cantonment in 1857), the novel informs us that he participated because his religion was threatened, *kyonki deen khatrey mein thaa*[21]. This is yet another evidence for the apologists of colonialism who put greater emphasis on the religious cause of the Rebellion. But simultaneously the narrative also says that this was a stir (*shorish*) of Mewatis and Banjaras, which is indicative of non-elite or subaltern participation in the rebellion. Greater detail has been quoted from Syed Ahmad's account of 1857 in Bijnor, *Tarikh e-Sarkashi-e-Bijnor*. Then, in the subsequent pages, as the narrative proceeds, one comes across contemplations about the causes of the failure of Indians in 1857. It clearly spells out that most of the rebel leaders had their own personal motives: Some of the feudal leaders such as the Nawab of Rampur, wanted back their crowns (*taaj wa takht*). (*Baghaawat ke beshtar qaideen ke zaati maqasid judagana they)*[22]. Contrary to much emphasis (in nationalist historiography) on the Hindu-Muslim unity during the uprising, this autobiographical novel records that in the Sherkot mohalla of Bijnor, religious hatred (*mazhabi adaawat*) had set in; Hindu and Muslim 'rebels' started plundering each other's mohallas after the Muslim 'rebels' insisted on carrying the Muslim flags (*Muhammadi Jhanda*). It is also to be noted that at one place her autobiographical novel *Kaar-e-Jahaan Daraaz Hai*, mentions that a senior British official attempted to bribe some Hindus with Rs 50,000 to create Hindu-Muslim dissension and violence. It says:

> In the month of June (1857), the command of the rebel army in Bareilly came under Subedar Bakht Khan. Khan Bahadur Khan, the old grandson of Hafiz Rahmat Khan was appointed the viceroy of the subah Katehar by Bahadur Shah Zafar. Bahadur Khan obtained the Rajputs' help. Shobha Ram Bena was appointed the Dewan.
>
> Now the British, in order to finish the joint independent administration of the Rajputs and Muslims, conspired for Hindu rebellion and for the purpose Rs 50,000 was given to Captain Godani. He failed but in Bijnor, the Hindu Chaudhrys, loyal to the British, stood up against Nawab Mahmood Khan.[23]

The novelist's creative imagination or perception (may be obtained through oral tradition) is corroborated from archival evidences. George Copper, Secretary and Chief Commissioner of Awadh received a letter (dated 1 December 1857) from the Governor General to sanction Rs 50,000 to the Hindus of Bareilly to create Hindu-Muslim tension in the town[24]. Amazingly, even the amount of bribe being distributed is so precisely accurate in the fictional description. The narration of the police hunt of Meer Ahmad Ali Tirmizi helps us get picturesque details of the effective state espionage, state repression and precision with which the rebels were sought to be caught and punished with the worst possible ruthlessness. The novel also informs us that Feroz Bakht, the grandson (*nawaasa*) of the Mughal Emperor Farrukhsiyar survived the catastrophe of 1857 by begging in Muradabad, and then he escaped to Iran from where he went to take shelter with the Czar of Russia.

Afterwards, it starts its comments about the consequences of 1857 on Muslim minds. It says: *Musalman ab sirf karamaat ki ummeed par zinda hai*. Muslims now survive only on the hope of miracles[25]. Decadence (*Inhetaat*) persists with greater intensity, superstitious beliefs and practices like the use of amulets abound. *Taaweez, gandey, jhaarh phoonk ki garm bazari hai*. *Khanqahs* and *dargah* have become dens (*addah*) of luxuries (*aiyaashi*) and evils (*shar baazi*), whereas the pre-existing centres of learning have declined owing to the decline of the feudal lords. While many elites have lost their *jagirs*, some have started taking pride in colonial honours and titles such as Khan Bahadur, Rai Bahadur and in the services like Deputy Collector. They are those who have taken up modern education and their aspiration to change the 'system' (*nizam*). Because, the novel pronounces its judgment: 'The civilized people have always survived on the hope that if the present system is changed, the new one will be better than the present one' (*mutamaddan insaan hamesha is ummeed par zinda rahaa hai ki agar maujoodah nizam badal diya jaye to naya nizam is se behtar hoga*)[26]. Such conversations recorded in the novel informs us how the educated middle class of late nineteenth century India was about to see the beginning of nationalism. This is a self-evident historical truth that those parts/social groups/classes of India witnessed the early rise of anti-colonial nationalism, which had an early formation of the educated middle class.

Hyder's other novel *Gardish-e-Rang-e-Chaman*, gives more picturesque details (touching the readers' sensibilities more deeply), about the pathetic, wretched conditions to which the princesses of the Red Fort were reduced in the wake of 1857[27]. Its two important characters Hajjan Bi and Mehru were the princesses in the Red Fort, who had to flee in 1857, to escape the colonial wrath but they, surviving many vicissitudes in their tragic lives, ended up becoming prostitutes[28]. The novel notes that '1857 was the year of the defeat of the Indo-Muslim feudal culture'; the post-*Ghadar* Victorian morality and the missionary propagation of Christianity gave rise to an orthodox society in colonial India'; the continuity of the Mughal cultural influences is testified by the fact that even in the late nineteenth century the descendants of the Mughals (like Akhtar Zamani Begum, the great granddaughter of Shah Alam II) despite having converted to Christianity and carrying the Bible in one hand, did take care of carrying their Urdu poetic collections (*bayaaz*) in another hand[29]. Despite the fact that the story of this novel starts with and in the context of 1857, it does not go into many details on the events of 1857. There is a need for deep academic enquiry into the reasons for relatively inadequate treatment of the theme of 1857 in her fiction. On the basis of the conversations recorded in her short story, Dareen Gard Sawaar-e-Baashad, and its sub-title, *Jo Rahi so Be-khabri Rahi* (only a 'blissful' ignorance was there), explain its reasons to an extent. Some dialogues have been mentioned earlier. Other dialogues in the story may help us explain the reason further. For instance, at one place in the story, a character, referring to the account of John Beames, a nineteenth century colonial bureaucrat, says that the 'Battle of Plassey (1757) was not merely a victory of a European merchant company over an Indian province, rather it was the victory of a combination of the native Hindu merchants and British financial classes. The reason for the decline of the Muslims' rule was their internal contradictions and bickering. The British had close connections with the Hindu merchants. Karl Marx has said this very differently, new mercantile capital registered victory over the feudal system'[30]. To substantiate it with historical evidence, the story narrates that a Marwari merchant capitalist established a jute mill on a part of the Nawab of Chaitpur, Reza Khan Muzaffar Jung's four thousand *bighas* of land. This incident in itself is a signifier (*alaamat*) of the victory of merchant capital over the feudal system'[31]. The narrative of the story does not express any sympathy for eighteenth-nineteenth century feudal elites. Regarding the dismissal of the eighteenth century Nawab Reza Khan Muzaffar Jung of Tirhut (Bihar), it says, '...but why should we have any sympathy for Md Reza Khan? He had neither modern science, technology nor did he have rationalism with which Clive and Hastings were equipped. When Muzaffar

Jung shook hands with Warren Hastings, it appeared that the medieval age of India was saluting the modern scientific age of Europe'[32].

Shameem Hanafi, therefore suggests, 'In the character sketches of Qurratulain Hyder we find an expanded horizon of moods and cultural norms which reveals that she is successfully capable of expressing the deep insights about different big civilizations in the context of contemporary situations of mankind. Study of individuals, in a way is also the study of various cultural and civilizational units. The existence of human and the realities about their history are often not as divergent as they might appear to be.'[33]

Conclusion

Thus, we find that the litterateurs' observations and sensitivities on a particular historical event are not less important to construct our past. The fictional works are another source which help us to discover and re-discover our past, as we see in the case of the novel *Gardish-e-Rang-e-Chaman*, a part of which has more picturesquely recreated/recorded some aspects of the impact of 1857 on the Mughal princesses. After 150 years of the event, when once again, the professional historians[34] have engaged in taking the pains of looking into the dust-loaded, moth-eaten archival evidences and popular memory is enthusiastically responding to such efforts, one hopes that the best fiction writers will join the inquisitive historians to collect stuff for their fictional creative productions. Moreover, a meticulous study and critical scrutiny of the fictional and poetic literature (which are collective memories and consciousness of society) may enrich our understanding of the growing ideas of nationalism in India, and this is how unending dialogue between the present and the past will continue endlessly.

Acknowledgements: I am grateful to my friends Najmul Hoda, IPS, Dr. Aftab Ahmad (Chicago) and a few others for their comments and suggestions. An early draft of it was presented at a seminar on 1857 in BHU, Varanasi, on

18 August 2007. I am also thankful to the participants of the seminar for their comments and suggestions.

Notes

1. I owe these points to Dr. Rizwan Qaiser, JMI, New Delhi.
2. Gayatri Chakravarty Spivak, 'A Literary Representation of the Subalterns: Mahasweta Devi's 'Stanadayini', in Ranajit Guha (ed.) *Subaltern Studies*, Vol. 5, OUP, Delhi, 1987, pp. 91-134.
3. Sudhir Chandra, *Oppressive Present:Literature and Social Consciousness in Colonial India*, OUP, Delhi, 1992. Also see Gayatri Chakravorty Spivak, 'A Literary Representation of the Subaltern: Mahasweta Devi's 'Stanadayini' in Ranajit Guha (ed.), *Subaltern Studies: Writings on South Asian History and Society*, OUP, Delhi, 1987, pp. 91-134.
4. Shameem Hanafi on *Gardish-e-Rang-e-Chaman* in Irtiza Karim (ed.), *Qurratulain Hyder: Ek Mutalea*, Educational Publishing House (EPH), Delhi, 1992, 2001, p. 375.
5. Fateh Muhammad Malik, *Qurratulain Hyder: Apni Talaash Mein*, cited by Shameem Hanafi, op. cit., p. 373.
6. Shameem Hanafi, op. cit., p. 377.
7. Ibid., p. 386.
8. Ibid., p. 373.
9. Ibid.
10. William Ray, *Story and History: Narrative Authority and Social Identity in the Eighteenth Century French and English Novel*, Basil Blackwell, Oxford, 1990.
11. Aishwarya Lakshmi, 'The Mutiny Novel: Creating the Domestic Body of the Empire', *Economic and Political Weekly*, vol. XLII, No. 19, 12 May 2007, pp. 1746-1753. Indrani Sen, 'The Great Rebellion of 1857 in the Nineteenth Century Colonial Novel', *People's Democracy*, Weekly, Vol. XXXI, No. 23, 10 June 2007.
12. Qurratulain Hyder, 'Dareen Gard Sawaar-e-Baashad' in her collection of Urdu short stories *Raushni Ki Raftaar*, Educational Book House, Aligarh, 1992. While critiquing the ideology of history, the story also says, *'Taareekh Khuda ka vision hai; Khuda Taareekh ke zariye apna plan work out karta hai'*, p. 275.
13. Ehtesham Husain, 'Urdu Adab: Inqilab-e-1857 Ke Pas Manzar Mein', in *Naya Daur*, Urdu Monthly, Lucknow, September 1957

and reprinted in the same periodical in April-May 2007.

14. I am thankful to Naved Masood for this point.

15. Shad Azimabadi's Urdu novel/novella, *Peer Ali*, consists of the contents taken from these two works by Shad Azimabadi.

16. Surendra Gopal, *Urdu Historiography in Bihar in the Nineteenth Century: Contribution of Hindu Authors*, KPJRI, Patna, 2004. For the details of the movement of 1857 in Tirhut, see, Mohammad Sajjad, Local Resistance and Colonial Reprisal: Tirhut Muslims in the Ghadar 1857-59, in *Contemporary Perspectives: History and Sociology of South Asia*, Vol. 2, No. 1, January-June 2008, pp. 25-44. Also see, S. Narain, 'The Role of Tirhoot in the Movement of 1857-59', in *Journal of Bihar Research Society* (JBRS), March 1954, pp. 55-73, and Vijay Kumar Thakur, 'Movement of 1857-58 in Tirhut and the Rebels' in *JBRS*, Vol. 61, 1975, pp. 105-22.

17. For a detailed study about these literary luminaries, see Mushirul Hasan, *Moral Reckoning: Muslim Intellectuals of Nineteenth Century Delhi*, OUP, Delhi, 2005.

18. Qurratulain Hyder, *Kaar-e-Jahaan Daraaz Hai*, Vols. I and II, EPH, Delhi, 2003 (Reprint), p. 156. The new print has combined the first two volumes.

19. Qurratulain Hyder, *Aag ka Darya*, EPH, Delhi, 1957, 2000 (Reprint), p. 221. For a detailed critical study of this novel, see Asloob Ahmad Ansari's essay in *Fikr-o-Nazar*, Urdu quarterly, Aligarh, October 1960. Also see Liyanage Amarakeerthi, '*River of Fire*: Critiquing the Ideology of History' in *Annual of Urdu Studies*, Vol. 18, 2003, pp. 25-44.

20. *Kaar-e-Jahaan Daraaz Hai*, p.108.

21. *Kaar-e-Jahaan Daraaz Hai*, pp. 43-44. In her other novel, *Gardish-e-Rang-e-Chaman*, there is a narration that the whites martyred those who battled crying *Deen! Deen!* p. 105.

22. Ibid., p. 50.

23. Ibid., p. 46.

24. S.M. Azizudin Husain, *1857 Revisited*, DSA in History, JMI, New Delhi, 2007, p. 85.

25. Ibid., p.68.

26. Ibid., p. 83.

27. Shameem Hanafi observes that this novel is relatively less burdened with history, op. cit., p. 384.

28. *Gardish-e-Rang-e-Chaman*, p. 138. I am grateful to my wife Nargis for sharing her views on the novel. The title of the novel has been taken from a lesser known couplet of Ghalib, *umr meri ho gayee sarf-e-bahaar-e-husn-e-yaar; Gardish-e-rang-e-chaman hai maah o saal-e-andaleeb*. This in itself is suggestive of the mercilessness of the time impacting upon the people (specially the upper middle class), which is the dominant theme in almost all Hyder's fiction.

29. *Gardish-e-Rang-e-Chaman*, p. 366.

30. Qurratulain Hyder, 'Dareen Gard Sawaar-e-Baashad' in her collection of Urdu short stories *Raushni Ki Raftaar*, Educational Book House, Aligarh, 1992, p. 277.

31. Ibid. Also see Abdul Majed Khan, *Transition in Bengal, 1756-75: A Study of Saiyid Md. Reza Khan*, Cambridge, 1969. Reza Khan Muzaffar Jung was the *Chakladar* of Chittagong and Nawab of Chaitpur in Bengal, and then he became the Jagirdar of Tirhut in north Bihar, founded the town of Muzaffarpur, Bihar. For details, see my essay on 1857 in Tirhut, in *Contemporary Perspectives*, January-June 2008 and Hyder, *Kaar e Jahaan Daraaz Hai*, Vol. I, Educational Publishing House (EPH), Delhi, 2003, p. 180.

32. Qurratulain Hyder, 'Dareen Gard Sawaar-e-Baashad' in her collection of Urdu short stories *Raushni Ki Raftaar*, Educational Book House, Aligarh, 1992, p. 278.

33. Shameem Hanafi on *Gardish-e-Rang-e-Chaman* in Irtiza Karim (ed.), *Qurratulain Hyder: Ek Mutalea*, Educational Publishing House (EPH), Delhi, 1992, 2001, pp. 368-95.

34. S.M. Azizuddin Husain's recently published collection of 150 documents sifted from the National Archives of India, New Delhi, and also from some provincial archives, with the title, *1857 Revisited*, is one such outcome.

10

The Creative Genius of Aini

SYED MOHD AHRAF

In 1994, Qurratulain Hyder wrote these lines in the Preface of a collection of stories:

> At the end of the twentieth century, we are faced with an ignorant, insensitive and criminal world. Man is reinventing himself.

Fourteen years on, things are even worse. Obscene style of anchoring on the entertainment channels of media, nauseating nudity in advertisements, guilelessness of teenagers and youth and ostrich-like behaviour of elders, fear of going out among decent people, terror and riots and insensitive politicking, violence on any pretext right or wrong, and the audacity to go to any extent to get luxurious things in life....

Today, in this ignorant, insensitive and criminally inclined world, such disgusting scenes, as pointed out by Qurratulain Hyder, are found everywhere. There is some satanic power that is slowly consuming our culture and our great values in an organized and puzzling manner. A lethal situation has been created as if one specific culture that is noisy, reprehensible and eye-scorching, defines the culture of the entire universe. More so, because Aini's literary legacy gives us precisely the message that the world should not have become what it is.

There were two major accusations against Aini's literature:

- Aini writes for the elite class and writes about them; and
- Aini's language is anglicized

It is surprising that these charges were aired and supported by very senior critics. What is more surprising is that even after 50 years, a few academic critics still harp on the same theme. Aini's texts, though, provide enough evidence against these charges. For instance, Firoza of *Nazarah Darmiyan Hai*, Surayya of *Housing Society*, the two sisters of *Agle Janam Mohe Bitiya Na Kijo*, Gracy of *Yaad Ki Dhanak Jale*, Chhammi of *Hasab Nasab*, Kallu Mehtar of *Darin Gard Saware Bashad*, the old man of *Dalan Wala*, the heroine of *Chandni Begum*, the dwarf girl of *Dekho Iss Tarha Se Bhi Raqse Fughan Hota Hai* — all these living-breathing characters of Urdu literature do not belong to the elite class of society. They are downtrodden, poor and much worse off than us.

As far as her language is concerned, friends have many misconceptions. Aini used to write dialogues in the lingua franca. Our lingua franca consists of many words in English. Yours truly also occasionally uses English words to pace up the story. And numerous earths, skies, countries and contexts, races and humans, cultures and civilizations and periods of time that Aini wanted to show was not perhaps possible in traditional Urdu. The change in themes naturally leads to a change in the language that serves as a vehicle for it. For example:

- The language in *Housing Society* is that of the elites of *qasbas* (towns) of UP.
- *Saint Flora Ke Eterafat* is written in the language of a nun where the first sentence itself is in praise of God and Jesus.

- *Agle Janam Mohe Bitiya Na Kijo* has pure Lucknowi dialect.
- The language of *Aag ka Darya* bears witness to the changes that language went through with changing times. The opening pages read as if Kalidas is writing Urdu prose.
- *Kaare Jahan Daraz Hai* uses the language of a news-daily where an attempt to finish the discourse in a precise manner can be felt in different chapters.
- The narration in *Qaid Khane Mein Talatum Hai Ke Hind Aati Hai* is close to poetic expression as the plotless subject or the subject of multiple plots could only be covered in that fashion.
- The language in *Chandni Begum* carries the influence of the mixed language of the last decade of the twentieth century.

I would like to conclude this point by saying that depending on situations, Aini could write in a wide range of styles. She wrote Persianized Urdu with authority. For example, in *Housing Society*, if one analyses the claimant lady Buta Begum's application to the District Collector, one would find line after line in Persianized and Arabic-intensive Urdu.

Aini had an authority over depiction of all kinds of details. Things, places, buildings, events, races, communities, languages, regions, movements, traditions, weathers, feelings, different moods of love — there was not a single narrow spot that Aini's pen could not bring alive. And there was no detail that she could not express through hints and suggestions.

> *Tumhen ghamzon mein asan hai maani ka ada karna*
> *Hamen lafzon mein mushkil hai bayan-e mudda'a karna*

You can convey meanings by mere suggestions
For us it is difficult to word our expressions.

Hyder's pen provides us with countless expressions of Indian feminism. Champa, Champak, Champa Ahmed, Surayya,

Chhoti Bitiya, Sita, Jamilan, Rashke Qamar, Gulzar Bai and many other memorable characters of *Agle Janam Mohe Bitiya Na Kijo* are fine examples. Hardly anyone has written with such detail and consistency on the deprivation of the woman and her fate. And so well.

Extensive knowledge of sociology, history and geography provided depth and breadth to Aini's literature. While her knowledge of history has often been talked about, there is need to discern her knowledge of geography as well. There is hardly any place on earth that has not found a direct or an indirect mention in her fiction. She discusses countries, cities, towns, villages, seas, rivers, plains, mountains and regions with mastery. She had vast knowledge of plants and animals of places she wrote about. This is clearly evident in her novels, short stories and even in reportages.

Qurratulain Hyder exercised creative freedom that is unheard of in the Urdu language. Fiction is usually confined to time and space but these fetters are often broken in Aini's world. In her short stories, one does not even feel the difference in the real and the surreal. At least three of her stories do not belong to routine affairs — 'Roshni Ki Raftar', 'Saint Flora Ke Eterafat' and 'Malfoozate Haji Gul Baba Bayktashi'. But Aini's craft was so powerful that her reader doesn't think for a moment how a skeleton can come to life after hundreds of years. How a Sufi can come out of his grave or how a woman, Dr. Padma, can enter a three thousand-year-old past, sitting in a ship. Apart from events, she exercised her freedom in matters of language as well. She would bring in a word or a piece of expression from anywhere and it would fit in the discourse as if it was meant only for that.

When Firdausi wrote *Shahnama*, a few envious people raised questions that such and such line is out of balance or a character is falling off at another place and that such and such word is out of rhyme. They gathered in the court of Mahmud Ghaznavi. Firdausi rose and uttered a single sentence:

Listen friends! The *Shahnama* was destined to be written by Firdausi so I did. Now you should all rectify your rhyme and rhythm according to the *Shahnama*.

I feel that if someone challenged Aini's free will, she too would have said:

Well, I had to write the story, so I did. Now you please fix your styles according to my story.

Now please bear another point of this rather hazy view:

In the last thirty years of the twentieth century, our society was reduced to such a pitiable condition where there was hardly any political or philosophical institution that could offer ideals for the youth. Such a situation demands literature of protest. Usually, literature of protest is not good literature. It becomes somewhat melodramatic and borders on sloganeering. Aini was quite successful on this front as well. One is often surprised that our committed progressive seniors, with the exception of Majrooh and Makhdoom could not manage to create superior literature through their writings of protest. The superior part of Ali Sardar Jafri's poetry is not that of protest, it is romantic in nature — for example the first half of 'Mera Safar' and 'Awadh ki Khake Hasin'. An unbiased assessment would prove that among the leading lights of our writers of twentieth century, there are only three who managed to blend the harsh pain of protest into their songs — Iqbal, Faiz and Qurratulain Hyder. Every single line of 'Qaid Khane Men Talatum Hai Ki Hind Aati Hai' is an example of superior literature of protest. 'Yeh Ghazi Yeh Tere Pur-israr Bande' is an example of literature of protest for its quintessence and style of expression.

The oppressive governments which advanced the theory of 'clash of civilizations' should get the literature of this Indian female translated into their languages — read it themselves and let their new generations read it too. The more I think about Aini's knowledge of history, the more my faith is reaffirmed that the consistent and detailed descriptions of history, geography, various countries and religions which are found in Aini's literature were not merely to show off her knowledge and authority. Instead, her real objective was to show the interactions, commonality, and shared values among various civilizations. In Aini's world, civilizations interact with each other in a way as two good neighbours ask about each other's welfare in the morning.

A brief excerpt from 'Saint Flora of Georgia':

> But it was strange that the new (Islamic) government treated us very well. They were heard saying that they were following the charter of their Prophet which he had shown to the priests of the church of Saint Catherine.

After the sunset, when anyone of us nuns went up to the dome to light the candle, we would see caravans going towards Lebanon, Palestine and Egypt ringing bells and following their respective lead singers. Once in a while, someone from them would call out, 'O followers of Prophet Jesus, the soul of God, may you live in peace! In response, we would stand there carrying the candles in the dome till those travellers were lost in the dark.'

In the same way, in 'Nazara Darmiyan Hain', two civilizations are in love with each other. It is another matter that they became a victim of the rival's evil eyes.

Similarly, in her Reportage, 'Dar Chaman Har Warqe', she proves the proximity of the language of Parsis' religious text with Sanskrit shlokas. This makes it clear that Aini not only tries to find commonalities between Muslim culture and other cultures. She did not reserve this for any single culture. Somewhere, she also tells us that, in America, there are cities with names like *Dilli*, *Lucknow* and *Madina*.

One can find two hundred such examples in the fiction of Qurratulain Hyder. I wish to say that, because she was rooted in India, mysticism, her personal broad-mindedness in issues of faith and after her study of three thousand years of history, Hyder had come to the conclusion that cultures actually encourage people to love each other. Cultures are fundamentally there to unite and not separate. Cultures form the platform for people to interact and not fight.

Hyder's novels and short stories are indeed on a very high pedestal. But even if we place any of her collection of reportages over the satanic book of clash of civilizations, the bones of the book underneath would start cracking. This has to be done by our young researchers. It should then be translated into many languages to let the world know that besides literature, Aini was a very valuable human being in the other affairs of the world too.

Translated from English by Nishat Zaidi

11

Qurratulain Hyder and the Partition Narrative

SHAMIM HANFI

The odyssey of Qurratulain Hyder's sensibility which started with *Mere Bhi Sanam-khane* (1949) passed through her second novel *Safina-e-Gham-e-Dil* (1952) before it found its culmination in *Aag ka Darya* (1959). Here, it is important and worth considering that unlike the common practice of the post-partition years, Qurratulain Hyder, as far as she could, refrained from taking up as her subject the political events and communal riots in a direct way. Contrary to the general impression, I think in *Aag ka Darya*, Qurratulain Hyder has tried to keep herself free of the determination of history. It's a meta-history level narrative.

Most short stories written against the background of the post-partition riots seem to be dominated by a mind in a hurry to pour itself out. It appears as though the writers did not get the time to think over and analyse their feelings. The tragedy of partition was so horrifying that it was not easy for the average writers of the time to be mindful of the demands of any stable creative value on a firm footing. The most rational interpretation of the post-partition literature is found in the writings of Mumtaz Shirin and Mohammad Hasan Askari. Mumtaz Shirin thinks that till that time:

The riots had not got into the frontier of intellectual experience after a proper assimilation in the mind. Those stories were written under the compulsion of instant writing. The writers took to a narrow path with utmost precaution. They had decided beforehand what could be the progressive analysis of the riots and their causes, what should be the attitude of the writers and what kind of stories should be written.[1]

The formula story of that period was a product of a certain lack of patience. Apart from those who reviewed the general situation of that time along religious and communal lines, even the writings of many progressive authors betray the writer in a hurry and the resultant sentimentalism and unequivocal treatment of the subject. In his article '*Fasadat Aur Hamara Adab*' (Riots and Our Literature), Mohammad Hasan Askari has raised the following question:

Can these happenings by themselves and just as events become the subject of literature? While contemporary answers to such questions we should forget for a while our personal and national miseries. If we want to find a satisfactory answer to our question, we should for the time being take leave of our feeling of being persecuted and oppressed.

Most of our writers were just not able to keep themselves emotionally detached from what was happening before them. In the context of a history and life besieged with collective calamity, the first question that a writer faces is about his own position against the backdrop of the entire situation. Then the immediate post-1947 happenings were surrounded together by a number of cultural, philosophical, psychological and emotional questions and it seemed as though there was no room for coming to terms with the collective fate in that atmosphere. It was a time marked more by a disintegration of dreams and ideas rather than one conducive to their growth. And though there is no end to the ifs and buts of history, it was becoming increasingly difficult even for the average human beings of that time to keep their senses in harmony and their thoughs organized. The dawn of independence had come like a nightmare and the feeling of anxiety and desperation gave way to a deep sense of defeat. Hence the following observation of Mumtaz Shirin has an objective and logical ring:

> Rather than the external trauma of the riots, the greater experience and event of that time was that exile and migration which came in the wake of the riots and this migration with its internal pain and sorrow became a creative experience. It was not just migration from one land to another; it was a migration from one time to another.[2]

The riots that broke out in the shadow of the 1947 partition bear the seal of history and their circle is so inflexible that any writer of fiction who takes up the riots as his subject would find it difficult to transgress the limits set upon him. More than any other writer of that time, Sadat Hasan Manto knew how to keep himself from being overwhelmed and intimidated by the external events. He neither allowed any room for sentimentality in his stories, nor assumed the pose of a reporter and chronicler of the communal case, nor that of its judge and propagator. Qurratulain Hyder's distinction also lies in the fact that from *Meray bhi Sanamkhane* to *Aag ka Darya*, she nowhere mortgaged her creative freedom to history. She is not as sanguine and emotionally detached in her creative stance as Manto but she seems to be quite successful in saving herself from the sweeping flow of history as she constructs a narrative with an epic dimension. In the context of the general narrative tradition of Urdu fiction it was an extraordinary creative endeavour, almost a quantum jump, which was difficult to sustain for her run of the mill contemporaries.

Aag ka Darya is neither an alternative to sociology nor will it be proper to deduce history from it. Its narrative space encompasses ancient Indian civilization, Indo-Islamic civilization of the middle period and the overall situation of our own time or what might be called the twentieth century scene. Its time frame is spread over a period of two thousand and five hundred years and its range is much more varied and inclusive than that of any other Urdu novel written till date. But the fiction that was written immediately after partition was written in a hurry as though with an anxiety to meet a deadline. Therefore not much of that fiction can save itself from getting dated and stand on a firm artistic and creative foundation as literature with an abiding interest. The big picture of India's partition and the events that accompanied it were very complex. Most of the fiction written against its background is one sided and superficial. Partition was undoubtedly a great tragedy but those who wrote about it could not measure up to it and were unable to break free of their stereotyped reaction. Even for Qurratulain Hyder it took some ten years to move away from the stage of *Meray bhi Sanamkhane* and come to *Aag ka Darya*. Before elaborating this point my mind is diverted to yet another important observation on the literature of that period. Writing in *Fasadat aur Hamara Adab*, Mohammad Hasan Askari notes:

> Man's history is twenty-five to thirty thousand years old. God knows what has already happened and what is still to happen. How far can literature take care of the sentiments of each individual and group? We will have to take leave for a while of our feeling of being oppressed if we want to find a satisfactory answer to our question.
>
> The 1914 war produced a great bulk of literature. But how much of that literature is alive today? W. B. Yeats with the characteristic cruelty and hard-heartedness of a true writer frankly declared that he had not included any poem about the war in his collection of new poems because passive suffering in itself is not a subject of literature.

It is necessary to 'de-historicize' *Aag ka Darya* in order to appreciate its true greatness. James Joyce says that the artist is both inside and outside his work. He is in the background and in front of it. And he is also seen in conflict with himself altogether unconcerned with his work. Over-dependence on the events of the external world results in the writer's relying on borrowed experiences rather than on his own. All his insight becomes subservient to collective aims and his general social consciousness. The greatest harm that comes from this tendency is that the writer's range of creative efforts gets narrowed down and sometimes his writing reads like journalism. The time-identity of *Aag ka Darya* is based on its not being a historical novel despite the fact that it apparently uses history as its point of reference. The spectacle of life that furnishes the foundation for this novel has in it not only the rhythm of a collective life spanning two thousand five hundred years but also the echo of the ever present time. History and that which is above and beyond it or historical time and mythical time are uniformly interwoven in the texture of this novel. Hence the central issue in *Aag ka Darya* is not characters but cultures.

Aag ka Darya can be regarded as a denial of the tradition of fiction inherited by Qurratulain Hyder as well as an affirmation of a new tradition. The blue print of this novel as it took shape in Hyder's mind was different not only from the fiction preceding her work but also from her own earlier novels, such as *Mere Bhi Sanamkhane* and *Safina-e-Gham-e-Dil*. The late Mujtaba Husain who regarded *Aag ka Darya* as a failure in terms of creativity says:

> *Mere bhi Sanamkhane* is Qurratulain Hyder's most successful, interesting, lively and cheerful novel. Here her style of writing is not cumbersome nor is it affected by the book's length. Apart from this, the theme which is found in two of her later novels, *Safina-e-Gham-e-Dil* and *Aag ka Darya,* appears to be new and attractive for being presented for the first time.[3]

There are several flaws in this assessment. First, it is not critically proper to term the length of *Aag ka Darya* a burden. Second, *Aag ka Darya* is not very different from Hyder's earlier novels as far as its style is concerned. And the third and most important point is that these three novels are not alike despite apparent similarities of theme and subject. Nature imprints only one book in the inner being of every great writer and throughout his life he searches the path of his expression with the help of the key elements of that book. Qurratulain Hyder had certain basic concerns, stances and commitments and she never deviated from those philosophical preferences, human sympathies and moral affinities right from *Mere bhi Sanamkhane* to her last novels *Kar-e-Jahan Daraz Hai* and *Chandni Begum*. The fact remains that it was *Aag ka Darya* that established her identity as a writer. Qurratulain Hyder did not accept this general preference (for *Aag ka Darya*) but it is not obligatory for us to agree with whatever a writer says about himself/herself. It is necessary to stress here an important fact which I mentioned earlier that instead of characters, culture and its related issues are of basic significance in *Aag ka Darya*.

Both politics and religion are relegated to a secondary position or become altogether meaningless in the story of civilizations. All of us know about the role of politics and religion in the context of the difficulties and problems faced by our shared ways of life throughout India's history. Qurratulain Hyder has used her memory as a symbol of protest in the journey from the past to the present. Before *Aag ka Darya*, this note of resistance and dejection was not so prominent in her writing nor was its perspective so vast. For instance, she wrote in *Safina-e-Gham-e-Dil:*

> Abba Mian (Father)! All your dreams of *inquilab* (revolution) have gone wrong somewhere. Now when we are here to say farewell to you close to your *mafia* shrubbery in *Aish Bagh*, perhaps you don't even know what we have been through and why we had to leave you. There will now be a distance of thousands of miles and the solitude of hundreds of years between us and the soil in which you were born and buried. Now we are foreigners to each other — because we are leaving our country — because we have proved utterly worthless. Our generation could not carry the burden which you, Abba Mian and your companions had handed to us.

There is no doubt that after 1857, the 1947 partition of India and the communal riots meant a great national calamity to our collective existence. It has affected the lives of us all and for many of us the fires of this great tragedy have not yet diminished. Hence its imprints can be seen even today on the output of the Urdu short story and novel. *Aag ka Darya* and Abdullah Hussain's *Udaas Naslain* and later Intezar Hussain's *Aagay Samundar Hai* and several other notable Urdu novels and short stories by several younger and older short story writers from Qurratulain Hyder and Intezar Husain to Surendar Prakash, Joginder Paul and Asif Farrukhi have as their subject the life that unfolded in the shadow of Partition. The entire scenario of Urdu fiction can be viewed with reference to the pre and post-Partition situation as parallel realities related to a common background. Migration, exile, collective memory, lack of direction, search for new lands, defeat and disintegration of an organized cultural system, decline of shared values, a past entrenched in the present and an uncertain future — many of our questions are linked to this very thread of history.

After *Mere bhi Sanamkhane* and *Safina-e-Gham-e-Dil* had given a new direction to her pain and melancholy it was *Aag ka Darya* that honed Qurratulain Hyder's sensibility to a new sharpness. The quotation from *Safina-e-Gham-e-Dil* cited above shows the protagonist moving in a narrow groove of thoughts even though the creative rhythm of the writing is extremely romantic and personal. It has a marked ring of autobiography and personal elegy. It does not express any deep insight perhaps because of a certain uncontained sentimentality and immature thought. Maybe because till that time, Qurratulain had viewed the whole trauma of Partition and migration in the light of her personal loss and she came to terms with the broader cultural and spiritual problems brought about by Partition only after casting away the cross of personal sorrows. By *Aag ka Darya*, she had moved from one shore of herself to another.

In *Aag ka Darya*, Qurratulain Hyder has brought to focus the interior landscape of a whole period, a whole society dying out in that period and a strong culture based on common civilizational values. Considered from this stance, the novel is the first great specimen in Urdu of a search for internal reality. Hence, it should be separated from such writing that deals with surface reality and relies on easy-going observation, and seen as a creative document founded on the realities of an internal world. The mark of a darkening quasi-tragic depth of insight that gives the works of Dostoevsky and Kafka their greatness may not be found in *Aag ka Darya* but *Aag ka Darya* also does not accord with that interesting but simplistic narrative which has held sway in Urdu from Ruswa and Ratan Nath Sarshar to Premchand. In a conversation, Qurratulain Hyder once observed: 'To present truth or not to present it has no meaning for a fiction writer because the fiction writer has an altogether different psyche.'

This conversation also contained the following remark which reflects the retaliatory reaction to a rather infirm academic observation on the mixing of fiction in truth with regard to *Aag ka Darya*:

> Truth? What truth? What is truth in the novel the creative writers are writing? The way truth is presented, is that truth? The truth that a fiction writer relates, is that truth?[4]

Compared to the earlier works of Qurratulain Hyder and the other Urdu novels that represent the narrative tradition before its appearance, *Aag ka Darya* is much more complex and sombre in terms of its form and stylistic framework. It makes a silent demand on the reader to be read as a representative work of a new creative value in accordance with the basic twentieth century currents of thought and the modern and global trends of fiction. In the context of the twentieth century Urdu fiction which rises above the unnatural divide of the East and the West and the prevalent popular modes of storytelling, *Aag ka Darya* is the first major novel which can be seen as a national allegory. Most of the criticism of this grand experiment is raw and ridiculous because many people simply could not contain the width of Qurratulain's vision and they remained prisoners of traditional critical jargon. This problem calls for a detailed critical exposition which is not possible within the limit of this essay.

Therefore I would like to conclude with the comments of two important critics on *Aag ka Darya*. The first quotation is from Mehmood Ayaz:

> All the three novels of Qurratulain Hyder *(Mere bhi Sanamkhane, Safina-e-Gham-e-Dil* and *Aag ka Darya)* are a great elegy on all those ideas and values which were nurtured by a certain way of living together and a concept of life...In *Aag ka Darya*, Qurratulain Hyder has projected the tragedy of Partition in the perspective of a cultural life of two thousand and five hundred years in a manner as if this event is not just the story of a particular country or class but a part of human history.

And the following lines from the memorable essay entitled *'Aag ka Darya par Wujoodiyaat Ke Asraat'* ('The Impact of Existentialism on *Aag ka Darya')* by Waheed Akhtar (included in a collection entitled *Urdu Fiction* edited by Ale Ahmad Suroor):

> *Aag ka Darya* is the first Urdu novel which throws full light on the man of the present age and the problems of his existence. A special feature of this novel is that Qurratulain Hyder has spread on its canvas a vast background spanning thousands of years. Hence the waves of this river carry along thousands of years of Indian culture, philosophy, conventions and customs....*Aag ka Darya* is a document of our civilization as well as a mirror for the contemporary modes of thought and feeling. Even if it is not regarded as the greatest Urdu novel, it will have to be conceded that it is one of the two or three great novels of Urdu. The other novel is definitely *Udaas Naslain* (by Abdullah Hussain). The Urdu novel has found its maturity in these two novels.

Waheed Akhtar is right in regarding *Aag ka Darya* as the first existential novel in Urdu. But its philosophical undercurrents also demand that it should be seen in the light of the social and humanistic concepts of existentialism. Only then can the meaning of its real individuality and value be determined. Here an observation by Mehmood Ayaz that Qurratulain

Hyder's intense emotionalism has at places turned the sublime into the ridiculous appears to be controversial. I think that as against the emotionalism of *Mere bhi Sanamkhane* and *Safina-e-Ghame-Dil, Aag ka Darya* contains a trained creative restraint and a deep awareness of culture. *Aag ka Darya* should be viewed outside the four walls of the author's preceding work *(Sitaron Se Aagay, Sheeshay kay Ghar, Mere bhi Sanamkhane,* and *Safina-e Gham-e-Dil).*

Qurratulain Hyder has woven the texture of the story in *Aag ka Darya* from the determinants of man's collective fate and the issues related to the general moral and cultural decline of the Indian subcontinent. The novel shows the same effort to rise above the level of reality which is often found in poetry. However, as far as Urdu fiction is concerned this effort is the first of its kind. This narrative based on the 1947 partition can mirror any age, any time. An important feature of this story is the fact that the writer wrote it on the other side of the border where for her everything past had become the chronicle of a lost world with little chance of recovery. Hence an abiding sense of a cultural loss is an unalienable part of this narrative texture.

Notes

1. *Fasadat Aur Hamaray Afsanay* included in *Zulmat-e-Neemroz*, Karachi, 1990.
2. *Zulmat-e-Neemroz*, p. 25.
3. Mujtaba Husain, *'Adab aur Aagahi',* in *Qurratulain Hyder Ek Mutalea,* ed. Irteza Karim,1960.
4. *Andaz-e-Bayan Aur,* p. 215, published 2005.

12

Lost/Found in Translation:
The Author as a Self-Translator

M. ASADUDDIN

The Book of Laughter and Forgetting was written in Czech
between 1976 and 1978. Between 1985 and 1987, I revised
the French translations of all my novels (and stories) so
deeply and completely that I was able to include, in the
subsequent new editions, a note affirming that the French
versions of these works 'are equal in authenticity to the
Czech texts.' My intervention in these French versions did
not result in variants of my original texts. I was led to it
only by a wish for accuracy. The French translations have
become, so to speak, more faithful to the Czech originals
than the originals themselves.
Milan Kundera, 'Author's Note' (1996)

The above declaration in the 'authorized' versions of
Kundera's books makes one realize the seriousness with
which translations of his work are treated by one of the
world's major writers.[1] The note that he refers to, appended
to all of his books published by Gallimard after 1987, runs in
the original as follows: *entièrement revue par l'auteur, a la même
valeur d'authenticité que le texte chèqueî* (entirely reviewed by
the author, having the same value of authenticity as the Czech
text). The revisions that he carried out in the French were so

significant that the Czech original text could no longer be considered original. Instead, it was the French translation that became the authorized text approved by Kundera. His assertions and his practice of reviewing and revising blur the distinction between the conventional notions of the original and the translation. In his author's note, he introduces two other terms, viz. 'authenticity' and 'accuracy', that fly in the face of his practice as a self-translator, even though he seems to swear by them. A certain kind of intentionality overrides the values of accuracy and authenticity that he endeavours to harness to his job in order to justify the alterations made in the French, and subsequently, in other versions.

Translation does constitute the 'afterlife', as the familiar trope goes, of a text in more senses than Walter Benjamin would have us believe (1969, 73). It allows writers to cross boundaries of language and culture and enjoy readerships larger and vastly different than texts in the original would have assumed, and thus assures the survival and dissemination of the text across time and space. Indeed, the two tests of greatness for a writer and his works are timelessness and translation. This being so, it is natural that every writer would like to be represented in other languages through translation, but as they may not read the languages in which they are translated, they are not always in a position to judge the quality of the work and how well they have been represented. We often read translated literature in an unselfconscious way, assuming that the translated version is a true representation of the original, and often implicitly trusting in the authority of the translator. History is replete with examples of how a writer's reputation has been made or marred because of the quality of translation.

A writer like Kundera can inhabit two or three languages/ cultures at the same time. But how about the many other languages and cultures into which his books are being translated? Can he possibly monitor how 'accurate' and 'authentic' these translations are? Certainly not. Under the circumstances, writers have to depend on translators for a wider dissemination of their works. And this relationship between writers and translators may not always be cordial. Indeed, it is often marked by tension and sometimes even hostility, unless the translator is of the status of say, Constance Garnett, who translated a massive volume of Russian literature into English in the first half of the twentieth century creating perhaps the first great wave of fiction rendition in the history of translation in world literature; or of Gregory Rabassa or Edith Grosson, who translated equally prolifically from Latin American languages into English in the second half of the twentieth century creating the second wave of fiction translation into English; or of William Weaver who contributed enormously to the body of Italian literature accessible to English-reading audiences worldwide, earning the highest tribute from no less a writer than Umberto Eco. However, if the translator is a lesser mortal, writers usually regard him or her as a useful but disposable appendage. If the work succeeds in translation, it is because of the inherent strength of the original, if it fails it fails because of bad translation. So, the poor translator has the worst of both worlds. Of course, the reverse can also be true. An incompetent translator can destroy the reputation of a writer beyond repair.

The fear of being misrepresented and the urge to reach a wider audience drive writers to translate their own works. They may also be driven by other motives, and these motives must be compelling enough to make them undertake the often painstaking exercise of rendering their own work into a language not their own. However, a self-translator's success or failure will depend on bilingual fluency — not mere competence — and the ability to inhabit two cultural worlds simultaneously. Writers often assume that they are the best translators of their work, but this assumption may not always be correct. We have examples of both successes and failures in this regard. The most pertinent and successful example, to my mind, is that of Samuel Beckett (Vladimir Nabokov would be a close second). Beckett translated most of his works between French and English. Sometimes he would begin to translate even before the original was completed. Readers are often struck by his ability to recreate the effect of the original in his translation, 'reinventing puns and compensating with new materials for anything which resists translation' (Connor 2006, 99). The original and translation are seen as near-identical twins 'organically continuous with one another,' existing in a relationship that characterizes the entire body of his self-translated works. On this same subject Tom Bishop remarked: 'The act of self-translation has given us the full texture of Beckett's oeuvre; each translation is not a superfluous addition, but an expansion of the work itself' (qtd. in ibid.). Beckett's apprenticeship under Joyce had made him aware of the extraordinary power and possibilities of words. The verbal economy that characterizes his style makes him a challenging writer to translate. The multiple versions of his translations (for example, *Waiting for Godot* has two well-known published versions in English) are often seen by critics as expansions of the original. The strategies adopted by Beckett in his practice of self-translation become an important means for helping readers uncover the meaning of the text and the intentionality of the author.

If Beckett's is a success story in the history of translation, there are failures as well. One known example is that of Rabindranath Tagore, the first and only Indian Nobel Laureate in literature and a great literary icon. Tagore saw translation as an instrument for projecting a particular image of himself in the West. The desire to fulfil the expectations of his Western readers and be understood in their own terms led him to mangle, mutilate and cannibalize his works in all sorts of ways while rendering them in English. Very few of his translations represent their Bengali original closely. More often than not, they are rearrangements, reworkings or rewritings. He was clear about the fact that a close translation of Bengali poetry into English would not work. 'I intend to carry the essential substance of my poetry in the English translation, and this means a wide divergence from the original,' wrote Tagore in a letter to Ajitkumar Chakravarty, the celebrated Bengali poet (qtd. in Mukherjee 2004, 119). The divergences often assumed such proportions that the poems became almost unrecognizable. They were neither Bengali poems rendered in English translation nor successful independent English poems. Furthermore, he selected only certain kinds of poems that would facilitate his image as an Eastern sage and seer in the West, an image that was seriously flawed as far as his total literary output was concerned. This image took a beating fairly quickly, resulting in a lack of interest in his work. He had realized his folly after the damage was done and his reputation suffered an eclipse in the West. In a letter to Edward Thompson written in 1935, Tagore wrote:

> While going through them [translations] as appearing in different books, I was startled with the slipshod character of most of their number and strongly felt the desire for a ruthless excision. I have done gross injustice to my original productions partly owing to my incompetence, partly to carelessness.
>
> (ibid., 120)

The above remarks are intended as a framework in which I would like to place my observations on Qurratulain Hyder as a self-translator. Posterity will judge whether Qurratulain Hyder has done herself good or harm by undertaking English translations of her own work. For the limited purpose of this paper, I will examine the deviations from the original in two of her novels and discuss the possible causes for these deviations as well as their implications for our notions of originality, textuality, authorship, and so on.

Hyder has translated both from English to Urdu and Urdu to English. She has translated Henry James's novel *Portrait of a Lady* into Urdu as *Hami Ciragh, Hami Parvane* and T.S. Eliot's poetic play *Murder in the Cathedral* as *Kallisa men Qatl*. There are significant issues that need to be addressed regarding these translations of English classics into Urdu, but they do not fall within the purview of the current discussion. From Urdu, in addition to her own work, she has translated Hasan Shah's *Nashtar* into English claiming that it was the first Indian novel. Her claim, as well as her translation, created a considerable stir in Urdu literary circles at the time.[2] A look at her translation of *Nashtar* will give us some clue to her translation practice. She adds a foreword and an afterword, the common translatorial devices for creating a context for the translated work. In the foreword she writes:

> *Nashtar* was translated by Sajad Hussain Kasmandavi into Urdu and serialized in the famous journal *Oudh Punch*. In 1893, it was published from Lucknow as a slim volume of 155 pages. The Persian book is extinct. I have translated Kasmandavi's edition. It is obvious that he has remained extremely faithful to the original and retains many passages and all Persian ghazals in his text. From time to time he makes his humorous comments on the author's views and actions. (1992, 5)[3]

It is not at all clear how it became obvious to Hyder that Kasmandavi had remained 'extremely faithful' to the original, particularly when he felt it was legitimate to comment freely on the author's views and actions in the body of the text. About her own translation of the Urdu version into English, Hyder says, 'I have been strictly faithful to the text and have not anywhere modernized either the narrative or the dialogue' (ibid., 8). Then she adds in the next breath, 'I have only cut down the ornate passages and have also omitted most of the ghazals of Hafiz quoted in the narrative...' (ibid.). It is evident that the definition of being 'strictly faithful' must be stretched considerably to accommodate all the deviations that Hyder herself admits to in her foreword. It is only when the English version is read alongside the Urdu original that the extent of her deviation from the original becomes apparent.

As far as the English translation of her own works is concerned, the following volumes have appeared: *Patjhar ki Avaz* (1965) as *The Sound of Falling Leaves* (1994), *Akhir-e Sahab ke Hamsafar* (1979) as *Fireflies in the Mist: A Novel* (1994), *Aag*

ka Darya (1959) as *River of Fire* (1998), and *Mere Bhi Sanamkane*
(1949) as *My Temples, too* (2004). She believed firmly that she
was the ideal English translator for her own works because
only she knew the meaning that she, as the author, intended.[4]
She understood that the job of a translator was difficult and
demanding. In an interview with Taqi Ali Mirza, she says:

> Translation requires both skill and creativity. The translator
> has a disciplined and responsible role. She has to be faithful to
> the text and at the same time interpret the original in a way to
> render the translation as readable as the original.   (1998, 217)

However, it seems from her practice that all these rules were
for others to follow, or were for those who were 'mere'
translators. A creative writer makes her own rules. Her
translations from Henry James and T.S. Eliot take
considerable liberty with the original. However, when she
translates her own work, it is not simply a question of taking
liberty here and there. Rather, it involves entirely refashioning
the work according to a new aesthetic. Here, she considers
herself totally free. There is no obligation to remain 'faithful
to the text' because it is her own and not somebody else's. In
the same interview she asserts:

> A translator has to be faithful to the text, and she doesn't have
> the freedom to make changes as it is somebody else's text. I
> being the writer, can do so. I do not merely translate, I don't
> even say that I transcreate. *I rewrite, and I rewrite with the English-
> knowing public in mind*.   (ibid., 216, emphasis added)

She rarely granted permission for anyone to translate her
work into English.[5] Perhaps the solitary example in this
regard is C.M. Naim who translated her novella *Sitaharan*
and one short story (see *Season of Betrayal*, 1999). And I have
it from very reliable sources that even a scholar-translator of
Naim's stature had a tough time getting that approval.

Before discussing *Aag ka Darya* (*River of Fire*) it would be
instructive to take a look at *Akhir-e Shab ke Hamsafar* and its
English translation. Major structural and other changes are
to be found in the English version. Hyder's creative impulse

takes hold right from the beginning. Indeed, it would be far-fetched to attempt to establish any kind of correspondence even between the title of the original and the title of the English translation, *Fireflies in the Mist*. They evoke distinctly different images in the mind of the reader. All the material has been organized anew in the English version, new chapters have been added, old chapters have been merged into one another, and new characters have even been introduced.

The first two chapters in the English version, 'Caledonia' and 'Golden Album,' are additions. These two chapters cover the prehistory of Deepali Sircar, the protagonist, by introducing her grandfather Romesh Baboo. The Urdu version starts with a description of Chandrakunj, where the protagonist Deepali Sircar lives with her family, placing her in her locale in the first chapter. The English version starts with a description of the Ganges and a brief history of Caledonia, a planter's house that was built in Dhaka by a Scotsman called MacDonnel Saheb. Then the reader is introduced to Romesh Baboo, the new owner of Caledonia. Descriptions of Caledonia are given in glowing terms and in purple prose. Romesh Baboo is presented as a thoroughly anglicized gentleman who composes heroic couplets in English. He may have been conceived on the real character of Michael Madhusudan Dutt, the flamboyant Bengali poet. The first two chapters also lay out in considerable detail the lives of Nawab Nurul Zaman and Nawab Fakhrul Zaman Choudhury, including the predominant passion of the latter's life—music and dance. The reader is also introduced to Nawab Syed Ahmad Ali's album which provides a vivid picture of the lives of the aristocrats of that time. All these details are completely absent in the Urdu novel.

Further into the novel there are several chapters that stand separately and independently in the Urdu version but have been merged into one in the English. For instance, the twelfth and fourteenth chapters of the original, 'Santiniketan' and 'Aamar Praner Aaram Moner Ananda' respectively, are combined in English under the title 'The Cloud Messenger.'

In a reverse case, Hyder has split the sixth chapter in the Urdu, 'Reverend Paul Mathew Banerjee,' into two chapters in English, 'The Rev. Paul Mathew Banerjee' and 'A Sari for Virgin Mary.' Besides this, there is a blending of the contents of some chapters into one another. The author-translator sometimes also adds or inflates some episodes in the translated text and this results in a certain shift of emphasis. There are omissions of segments of the original text as well. For example, about two pages of the original Urdu text that deal with the activities of the famed Bengali terrorists during the freedom movement of India have been deleted from the English text. Finally, the English version has been divided into three parts, whereas the original does not have this division of the content.

Apart from these kinds of structural changes, Hyder's general practice of self-translation has two major components—rewriting and recontextualization. To some extent, one follows from the other. Rewriting involves both compression and amplification and the introduction of a certain terseness and concreteness in the English version. A close analysis of Chapter 23, 'Ganga and Brahmaputra,' reading the translation alongside the original, demonstrates this.

Urdu original:

> [....] *'Accha, kahin se machis le kar a'o.'*
> *Kis maze se hukm calate hain, main kaniz hun un ki, zarkharid, carnon ki dasi. Kitne hi kamred ban ja'en asliyat men rahenge vohi nakhalis Hindustani lard aind masmar. Main nahin lati macis-vacis.*
> *'Are bha'i zara bhag kar ek le a'o na kahin se—'Abdu'l-Qadir miyan se mang lo. Voh zarur biri pite honge.'*
> *'Main un se ja kar kahun zara diyasala'i dena jo mere ek 'aziz dost ko cahiye jo mujhe bhaga le jane ka progaram bang rahe haie.'*
> *'Jab tum ('anqarib insha'-allah) bhagogi to Binay Babu la-muhala yehi shubah karenge ke un ke zarie hi tum ek miyan bha'i ke sath uranchu'in.'*
> *'Is khayal men bhi na rahiyega. 'Abdu'l-Qadir miyan men intiha'i fiyudal vafadari hai. Voh ap ke Maulavi Abu'l-Hashim nahin hain.'*
> *Daf'atan voh cup ho ga'i.*

'*Voh—voh ham ne ek suhana—na-qabile yaqin khvab dekha tha na...*'

'*Han.....' larki ne ahista se kaha.*   (1979, 183-84)

English version:

'Get me a box of matches from somewhere.'

'I am no longer your courier for the underground. Sorry, wrong number. Besides, an Indian male, even if he calls himself a comrade, would always consider himself a woman's lord and master....'

'So you have become a feminist and are upholding the middle-class norms at the same time!' He laughed.

(1994a, 169)

Urdu original:

Burhe nakhuda ne kan khare kiye aur nazdik ho kar dilcaspi se bat sunne laga. Aur ek dafa' mur kar naujavgn ko dekha. Naujavan ne muskura kar use 'As-salamu'alaikum' kaha aur bat jari rakhi. 'Bangal Muslim aksariyat ka suba hai. Yahan ki Muslim janata pregresiv lidarship ki muntazir hai.'

'*Navab log to progresiv lidarship nahin hain.*'

'*Progresiv lidarship hamari hogi. Hamen lig ke qarib ana hoga.*'

[...]   (1979, 184)

English version:

The bearded skipper pricked his ears and moved a bit closer to hear the conversation.

'Isn't he the ancient spirit of the river?' she whispered.

'Don't romanticize everything. He may be the Ancient Mariner and all that. What interests me right now is that he may be a staunch follower of the Muslim League, hoping that soon these Indian rivers would turn into Pakistani rivers. Geography is changed by human beings.'

The shipmaster turned round and was greeted by an enthusiastic *Assalam Aleikum* by the young man. He was now telling his companion, 'Bengal is a Muslim majority province and the Muslim masses are waiting for progressive leadership.'

'The nawabs of Bengal are Muslim League leaders. And they are so reactionary,' she hotly replied. With his keen river-eye the captain noticed that the heathen woman was very much

in love with this upright follower of the Lord Prophet. But it
distressed the Ole Man of the River when the fellow declared,
'We, the communists, shall have to come close to the Muslim
League. We shall provide progressive leadership to our
masses.'[...]   (1994a, 170)

The following are the additions in the English version:

Arjumand Manzil was no Gothic castle. It was quite a normal
household. But why didn't Jehan Ara ever mention him? Why
didn't he ever talk about her? This man is a double-crosser. A
two-timing crook. Sudden tears filled her eyes. She bent over
the railing and stared hard at the dark waves. She remembered
the nightmare she had had in Santiniketan. On waking up she
had decided never to meet him again. She had not answered
his letters. Still, he had chased her down the Ganges and here
he was, smiling away so cheekily.   (ibid., 171)

A military flotilla passed by. She walked down along the first-
class cabins and spotted a figure in white. Lone White girl in a
flowing milky-white nightgown. Dejected and pensive. Flaxen
hair streaming in the wind. Diana of the Uplands. Perhaps the
daughter of a top executive of the Scottish steamship company.
Perhaps boyfriend Duncan was also aboard one of those
troopships, and was worried about him.   (ibid., 172)

These excerpts present a fair sampling of what goes on in
the process of Hyder's intertextual transfer. As she explains
in her interview with Taqi Ali Mirza, the process is more in
the nature of rewriting than simple translation as we
conventionally understand it (1998, 216). The first pair of
excerpts demonstrates how the English version attenuates
the original Urdu by deleting a substantial part of the Urdu
text containing details about local colour, behaviour patterns
of the local people (i.e. asking for matches from strangers to
light up cigarettes, which is quite common in this part of the
world), etc. The English version also introduces a discourse
on feminism which is absent in Urdu. The second pair of
excerpts is indicative of the reverse process. Here the English
version not only amplifies the original, by stating explicitly
what was only implicit in the original, it also adds details

not even suggested by the original. The indigent, nondescript boatman of the original Urdu is transformed into the 'Ancient Mariner,' 'shipmaster,' 'captain,' and 'Ole Man of the River,' creating new echoes and resonances. What is 'not progressive' in the original becomes 'reactionary' in English. The historical details are also fleshed out in the English version. The two excerpts which are new additions in the English — one characterizing Arjumand Manzil as a Gothic castle and introducing the concepts of 'double-crossing' and 'two-timing,' and the other, introducing the irresistible figure of a 'Lone White girl in a flowing milky-white nightgown' in arresting detail — are attempts at recontextualization so that the English version seems more 'natural' to English readers. To a lesser extent, Kundera did the same in order to make the French versions of his Czech works more accessible to the French audience.

Hyder has tried to get rid of the nagging questions of authenticity and translatorial responsibility in a single stroke by calling *River of Fire* a 'transcreation,' not a translation. However, this should not deter us from examining closely the kind of changes the original text has undergone in this process of transcreation that separates the original Urdu from the English version. In her brilliant essay, 'The Configural Mode: *Aag ka Darya*,' Kumkum Sangari, examines the varieties of genres — such as the Buddhist Jataka tales, the tales of the *dastan* tradition, Hindustani music, and so on, that, according to her, informed the composition of the novel.[6] She regards the English version as a 'recomposition,' arguing that 'the two novels [i.e. the Urdu and English versions] have now to be read against each other and grasped together as part of a single configuration, rather than in the banalities of mistranslation or of the authorial hubris of recreation' (2005, 22). I would agree with the view that the two versions (of course, there are other versions done in other languages, including the Hindi version which the author supervised) together encompass the textuality of the novel and a reading of the novel will be infinitely more nuanced if a person has access to all versions rather than a single version. Nevertheless, an analysis of the process of translation (or mistranslation) from one version to another does give important clues regarding the changed perception of the author about her text, and an examination of this process certainly cannot be termed banal. The ruthless excision the original text undergoes in its English avatar, and the process of editing and inserting new short as well as long passages may conceal the politics of the author, and, as Sangari herself avers, they may indicate that 'some concerns had gradually receded or become less pressing' (ibid.). They may also shed light on the author's personal history of migration to Pakistan, and reverse migration to India, and the implications of these migrations for her literary career. There is a great deal of sense in Michèle Barett's assertion that 'the politics of translation takes on a massive life of its own if you see language as the process of meaning construction' (qtd. in Spivak 2004, 369).

Apart from the fact that the target audience for the two versions is entirely different, during the forty odd years that separate the original from its transcreation, the author must have evolved along with the literary fashions and sensibilities. The first casualty of these changed sensibilities seems to have been the epigraph of the original novel, which was taken, selectively, from T.S. Eliot's *Four Quartets*. This epigraph foregrounded the particular historical vision projected by the work. It survives in the translations into the different Indian languages that were brought out by the National Book Trust, but not in English. Sangari recounts how she asked the author why she had left out the epigraph in the English version and was told dismissively, *'chhut gaya hoga'* (it may have been left out inadvertently), and Hyder refused to discuss the issue. But it would be naïve on our part to simply take such responses at face value without considering such changes. A writer of Qurratulain Hyder's calibre would not append a lengthy epigraph to her most important work without sufficient reflection, nor would she omit it without sufficient reason. It can be viewed as an inalienable part of the author's politics, an attempt to influence the reception of her novel in the English-speaking world. Was it because literary fashions had changed and newer modes of viewing history had come into being, or was it because Eliot was no longer the rage, or because what was good for an Urdu readership on the Indian subcontinent might not necessarily be good for a global readership in English? Had Hyder stopped believing in a circular notion of historical epochs? That cannot be since the novel in the English version still endorses and encourages such a notion.

As for structural changes, compression seems to be the guiding principle that determines the reorganization of the original material, though there are instances of elaboration and amplification as well. The Urdu novel contains 101 chapters, while the English version has only seventy-three. If we divide the text into the four historical epochs the novel encompasses, we find that, while the author devotes the first sixteen chapters spanning nearly 116 pages of *Aag ka Darya* to Shravasti, or the period of Buddha, in *River of Fire* the period has been wrapped up in the first nine chapters spanning barely fifty pages. The second historical epoch, the time of Kabir in the late fifteenth and early sixteenth centuries, has been covered in nine chapters in both versions (chapters seventeen to twenty-five in *Aag ka Darya* and chapters nine to seventeen in *River of Fire*). The third epoch, the British colonial period, takes up nine chapters in *Aag ka Darya* while *River of Fire* devotes as many as thirteen chapters to it. The fourth part, dealing with the freedom struggle and the agonies of partition and its aftermath, is the most substantial. In the Urdu original it is covered in fifty-seven chapters spanning nearly 400 pages, while in the English it has been dealt with in forty-three chapters spanning nearly 250 pages. Within this skeletal framework of the transmutation from Urdu to English, chapters have been reorganized, contents changed, blended and reorganized, characters have been changed and added, new attributes have been given to characters, and narrative devices have been tinkered with.[7] Further, whereas in *Aag ka Darya* the chapters are indicated simply by numerals, in *River of Fire* they have been given individual titles, and these titles have been chosen quite consciously in a manner that suggests the author had a very different readership in mind. Titles such as 'Birdman of the Crossways,' 'A Farewell to Camelot,' 'The Forest of Arden,' and 'La Paloma' have echoes and associations that can be understood by someone steeped in Western tradition and culture. Hyder was a writer endowed with a dual vision and plural sensibilities. It might be reasonable to suggest that when she translates into English, it is her anglophone sensibility and her notion of the novelistic tradition as it developed in the West that appears to modulate her text. Thus, in the 'transcreation' of *Aag ka Darya* into *River of Fire* there is an overall change in tonality; the Urdu version sounds lyrical and philosophical, while the English version sounds more earthy and sinuous. A comparison of the opening paragraphs from the original Urdu and the English version would amply illustrate the different orientation the writer wanted to convey in the 'transcreated' version.

It is quite natural for anyone interested in translation studies to speculate on the reasons for such changes. The most important factor seems to be the anticipated readership. Qurratulain Hyder had a different readership in mind for the English version and she appears to have made changes to satisfy the anticipated expectations of this new readership. A second reason may have been a desire to improve the original Urdu novel. Writers constantly evolve in their art. When going back to their work after a considerable gap of time, there is a natural desire to improve and refashion the work in line with the author's latest thinking. A third reason could be an author's creative impulse that just refuses to reproduce something in a derivative way, even if it is in a different language. It may be difficult for a creative writer such as Qurratulain Hyder to stop being creative and tinkering with incidents, characters, and turns of phrase.[8]

Finally, there is also a notion that some languages, particularly Eastern languages, can tolerate slight verbosity, prolixity, ornate writing, purple prose, etc. All these just do not work in English. English has to be sparse and bare, unadorned, understated, sinewy and tactile, shorn of any kind of airy-fairy prose. If there is wit, it has to be subtle; if there is humour, it must be tongue-in-cheek and self-deprecating. Thus, the seemingly rotund and baroque narrative fictions in our languages should be suitably laundered and pressed, with all of the wrinkles evened out in English so that the folds fall neatly into place. One wonders if Qurratulain Hyder shared such a view. All the same, there is no neat pattern in her deletions and insertions. In *River of Fire* these have achieved a certain crispness and compression stylistically, but have also resulted in an altenuation of the local flavour and a loss of the cultural nuances.

The above discussion demonstrates that Hyder's practice of self-translation, or 'transcreation,' raises complex questions regarding originality, textuality and authorship. In the case of *Akhir-e Shab ke Hamsafar* and *Fireflies in the Mist*, which one should be taken as original and which one as translation? The title page of the English version simply says *Fireflies in the Mist: A Novel*. In her author's note on the following page, Hyder says, 'This novel has already been published in a slightly abridged form in Urdu, Hindi and Russian' (1994a, vi). In literary convention, abridgements are generally produced from larger original versions, but here, the case is the exact opposite. Should the two works be taken separately and independently? This also cannot be reasonably done since the basic plot and core characters are the same, and both have the same manuscript material as their primary source. Which one, then, is the master text and which the secondary? We might try to wriggle out of the situation by asserting that the two versions constitute a composite text. But there are practical problems in that case too. It cannot be expected that every reader will be able or willing to read the texts in both versions. If that is so, the readers' impression of the writer remains skewed by reading only the English version, or only the Urdu version, or the Hindi. Furthermore, if someone wants to translate it into another language other than Urdu or English, which version should be taken as the original, Urdu or English? How should these versions be arranged in libraries, research bibliographies, and so on? Hyder herself seemed to have this uncertainty and confusion in her mind. In a paper presented at the Sahitya Akademi in 1990, she refers to *Akhir-e Shab ke Hamsafar* in English as *Travellers at the End of Night*, not as *Fireflies in the Mist* (n.p.).

Aag ka Darya is now being translated into several European languages. In every case, it is *River of Fire* that is being used as the original or master text. Like the French translations of Kundera's works, the English translation of *Aag ka Darya* has assumed the status of the original. In the not too distant future we may have an Urdu version of the novel produced from *River of Fire*. Then the wheel will have come full circle and we will be engaged in an eternal chase tracking down the 'real original.' Shall we then determine the original text according to anteriority and posteriority, or the larger or smaller version, or shall we take both of them together as a composite text? Or, having failed to resolve the issue conclusively either way, shall we pronounce, with a Derridean flourish, that it does not really matter because the original is always already fissured? Perhaps the way out is to consider a new genre consisting of self-translation. What Elizabeth Klosty Beaujour says about self-translation in general is valid for Qurratulain Hyder's texts as well: 'Because self-translation makes a text retrospectively incomplete, both versions become avatars of a hypothetical total text in which the versions of both languages would rejoin each other and be reconciled' (qtd. in Anderson 2000, 1251). The two texts cannot be substituted for one another. They remain complementary despite belonging to their own fictive universes.

It would be naïve to suggest that the issues raised by Hyder's practice of self-translation make her a lesser writer, or that the issues can be resolved easily, or that they are resolvable at all, but a keen reader of Hyder must be aware of all these nuances of her practice as an author and translator that challenge traditional notions of originality, the singularity of texts, and authorship. We are now at a stage in translation studies where the terms of debate should really shift from questions of linguistic equivalence, the loyalty-betrayal paradigm, etc., to these larger issues.

Credit: Annaul of Urdu Studies, No. 23 (2008)

Works Cited

Ahmad, Aijaz. 1993. *In the Mirror of Urdu*. Shimla: Indian Institute of Advanced Study.

Anderson, Kristine J. 2000. 'Self-translators.' In *Encyclopaedia of Literary Translation into English*, Vol. 2. Edited by Olive Classe. Chicago: Fitzroy Dearborn.

Benjamin, Walter. 1969. 'The Task of the Translator.' In *Illuminations*. Edited by H. Arendt. Trans. by Harry Zohn. New York: Shocken.

Connor, Steven. 2006. *Samuel Beckett: Repetition, Theory and Text*. Revised edition. Colorado: Davis Group Publishers.

Hyder, Qurratulain. 1979. *Akhir-e Shab ke Hamsafar*. Bombay: Alavi Book Depot.

———. 1990. Novel and Short Story: Modern Narratives. Paper presented at the International Seminar on 'Narrative' organized by the Sahitya Akademi, Delhi, February 22.25.

———. 1992. Foreword to *The Nautch Girl: A Novel*. New Delhi: Sterling.

———. 1994a. *Fireflies in the Mist: A Novel*. New Delhi: Sterling.

———. 1994b. 'Khanam Jan ka Safar: Afsana-e Rangin se Dansing Garl Tak.' *Jamia* (Delhi) 91(8/9) (August-September):18.32.

———. 1995. 'Khanam Jan ka Tauba.' *Jamia* (Delhi) 92(1.3) (January-March): 21.55.

———.1998. *River of Fire (Aag ka Darya)*. Delhi: Kali for Women.

———.2005 [1990]. *Aag ka Darya*. Delhi: Educational Publishing House.

Mirza, Taqi Ali. 1998. 'Rigours of Translation.' In *Translation: From Periphery to Centrestage*. Edited by Tutun Mukherjee. New Delhi: Prestige Books.

Mukherjee, Sujit. 2004. 'Rabindranath Tagore: The Translated Poet.'
    In *Translation as Recovery*. Edited by Meenakshi Mukherjee.
    New Delhi: Pencraft International.
Sangari, Kumkum. 2005. 'The Configural Mode: Aag ka Darya.' In
    *A Wilderness of Possibilities: Urdu Studies in Transnational
    Perspective*. Edited by Kathryn Hansen and David Lelyveld.
    New Delhi: Oxford University Press.
Sarmast, Yusuf. 1993. '*Nashtar*: Pahlā Hindustani Navil.' *Saughat*
    (Bangalore) 5: 455-63.
Siddiqi, 'Azimu's-Shan. 1995. 'Afsana-e Rangi se Dansing Garl tak:
    Afsana ya Haqiqat.' *Jamia* 92(1-3) (January-March):7-20.
Spivak, Gayatri Chakravorty. 2004. 'The Politics of Translation.' In
    The Translation Reader. Edited by Lawrence Venuti. Second
    edition. New York: Routledge.

Notes

1. Kundera's serious reflections on translation can also be seen in his incisive comments on the translation of Kafka's works into English, where the translators, according to him, have falsified the original in their efforts to render his works in idiomatic English by eliminating repetition and the apparent roughness and sloppiness of style in the original. See his *Testaments Betrayed: An Essay in Nine Parts*. Translated from the French by Linda Asher. New York: HarperCollins, 1995. 100–115.
2. For a detailed account of this debate, see Hyder (1994), Siddiqi (1995), and Sarmast (1993).
3. The title of the American edition is *Dancing Girl*. The Persian original by Hasan Shâh is known as *Qissa-e Rangin* or *Afsana-e Rangin*. *Nashtar* is the title of its Urdu translation/adaptation by Kasmandavî (ca. 1894).
4. In my personal conversations with her, whenever the issue of translation came up, she always asserted forcefully that no one else could translate her work as well as she herself could.
5. When the National Book Trust, India took up the project of translating *Aag ka Darya* into fourteen Indian languages, she was apprehensive about the quality of the translations. She tells Taqi Ali Mirza: 'You see I have suffered a great deal on this account. They sought my permission to get my so-called

great novel, *Aag ka Darya*, translated into fourteen Indian languages and I was told by readers of those languages that all these translations were terrible. My language is not easy to render into Hindi, and one sentence, one word can make all the difference. The meaning is lost, the atmosphere is lost' (*ibid.*).

6. Aijaz Ahmad holds a contrary view in that he regards *Aag ka Darya* as displaying elements of pastiche from other works, 'the borrowings from a number of Orientalist texts, such as Basham's *The Wonder that Was India* and Herman Hesse's *Siddhartha* are much too obvious and undigested.' Nevertheless, he admits the novel is a central document in the larger ideological ensemble of Urdu literature as it existed between the Partition of 1947 and the Indo-Pak War of 1965. See, Ahmad (1993, 6).

7. As for the characters, Champa's maid in the Shravasti period has been changed from Sarojini to Jamuna, Shahzadi Banu Begam of Jaunpur has been changed to Ruqaiyya, Cyril's native wife Shunila Devi has become Sujata, Professor Sabzjeevan has become Professor Banerjee, and so on. As for narrative modes, there are several major shifts from the Urdu original to the English.

8. At an international seminar held at Jamia Millia Islamia (Delhi) on 'Qurratulain Hyder and the *River of Fire*: The Meaning, Scope and Significance of Her Legacy' (5-6 February, 2008), Ritu Menon, Hyder's publisher from Kali for Women/Women Unlimited, narrated her experience working with Qurratulain Hyder to arrive at the final version of *River of Fire*: 'Aini Aapa would have several versions in English for the same chapter in Urdu. She would pull them out of a big box and say tantalizingly, 'Shall we take this one, this one, or this one?' ' This is certainly an unusual practice in translation history. It also indicates that Hyder, unlike Beckett, who considered self-translation a dismal drudgery, really liked the job of translating her own work, perhaps as a way to test newer facets of her writing genius.

TEXTUAL APPRAISALS

13

Imagining India:
In and as the River of Fire

RAKHSHANDA JALIL

As a student of literature, and more recently of literary
histories, I have long been tempted by the idea of exploring
ideas through literature. I attempted that first with the idea
of revolt in the poetry produced in Urdu in the immediate
aftermath of the Revolt of 1857. I tried that again by exploring
the idea of protest in the work of the Progressives. It was
tempting to explore both the idea of India and of nationhood
as reflected in Urdu literature. I found there was much in
both Urdu prose and poetry that dwelt on the idea of a nation,
much of it was written in moments of crisis, whether it was
in response to the atrocities of the colonial oppressor or the
horrific genocide during the Partition or every time the threat
of war loomed on the horizon. But much of it was concerned
with the here and now, the immediate and topical; it was
almost necessitated by a hair-trigger response to a threat
perception. I looked for something that explored the idea of
nationhood in a larger, broader, more panoramic sense. I
found nothing could serve my purpose better than *Aag ka
Darya* written by Qurratulain Hyder.

Aag ka Darya, written in Urdu in 1959 and transcreated
into English by Hyder herself some 40 years later, traces the

trajectory of the Indian people from the Mauryan period to modern times. *Aag ka Darya* is, to my mind, a classic instance of Imagining India, an India from ancient times to the modern age, an India which as I shall attempt to show is changing yet constant. Putting four sub-stories into one composite whole, this *magnum opus* portrays an immense and complex smorgasbord of cultures and identities while remaining true to the spirit of liberal humanism that was the hallmark of both Hyder's writing and her personality. Hyder published the Urdu version when she was a mere 28 years old and in it not only does she present 2500 years of Indian history, but more importantly, gifts us—perhaps unwittingly—with a timeless metaphor for imagining India in the form of a ceaselessly flowing river. Through it she also shows how history is a continuum, a coming together of many small rivulets and tributaries that together make one sweeping river. Somewhere, she also rebukes those who go looking for important and not-so-important bits and pieces of history for they fail to see its totality.[1] The River of Fire is the River of Time and Time, like the river, any river or a river anywhere known by any name, is by its very nature ceaselessly flowing. Those who stand, or live beside its banks, occasionally watch it pass by; but very few stop to listen to its wordless story. The river urges those who stand on the banks to travel with it; some do and some don't. Even those who travel on the river do so only for a short while; then they must either get off or drown. Some travel on the river on barges big and small, modest and stately; some succeed in travelling a short distance, while some are carried off on strong currents and are lost forever within its waters. And while men and women carry on with the business of their lives, while wars are waged, empires rise and fall, Time is flowing too as ceaselessly as the river. One can neither hold it nor ride it; one can however try and hear it as it passes by in the soft ripples of the waters.

Before we look at Hyder's *River of Fire*, it might be interesting to first look at the metaphor of the river itself and how it has served Indian poets and writers down the ages. The mystically inclined Amir Khusrau spoke of love as a river:

> *Khusrau darya prem ka, ulti wa ki dhaar,*
> *Jo utra so doob gaya, jo dooba so paar*
> Oh Khusrau, love is a river, it runs the other way
> He who jumps in it drowns, and who drowns, gets across

Invoking the river Ganges to bear witness to the arrival of those from other lands who set up home here, the revolutionary Urdu poet Iqbal asks:

> *Ai aabrood-e-Ganga woh din hai yaad tujhko*
> *Utara tere kinare jab caravan hamara*
> O waters of the Ganga, do you remember that day
> When our caravan had stopped beside your bank?

The river, for the poet, becomes both Time and Witness to Time. By the time Hyder decided to use it as the title of her epic, both the *darya* and the *aag ka darya* had become accepted metaphors in the Urdu lexicon. Jigar Moradabadi had already written his famous ghazal which ended with these lines:

> *Yeh ishq nahi aasan, bas itna samajh lije*
> *Ik aag ka dariya hai aur doob ke jaana hai*
> Love is not easy; however it is enough to understand
> That it is like a river of fire and you must drown in it

However, it was Hyder who wrenched the metaphor from its philosophical-mystical mooring and located it in an altogether different, *sui genesis* context. Hyder reinforces the sense of continuity borne by her central motif — that of the river — in several other ingenious ways all through the book. Everywhere in the *River of Fire*, the adage holds true — the more things change, the more they remain the same. Characters keep reappearing in different guises but with the same names in episodes spanning several thousand years. We first encounter Gautam Nilambar, a final year student of the Forest University of Shravasti in a spot not far from the Buddhist vihara at Jetvan. As he is waiting to cross a swollen river, he sees Kumari Champak, the daughter of the Chief Minister, and is inexorably drawn towards her. Soon he meets a motley set of dramatis personae: the princess Nirmala, her brother Hari Shankar, and the low caste milkmaid Sujata. The time is 150 years after the Buddha, the place is Shravasti in the Bahraich region, and the river is the Saryu. Hyder uses her characters to make several sweeping statements about the time: about Shudras converting to Buddhism and thus incurring the wrath of the powerful Brahmins; about the prejudice against the newly emergent Buddhism from orthodox Brahminism. Gautam, Champa, Nirmala, Hari Shankar, Sujata will reappear in many reincarnations as the novel hurtles across the centuries. They will be accompanied by a motley cast of characters bearing the same name in each reincarnation — Englishmen called Cyril Ashley, coachmen called Ganga Din, maids called Jamuna, and so on. Kumari Champak becomes Champavati, the Brahmin girl, then Champa Jan the courtesan in Oudh; she resurfaces as Champa Ahmed. Somewhere these are manifestations of a syncretism, the Ganga-Jamuni culture as it was called. These reincarnations are handled imaginatively and make for an interesting sense of continuity.

Continuity is maintained in other things too. While the landscape changes – as the narrative traverses the length and breadth of the Indo-Gangetic plain, sometimes upstream sometimes downstream — a river runs all through it. While its name might change, it is — both literally and figuratively the same river. The Saryu of the opening anecdote becomes the Jamuna, or the Ganga, the Gomti, or the Padma. No matter what the name of the river or of those who dwell beside its banks, there is always a wandering mendicant somewhere nearby — an incarnation of Khwaja Khizr who had drunk from the fount of immortality and, like Saint Christopher, appears as a guide before travellers who have lost their way. Like everyone else in this novel, he is called by different names and takes different guises. Called Satyapir Satyanarayan in rural Bengal, this wandering mendicant appears in the guise of a sufi or a yogi, a nun or a monk, and shows the way both literally and metaphorically to those who are lost.

The novel opens in the season of *beerbahutis* (tiny velvety red insects called the Bride of Indra) and rain clouds, some time in the fourth century BC when Gautam Nilambar, chances upon Hari Shankar, an absconding prince yearning to be a Buddhist monk. And thus begins a magnificent tale that flows through Time, through Pataliputra during the reign of Chandragupta Maurya, then the Sharqi Empire of Jaunpur, the Kingdom of Oudh, the British Raj till finally the night-bitten dawn of Independence ushers in Free India. While the same set of characters are born and reborn in different circumstances in different times, they are destined to be forever grappling with the same set of emotions – love, wanderlust, the yearning for something indefinable yet inexorable. The fiery river of Time flows along the banks of their lives as they are reborn and recreated, weaving through the twists and turns, the flows and eddies, keeping them together, keeping them apart. The story comes full circle in post-Partition India when Hari Shankar and his friend Gautam Nilambar Dutt meet yet again, beside the same river Saryu, and mourn the passing of their lives into meaninglessness, their friends who have left for Pakistan, and what remains of their country of which they were once so passionately proud. Have those who have left betrayed them, or have the ones left behind betrayed those who have left? In answer there are only more questions.

What happens between then and now — between that first meeting 2500 years ago and now in 1955 — is history, full of clamour and conflict, the deviousness of rulers and apathy of the ruled, and the irrelevance of religion in defining Indianness. Interspersed with the human drama involving the main cast of dramatis personae, the narrative throws up many questions. It is these questions that look at the 'idea' of India from different points of view at different times in history. The earliest indication of this interest in the notion of a nation-state that will continue to preoccupy the protagonists all through comes in the first episode when a group of travelling Persians tells Gautam Nilambar that they have come to Hind to seek a livelihood. A perplexed Gautam asks: 'Where is Hind?'[2] 'The country in which you live!' the Persian answers. He then goes on to list the similarities between Persian and the languages of Hind. To which Gautam cynically remarks, 'Affinity in language does not keep people from fighting and hating one another.' His words are prophetic as we will see later.

Gautam dies while trying to cross a river in full spate. Chandragupta Maurya's army invades peaceful Shravasti, a small, semi-pastoral outpost ruled by a weak *rajan* because the Prime Minister of the great Mauryan empire doesn't want weak feudatories. As Chandragupta becomes the first *samrat*, emperor of the state of Bharat, Hyder muses when 'Death cancels all conflicts of Rup and Arup' is there any place for pacifists and theorists? She recalls the words of the Buddha: Victory breeds hatred because the vanquished sleep in sorrow, and only that person is peaceful who is above victory and defeat and happiness.'[3] The narrative jumps 1500 years and Gautam's place is taken by Abul Mansur Kamaluddin of Nishapur. Born of an Iranian Shia mother and a Sunni Arab father, he has come to India in search of fortune. It is the year 1476 and at the crossroads of the world India is being touted as the land of tomorrow. Sufis, scholars, merchants, scribes, people of all faiths and classes are flocking to this land of opportunity. One of them is Kamaluddin or Kamal who is headed to Jaunpur, the academic capital of India, aglitter with the lamp of learning lit by the enlightened Sharqi rulers. 'The Sultan business is good business,' a wandering dervish tells Kamal as he trots along on the high road to a new life in a new land:

> The modus operandi is simple and to the point. Wherever the government at the centre loses its grip over the provinces you gather enough military strength and a few allies, usually Hindu Rajput chieftains, and declare your independence. Then you

obtain a firman from the nominal caliph of Islam who resides in Cairo. According to this decree of the figurehead pontiff you become his deputy caliph and the Friday sermon in the cathedral mosque and all the mosques of your realm is read in your name, instead of the reigning monarch's at Delhi. You mint your own currency and send out your envoys. You assume the grandiose titles of the ancient Kings of Iran till you are replaced, often violently, by another dynasty.[4]

And, indeed, every power-hungry militiaman of Turko-Iranian descent wants to proclaim himself sultan and capture Delhi, the beating heart of the country called Hind. Towards this end they make and break alliances, wage wars, buy peace, extend the borders of their ever-changing kingdoms. And what of the people of Hind? They seem happy enough with whoever rules over them as long as they are allowed to indulge their one grand passion, namely, Religion. They are happy as long as they have the time to indulge it and to celebrate their many fairs and festivals all through the year. Qalandars hobnob with yogis, exchanging ideas and practices from each other, bhakta cults flourish side by side with Sufi silsilas, and the countryside is awash with wandering mendicants of different faiths and orders. In the midst of all this, Gautam reborn as Kamal meets Champavati, the sister of a learned Brahmin in Ayodhya. Fated as they are to be forever separated, he moves on, across the breadth of Hindustan, witnessing the rise and fall of empires.

In 1484 Bahlol Lodi captures Jaunpur and in 1500 the city of colleges and universities, the academic capital of Hind, home to thousands of ulema, Sufi lodges and writers, is razed to the ground by his son, Sikandar Lodi. 'Every age produces a liberal,' writes Hyder, 'who behaves like a barbarian due to the exigencies of the times.' Kamaluddin witnesses the destruction of the great and liberal civilization of Jaunpur nurtured by the Ganga-Jamuni Sharqi rulers at the hands of Sikandar Lodi. Though he is himself a poet, scholar and educationist, Sikandar Lodi orders the scholars of the Sharqi court to be presented before him 'tied by their turbans.'

Sikandar Lodi also bans the annual *urs* of Salar Baba at Behraich and the worship of Seetla Mata; he also declares the weaver-poet Kabir a heretic. Stirring things were happening all through the medieval age but Sikandar Lodi's reign was especially tumultuous. Kabir was singing his songs of heresy and irreverence when a child called Nanak was born in a Khatri household in Punjab; he was destined to lay the foundations of a new syncretic religion. Kabir reminds Kamal of Rumi, who had lived two hundred years ago. 'They all say the same thing,' rues Kamal, 'but it doesn't help.' Meanwhile, in the far eastern arm of Hindustan, the Suhrawardy order was busy enticing the lower castes of Bengal:

> Everybody seemed to be a singer in Bengal. Storytellers chanted roop-kathas; ferrymen, snake-charmers and elephant-trappers sang their ballads. They sang of Allah, Mohammed or Radha-Krishna. Vaishnavism was flourishing. Kamal rowed his boat from dargah to dargah, also singing... Mosques and temples lay hidden in bamboo groves.[5]

Kamal, the wanderer from Nishapur, eventually marries the low-caste Sujata Debi, settles down in a village beside a river and becomes the writer of innumerable ballads and folk songs that are sung in rural Bengal long after he is dead and gone. An unwilling pawn in the great game between Afghan and Mughal forces, he dies with these words from the Holy Quran on his lips: 'Return, O Soul, to thy Lord, accepted, and accepting –'

The next episode begins with Cyril Ashley as its 'hero'. It is the year 1797. The Battle of Plassey is over and the English have long shed their garb of traders. The once-mighty Mughal empire is divided into 22 provinces each governed by a provincial viceroy. Delhi has been ravaged by Nadir Shah. Famines stalk the once-fertile land from Bengal to Oudh. The Nawab Vazirs of Oudh are holding on to the last vestiges of high culture. They celebrate Holi and Basant with as much fervour as their Hindu subjects. But the Court of Nawab

Wajid Ali Shah is like Camelot; its candle burning at both ends gives out a lovely light. Like Baz Bahadur of Malwa and Hussain Shah Nayak of Jaunpur, Wajid Ali Shah is an accomplished musician, an exponent of *thumri* and *dadra*, a master-stylist of Kathak, creator of Ras Lila in which he himself danced as Krishna. This most unusual of rulers was known to his people as Akhtar Piya or Jan-i-Alam — the life and soul of the world. In this fairy kingdom, Kamal reappears as Kamal Ali Raza Bahadur alias Nawab Kamman and Champa as the courtesan Champa bai — lovers destined never to meet. Gautam appears as Gautam Nilambar Dutt, a fine specimen of *bhadralok* gentility who regards the Uprising of 1857 as a quixotic impulse. 'The solid fact remains, thought Gautam, that after 1857 the English ushered India into the modern age.'[6] Kamal, on the other hand, cannot reconcile the atrocities committed by the English upon the Indian people with their otherwise modern and liberal outlook. Having spent two years in England and France, Kamal says, 'The English are a fine people in their own country; they become a different species as soon as they cross the Suez.'[7]

The narrative takes another leap forward. The year is 1940 and the setting once again Lucknow but a Lucknow seething with political unrest. And it is here, in the fourth and last section that the terrain becomes more contested, the dualities sharper; what is more, there are no longer clear-cut answers to any questions. The same set of characters reappears in different guises. Hari Shankar and his sister Nirmala Raizada live in Singharewali Kothi on the banks of the Gomti. Their friends and neighbours are the equally genteel, well-born, well-educated Kamal, Talat and Tehmina. Kamal is Hari Shankar's alter ego, his *hum zaad*. Together, they listen to Pahari Sanyal songs on the radio, and along with the girls enact scenes from *Midsummer Night's Dreams* and go 'ganjing' in the tony Hazrat Ganj. The girls play the sitar and learn to dance, while the boys play tennis at the club and spout poetry. A cocktail of Indian society — from different parts of the country, of different classes and castes — is found in the campuses and coffeehouses of Lucknow. In the midst of all this, Hyder throws a googly:

> There was yet another aspect of the new nationalist movement that was making its presence felt — some people had openly begun talking of Ancient Hindu Culture and the Glory-that-was-Islam. How was Indian culture to be defined? Was it a ruse for Hindus to enslave the Muslims? Could 'real' Indians only be Hindus? Were Muslims unholy intruders who should be treated as such?[8]

Every now and then the characters go inwards and resume their journey through Time in their imagination. That is when Hyder steps in and takes us on a conducted tour of history. That is when some of the most significant questions get asked — questions about religion, culture and identity and the over-riding question of Indianness. Who are 'real' Indians? Can 'real' Indians only be Hindu? Can culture be pure Hindu or pure Muslim? Who will decide its purity and content — the Hindu Mahasabha or the Muslim League? The Muslim thread, Hyder says repeatedly, has been present in every pattern of the Indian tapestry. Can this thread be destroyed, pulled out by the root and obliterated by the demand for Pakistan? And, is the demand for Pakistan a threat to the idea of India?

Through certain members of the extended family like the staunch Congressi Asad Mamu and his diametrically opposed Muslim League Zaki Chacha, through Gunga Din the coachman and Ram Autar the gardener, and their illiterate but enlightened wives, Hyder tries to explore why some families hitched their wagon to the Muslim League and others put their faith in the Congress, and why the Muslim League enamoured some Muslims and left others cold. When the Leaguers first spoke of protecting the rights of the Muslims by securing fair representation in the legislature, they gave voice to a long-felt need to recognize the Muslims as a distinct religious and political unit. On the face of it these seemed perfectly legitimate aspirations; the problem, Hyder muses, lay in the manner in which the League went about its business. It employed a combination of rhetoric and religion to bludgeon its way. It used fear as a campaign tool, making Muslims view all Hindus as a 'threat' to their survival once the protective presence of the British was removed. The League's final unequivocal demand — a separate homeland — did not appeal to some Muslims for the same reasons of faulty logic. Jinnah's assurance of providing constitutional safeguards to minorities appeared humbug in the face of his proclamation of a Pakistan that would be a hundred per cent Muslim. When Pakistan is eventually formed, it leaves many wondering if the cleavage of hearts and land was truly inevitable, or could it have been averted? What went so wrong between the two major communities of the subcontinent? What caused the disenchantment with the Congress? What made some staunch Congressmen rally around the once-derided Muslim League? What cooled the Muslim's ardour to join nationalistic mainstream politics? For that matter, why was the Muslim suddenly regarded as a toady and a coward content to let the Hindus fight for freedom from the imperial yoke? Why was he suddenly beyond the pale? How did he become the 'other'? And what of the dream of the Muslim Renaissance spelt out in such soul-stirring verse by the visionary poet Iqbal? In turn, why did the Congress baulk at the issue of separate electorates, calling it absurd and retrograde? Why did it do nothing to allay the Muslim fear that the freedom promised by the Congress meant freedom for Hindus alone, not freedom for all? Seen from the Muslim point of view, the Congress appeared guilty of many sins of omission and some of commission. 'Nationalism' increasingly began to mean thinking and living in the Congress way and none other. Those who lived or thought another way came to be regarded as anti-national, especially in the years immediately after independence.

Finally, I want to raise the question of progressivism. Who or what is a progressive? Only those who belong to schools of thought and subscribe to well-established ideologies, or those who are willing to look ahead? Those critics of Hyder who have called her, among other things a Pompom Darling and a reactionary, would do well to remember that she admitted there was blood on the hands of the beautiful people of Camelot:

> One morning we discovered that our own hands were drenched in blood, and we saw that all those fine people — intellectuals and authors and leaders — many of them had blood-stained hands too. Most of them were not willing to atone. They ran away, or took different avatars, but there were some genuine human beings, as well.[9]

And who are these genuine people? They are humble folk, gardeners, farmers, peasants and betel-leaf sellers, *chikan* embroiderers — the 'real' backbone of India. For all her talk of expatriates living in St John's Woods, of high tea on manicured lawns, of young men playing tennis and girls reciting Shakespeare in the sylvan surroundings of IT College, in short, for all her talk of people who live in houses with quaint names like Singharewali Kothi who traipse through Moon Garden (Chand Bagh!), there is in Hyder's literary sensibility a profound understanding of the real India that lived on the fringes of the Camelot she knew and inhabited.

A large part of the last section of the novel is located in England where the diaspora of young intellectuals from the Indian subcontinent congregates — in search of higher education, better jobs, a more cosmopolitan outlook. But like birds of passage, they must eventually fly back home — either their old home in India or in search of a new home in Pakistan. Kamal, a highly qualified scientist, returns to India and finds his home declared evacuee property. He looks for a job but can't find one in a new country grappling with rampant unemployment. Defeated, he leaves for Pakistan with his aged parents. The staunch nationalist who had once declared, 'I don't want religion; India needs peace and bread' capitulates. Millions of families cross the border in search of new lives; others stayed back, often to an uncertain future.

Hyder too left for Pakistan where, incidentally she wrote *Aag ka Darya*. She returned to India in 1961 and never discussed her reasons for going away or returning. Perhaps because she had already given her answers and had no further desire to rake the ashes; her answers can be found scattered not just in *Aag ka Darya* but in her entire corpus of writing which is one long ode to syncretism, pluralism, liberalism and secularism.

Notes

1. The question being asked all the time by some character or the other in *River of Fire* is: Do people cease to be relevant? Did Beethoven become irrelevant after the Second World War? Why then have historically important personages such as Baz Bahadur, Husain Shah Nayak and Wajid Ali Shah become irrelevant in modern India?
2. *River of Fire*, Qurratulain Hyder, Women Unlimited, 1998, p. 43.
3. *River of Fire*, op. cit., p. 42.
4. Ibid., p. 63.
5. Ibid., p. 99.
6. Ibid., p. 170.
7. Ibid., p. 171.
8. Ibid., pp. 202-203.
9. Ibid., p. 310.

14

Representation of the Female Psyche: The Champa of *Aag ka Darya*

SAMI RAFIQ

Champa is the main female character in *Aag ka Darya*. Champa is a complicated and multi-faceted character and it is her journey or quest that helps in understanding her personality. Her journey — spanning centuries in the quest of knowledge, freedom, love and power — is shown through a series of rebirths in various time periods in Indian history. She has been referred to as Champak, Champavati and Champa at different times. However her journey is not an isolated subjective phenomenon; rather she is part of the flowing river of time or what has been referred to as Aag ka Darya or the river of fire. The novel opens with the scene of Gautam swimming across a river. The river of fire is representative of time that carries in its drift and spate human lives and human history and its waters are creative and destructive. She floats along the river of time along with other companions who drift in and out of her many lives, such as Kamal, Hari Shankar, Tehmina, Talat, etc. The symbolic river is always in the background whether it is the Champak of Shravasti or the Champavati who sits beside the river as Kamal deserts her or the Champa Ahmad who watches the boats on the Gomti river in Lucknow. Her journey begins

with her encounter with Buddhism. Her meeting with
Suman, a Buddhist nun who was born a princess, makes
Champak question Suman about her choices.

> Suman had renounced her royal life at the age of eighteen to
> join the Buddhist Sangh. She was twenty years old when
> Buddha gained enlightenment. It was eighty years since
> Buddha passed away. At eighteen years word of Suman's
> beauty had spread far and wide. Now a 98-year-old woman
> was sitting before her dressed in coarse saffron coloured clothes.
> What did she get by renouncing the world? A thief seemed to
> question Champak thus—'If I renounce the world will I get
> peace? And if I do not get peace even by that, then'?[1]

Champak's questioning leads her on a long journey where
rather than renounce life she wants to live it and find the
purpose of her existence. By representing icons of great
women in epics, a restrictive, traditional world is shown in
which Champak is born. Though the *Mahabharata* presents
noble women like Gandhari who blinded herself because her
husband was blind and Anusuyya who got a second wife
for her own husband yet the prevailing attitude towards
women is one of contempt and distrust. It is this inequality
that Champak tries to oppose as her personality emerges.

The first meeting between Champak and Gautam
Nilambar is very significant considering that Gautam is an
ascetic, writer, and artist who breaks all the rules of his
ashram to be with her. However, the love between them is
unrequited and the relationship that they share spans several
centuries and births. Love rather than being a quest to unite
becomes a canvas on which the inequalities between Gautam
and Champak are displayed. Though the sexual side of their
relationship never develops till the end, their relationship is
constant. Champa's other romantic and sexual encounters
may be failures or successes but her relationship with Gautam
continues interminably. They first meet each other at a dance
and the dance is symbolic of the twists and turns of their
relationship down the centuries. He quietly leaves his ashram
and goes to the *mahua* garden where the royal court has set

up a stage and dance and music are being enjoyed. He joins the dancers and dances beside Champak. For Gautam Champak is symbolic of womanhood and he equates her with various goddesses and the dance with a celestial dance:

> Life is the greatest truth. Creation is the greatest reality. Hold shakti as sacred which is the mother of creation. Revere the goddess who is a mother-Uma-Gauri-Laxmi and whose other name is Asha — whose name is Kamala — who can be compared to lotus flowers. She is pleasant like the Champa flowers, she is a mother like the earth, a mother like the river. A mother is forebearing. A woman is forebearing because she is a mother. Champak is forebearing. Revere her. Worship her and bow before her...[2]

Champak in the earliest phase of the novel is for Gautam the embodiment of essential mythical womanhood. But while the dance goes on he falls asleep and in the morning the royal camp moves on. Champak as she passes by finds him asleep. The author's intention appears to have been to bring Gautam in touch with a dream-like reverie of perfect love but which he loses when he falls asleep. Champak arrogantly condemns Gautam who is fast asleep in the garden thus and then moves on:

> The one who is awake one day will fall asleep and the one who is asleep shall awake one day.[3]

The underlying meaning of these lines is revealed as Champak and Gautam continue to meet and separate in different periods. It also augurs that their love cannot be fulfilled till they can understand each other and Champa can create a place of value for herself in the patriarchic set-up which continues to dictate and confine women in a narrow world view.

The second meeting between Gautam and Champa is after a certain period of time and circumstances for both have changed. After her hometown Ayodhya was raided, she was captured along with the other girls of the household and forcibly married off to an officer in Chandragupta Maurya's court, who is twice her age and old and unsightly. But Champak is conscious of the word *pativrata* so she cannot now accept Gautam even if she wants to. Gautam who had escaped from the life of an ascetic and joined the theatre group in order to be with Champak returns once more to his old life. Champak repeats lines that she had uttered earlier:

> The one who is awake one day will fall asleep and the one who is asleep shall awake one day. [4]

This awakening and slumbering and vice versa is symbolic of a woman's quest or journey from a lower consciousness to a higher consciousness that is analogous to the development of character in a *bildungsroman* novel. Champa's character begins to take a definite shape when she, in the form of Champavati, meets her lover in the form of Kamaluddin in another birth. Here Champavati is a native girl from Ayodhya and Kamaluddin is an Arab soldier in the Mughal courts who sings praises of the valour and learning of the Mughal courts. Champavati is against war and desires that Kamal should give up war but he only laughs at her beliefs and moves on. A procession of wandering monks passes by; this is used repetitively in the novel as perhaps a representation of Champa's spiritual quest.

But the ideas that are dear to Champak are expressive of the female view of the world, which stands for harmony, love and peace. The very fact that Champak is on a journey of personal and spiritual growth is revealed when she retorts at his mockery of her interests saying:

> What else should we do...should we play chess in palaces like your princesses of Jaunpur?

He replies ironically:

> Of course...and our palaces have, besides chess, countless books, but you are yourself so learned .....[5]

This is a comment on Champavati's inadequacies in the eyes of Kamaluddin and which required more understanding and effort on her part. This is also the reason why she is unable to stop him and is left weeping on the shore of the river as he rides away into a haze of dust.

A comparison is brought about between the two men's (Gautam Nilambar and Kamaluddin) attitude towards women. While Gautam worshipped Champa in one birth, Kamaluddin is worshipped by her in another birth. Kamaluddin remembers all the women he loved while he travelled across the Arab world. He found that though they were sold, held captive by men, dominated by them and treated as having no identity or voice, they were icons celebrated and worshipped by poets. However, in Hindustan he found that women devotees sang *bhajans* in praise of Krishna showing that man had to acquire the stature of God to be worshipped by women. As can be perceived on the departure of Kamaluddin, Champavati's social status is revealed when she returns to her small tightly enclosed home. Ironically enough, the statue of Goddess Kali is placed on a small shelf and represents Champavati's limited and restricted world:

> On a shelf near the door a small statue of Bhavani was kept before which the smoke from an incense stick was rising in a thin quivering stream. Champa watched this peaceful atmosphere from the doorway and after drying her tears came into the door.[6]

Gautam Nilambar meets Champa again as a courtesan in the period of the British rule in India where he is a clerk under the British officer Cyril. The position that Champa acquires is of great respectability and learning and though Gautam thought that she was in a degraded position, a courtesan of those times, she enjoyed the admiration and respect of men. By being in the role of a courtesan, Champa escapes the stranglehold of social tradition which she experienced in earlier births and which made her subservient to men. She has the freedom to develop her personality in which ever direction she chooses. However, her love for Gautam remains unrequited as Gautam refuses to be held back by her charms.

He leaves Lucknow as a youth and returns to it as an old man. The period of Gautam's return is after the revolt of 1857 and both he and Champa have aged. But the aftermath of the revolt has ruined her and she becomes a beggar whom the lordly Gautam meets after a number of decades. It is clear that Champa is not spared suffering and agony in this birth too as she spreads her hands before Gautam begging for a few coins.

While Champa may have recognized him as her past love, she makes no demands of him and only blesses him. Gautam's musings at that moment reflect a typically patriarchal way of perceiving women. He muses thus:

> Where does Beauty go after it slides off the face of a lovely woman? Does old age turn women into a different species? Why are old men venerated and women ridiculed as hags? Why didn't I run after her and ask her to sit beside me in this carriage and take her home?[7]

Through Gautam's mindset the author shows the patriarchal attitude towards women that it is not the inner beauty of a woman that matters but her external appearance. However, Champa's personality undergoes greater changes and develops more complexities as she reappears in the pre-independence era of 1941. She experiences a sense of freedom that she had never experienced in previous births and this freedom can be understood as a freedom to love any man she chooses:

> Suddenly something strange happened. Champa felt an inexplicable elation. There was freedom in the wind, joyous contentment was palpable in the rustling of the leaves. Did others also experience this sense of liberation? Poor Tehmina, for instance, or foolish Gautam?[8]

Champa is romantically involved with Amir Reza (Tehmina's fiancé), Cyril Ashley, Gautam (who is involved with Shanta) and Bill Craig (who Shanta intends to marry after her divorce). But in all these episodes Champa does not see herself as flighty and she tells Gautam that it was not Cyril who deserted her but she who refused him. Gautam's ironical comment on Champa's indecisiveness reveals Champa's irrepressible desire for freedom:

> 'It seems to have become your pastime, refusing offers of marriage.'
> 'He wanted to divorce his wife and marry me, but I am not a home-breaker so I said, no.'
> 'Home-breaker, you mean,' he said gently, 'I'm sorry, I didn't know that. So once again you sacrificed your personal happiness for the sake of another woman. Tell me, then why are you trying to entice poor Bill?'[9]

To this Champa replies that she is jealous of Gautam's relationship with Shanta and therefore out of jealousy, she wants to hurt Shanta. Champa is part of a complicated web of relationships for though there is a subtle bond between her and Gautam is romantically involved with Shanta, a married woman and his cousin. He wants Shanta to be free of her unhappy marriage and be free to marry Bill Craig. Just as Champa cannot understand how Gautam can tolerate the fact that Shanta actually loves another man, so also Gautam cannot understand why she cannot commit herself to any man. But Gautam also affirms his complicated bond with Champa towards the end of the novel when the group of students is separating after having completed their education at Cambridge.

> Gautam said, 'Two distinct worlds are present in me all the time. One of them includes these people,' he pointed towards the room with its photographs and books, 'in the other there are only you and me, by ourselves. Both worlds are connected to each other through a bridge. What'll happen when this flimsy bridge breaks down?'[10]

Champa's personality finds wholeness only when she is back to the place where she had started her journey, a small town called Moradabad. When Kamal travels from Pakistan to Moradabad to meet Champa, his illusions about himself and his progress are shattered. He realizes that the Champa whom he thought was always far behind him was way ahead for she had found what her heart was seeking:

> Kamal had seen Champa today perched on another rung of her ladder, against another backdrop, another set, another set of props. At least this was her real milieu. He closed his eyes. The Champa of Lucknow, Paris, Cambridge and London, and now the Champa of this joyless, half-lit house in Moradabad. The sadder and wiser, the serene Champa of new India.[11]

References

1. Hyder, Qurratulain, 2003, *Aag ka Darya*, Educational Publishing House, New Delhi, p. 82.
2. Ibid., pp. 87-88.
3. Ibid., p. 90.
4. Ibid., p. 90.
5. Ibid., p. 120.
6. Ibid., p. 120.
7. Hyder, Qurratulain, 1998, 99, 2002, *River of Fire*, Women Unlimited, New Delhi p. 178.
8. Ibid., pp. 266-67.
9. Ibid., p. 325.
10. Ibid., p. 342.
11. Ibid., p. 401.

15

The Configural Mode: *Aag ka Darya*

KUMKUM SANGARI

When it appeared in 1959, Qurratulain Hyder's *Aag ka Darya* created a sensation. It received a Sahitya Akademi Award and was translated into 14 Indian languages within a decade. Yet this enthusiastic, somewhat astonished reception, the general acknowledgement of her stature (compared to Garcia Marquez), her 'historical sweep' and invocation of an inclusive syncretic culture, did not result in serious critical attention to the way the novel had cast the pain and promise of a secular-nationalist imaginaire into a unique literary-historical form.

The structural innovation of *Aag ka Darya* lay in the staging of four historical periods: the fourth century BC and the inception of the Mauryan empire by Chandragupta, the end of the Lodi dynasty and the beginning of Mughal rule in the late-fifteeenth and early-sixteenth centuries, the late-eighteenth century beginnings of East India Company rule upto its consolidation in the 1870s, the two decades ending in the 1950s that encompassed nationalist struggle, partition and independence. These constitute four sequential yet discrete experiential moments that can neither be made amenable to a causal and teleological reading, nor slotted as the discontinuous fragments characteristic of a high modernism. They are more readily grasped as a single constellation, as an individual attempt to apprehend a 'civilization', and as a doubled gesture, repeated in a different conjuncture when Hyder's own English version, *River of Fire*, appeared in 1998. This was a fifth moment, rendered invisible by labels of mistranslation or transliteration, yet so powerful, that I was compelled to re-read *Aag ka Darya* backwards from *River of Fire*, very much in the manner of the eponymous 'river' which, in the author's own words, is a metaphor for time that flows forward and backward.[1]

River of Fire is a novel recomposed by the author (she calls it transcreation). *Aag ka Darya* carried multiple generic possibilities that span much of the history of the Indian novel: a 'researched' historical novel, a 'mutiny' novel (an antidote to Raj fantasies), a regional novel in the *shahr ashob* tradition (lamenting the repeated decline and destruction of Awadh), a political 'discussion' novel (which evolved from the dialogues in reformist polemical treatises), an historical romance, an inter-racial romance (an ironic replay of Anglo-Indian fiction), a courtesan novel, an urban Lucknow-centred 'college' story, a fictionalized female autobiography, a cosmopolitan novel (on emigres and expatriates). Some of these become less vivid in *River of Fire*; some narrative sequences and narrative voices also change; each revision or reorganization remodulates it in intention and effect, in motif, theme, and reference; there is an overall abridgement that clips character and dialogue. This abbreviating process began in the author-approved translation into Hindi in 1968; it may have been a consequence of editorial interventions, yet it indicates that some concerns had gradually receded or become less pressing. Though the basic spatial and temporal structure remains unchanged, this 'final' version interferes so substantively with the earlier that it blocks any unproblematic return to the 'original'. The two novels have now to be read against each other and grasped together as part of a single configuration (to which I will return), rather than in the banalities of mistranslation or of the authorial hubris of recreation.

Since I cannot do justice to even one of these novels here, nor undertake a comparative study, I will, working backwards from *River of Fire*, try to convey how the four moments remain linked to each other through succession, sedimentation and retrieval, and discuss some of the literary and historical coordinates of Hyder's chosen form.

The Emplotment of Character

In each of these moments a central set of characters reappear with partly altered names either as different people or in recognizably similar situations. Scholars, historians, travellers, seekers, (potential) artists and writers, they relive individual trajectories of mutilation, desertion, uprooting, exile, wandering and settlement, often repeating a 'cycle' of withdrawal into personal and/or spiritual, resolutions in the face of gross political violence.

Champak in the first story is deserted by her fiancee Hari Shankar who becomes a Buddhist *bhikshu*; she rejects the same option for herself and shifts her affection to Gautam Nilambar; captured in war, she is forced to join the harem of an old *mantri* but still desires Gautam. Champavati in the second story, the sister of a learned *Brahmin* in Ayodhya, agrees to wed Syed Abul Mansur Kamaluddin and seems ready to convert to Islam but Kamal, a travelling scholar, never returns; she searches for him, then joins a band of Vaisnav *sannyasins* and retires to Brindaban. Champa Jan in the third story is a rich, intelligent courtesan in Lucknow who dallies with a British nabob and members of the landowning elite but falls in love with the *bhadro* Gautam Nilambar Dutt, and waits for him to return from Calcutta. Her middle age is spent as a *chowdhrain* of *tawaifs*; she eventually becomes an old beggar who lurks at the railway station, still in love with an ultimately indifferent man. Champa Ahmed in the fourth story, daughter of a genteel lawyer who supports the Muslim League, is a petit bourgeois, self-fictionalizing social climber, who plays out a series of relationships with various men including Gautam Nilambar, does not marry any of them, works in England for some years and returns to set up a legal practice with her father in her home town, Benares.

Nirmala in the first story is a princess who, captured in war, escapes from her captor's harem and becomes a Buddhist nun. In the second story, Nirmala's renunciation seems to be re-enacted by Champavati; Nirmala also lingers in Ruqqaiya Bano Begum, the aristocratic woman scholar, who is captured in war and never gets to marry Kamaluddin, the man she loves. In the third story, Nirmala can be glimpsed in the nun Annabella, the illegitimate daughter of Maria Theresa and Cyril Ashley. In the fourth story, Nirmala reappears as a bright, educated girl from Lucknow who enrols in Cambridge. In love with Gautam, who is also attracted to Champa Ahmed, Nirmala refuses to marry him; she dies of tuberculosis in England.

The parallel men are the Gautam Nilambars, Hari Shankars, Kamaluddins and Cyril Ashleys. Gautam Nilambar in the first story, a student at Shravasti, is the son of a rich Brahmin but not inclined to priesthood; his home destroyed, his hand mutilated in war, he is forced to give up sculpture and becomes an actor. He searches for the lost Champak, but when he does find her, he rejects her; he dies a wanderer. Gautam Nilambar Dutt in the third story is an English-educated Bengali in British service. Though fascinated with the Lukhnavi *tawaif*, Champa Jan, Dutt rejects her; he gives up his government job to teach in a Brahmo school, and eventually becomes a prosperous publisher. Gautam Nilambar in the fourth story, son of a Allahabad high court judge, is a bohemian artist at Santiniketan, who travels abroad, joins the Indian Foreign Service, settles restlessly into a bureaucratic job, and participates in the museumization of 'culture'.

Hari Shankar in the first story is a prince who, disguised as a Greek, travels widely over Central Asia, then renounces his kingdom and his fiancee to become a Buddhist monk. (Hari Shankar appears in the second story of *Aag ka Darya* as a soldier who fights alongside Kamaluddin to defend Jaunpur from the Afghans, but he disappears from the second story of *River of Fire*). Munshi Hari Shankar in the third story is a native clerk who introduces Gautam Nilambar Dutt to Lucknow, upholds both *purdah* as a status symbol and the *Manusmriti's* strictures against freedom for women. Hari Shankar Raizada in the fourth story, son of a Congress-I barrister who writes Urdu poetry, the childhood friend and professed alter-ego of the scientist Kamal Reza, works in the USA for a while and returns to a government job in India.

Abul Mansur Kamaluddin of Nishapur appears for the first time in the second story. The son of a Persian mother and an Arab father, he comes to 'Hindustan' in 1476 in search of fortune on the advice of a Phoenician Jew, becomes a court translator in Jaunpur. He passes through an 'intellectual' romance with the learned Ruqqaiya, a kinswoman of his patron Sultan Hussain Shah 'Nayak', then falls in love with Champavati. Separated by war, he makes no concerted attempt to find her till it is too late. When Jaunpur is destroyed by Sikandar Lodi, he deserts the sultan he serves, encounters Chistiya Sufis, Buddhist bhikshus and Kabir, and finally settles down in Bengal, tills the land, and marries the *Sudra* Sujata Debi. His elder son enters Mughal service, and because of this, Kamaluddin is dubbed a traitor, beaten, and left to die by Sher Shah's soldiers. In the third story, he is symbolically split between two characters who may or may not be his descendants: the impoverished Bengali ferryman Abdul Mansur, and Abul Mansur Kamaluddin Ali Reza Bahadur (known as Nawab Kamman), a hereditary landowner in Awadh. Nawab Kamman, though married, is an admirer of Champa Jan. He goes to England with Malika Kishwar's party to plead against her deposition. When he returns two years later, after the revolt, he finds his city, Lucknow, in ruins. In the fourth story Kamaluddin is split between two cousins: the Switzerland returned Amir Raza who does not marry Champa Ahmed, and the ardently socialist and nationalist Kamal Reza who studies at Cambridge, returns to a derelict Lucknow but cannot find a job; the land reforms impoverish Kamal's parents, their ancestral property is unfairly confiscated as evacuee property, dispossessed, they are compelled to emigrate to Pakistan.

Cyril Ashley appears in the third story. The son of an indigent clergyman, he makes his fortune in India, becomes a hookah-smoking nabob, seduces the Eurasian Maria Theresa and then deserts her. He takes Sujata for his 'bibi', makes a fortune, gets a knighthood, marries a British woman, dies lonely but founds a colonial 'dynasty'. His great-grandson, Cyril Ashley of the fourth story, is a member of the fashionable left at Cambridge, dabbles in Socialism, researches Anglo-French relations in India, and falls in love with Champa Ahmed. He joins the family tea plantations in Sylhet, East Pakistan, leaves Socialism behind, renovates the 'traditional' white burra sahib hierarchy into a neo-colonial enterprise that once again exploits the labour of the poor.

In each part the characters become more complex as they are inflected by their previous persona — they are distant from yet related to the earlier characters. For instance, in the second story, Kamaluddin is a travel writer, scholar of comparative religions, translator and composer of popular Bengali devotional poetry: as a historian, exile, wanderer, seeker, and (ironically) in the male privilege of deferral, he is a counterpart of Gautam of the first story; as a multilingual cosmopolite and a potential renunciate, Kamaluddin also bears traces of the Buddhist prince, Hari Shankar, of the first story. The novels, then, become a 'family' history without, necessarily, blood descent. Caught in political calamities, connected to each other through relations of love and friendship, the characters exist in the fullness of each historical moment as well as across the stretch of time.

The Champa, Gautam and Kamal characters remain central, Nirmala and Hari Shankar are adjuncts or 'weak' characters. In *River of Fire* Hari Shankar disappears from the second story; Margaret Teasdale, the great-granddaughter of the first Cyril Ashley's *liason* with Shunila, is dropped in the fourth. The relationship of Kamaluddin with Ruqqaiya is more detailed in the second story but Talat (an author surrogate figure), an irreverent journalist and self-appointed *daastan goh,* is attenuated in the fourth. Yet, in *River of Fire,* even as the characters become less full-bodied and somewhat enigmatic, the connections between them become sharper. This reshuffling of narrative arrogates the familiar liberty of the *dastaan goh*: characters, situations, episodes can disappear, change or be reinflected, details can be dropped or added, some sequences abbreviated and others expanded depending on the mood and context of narration. The narrative grid is stable, the embellishments alter: it has a fixed core and a floating text of elaboration. Such performative restructuring, which rehearses the interplay between orality and writing, was not only common in oral narrative but resembles musical improvisation as well. The possibility of housing many narrative variants in the same structure is analogous to setting a different *raga* to the same *bandish* or the same *bandish* to a different *raga.*

The serving classes are more individualized in their relationships, hybridities, migrations and politics in *Aag ka Darya.* They acquire a somewhat choric and static character in *River of Fire,* return more often as a set of functions — maids, innkeepers, ferrymen — and as generic or metaphoric names that indicate a set of recurring and massified social relationships. Gungadin the coachman appears in the third and fourth story while the equally typified Abdul appears as a ferryman and as a servant of Cyril. A milkmaid, Sujatha, helps the injured Gautam in the first story; in the second, Sujata Debi is the *Sudra* girl who Kamaluddin marries; in the third, Sujata, the daughter of impoverished gentility till now in the service of Awadh rulers, becomes the *bibi* of Cyril Ashley; in the fourth story, a beautiful *purbi* Sujata labours on Cyril Ashley's tea plantation. The Shunilas of the second and third story of *Aag ka Darya* are renamed Sujata in *River of*

Fire (Bimal Roy's famous film *Sujata* may have fixed it as a generic name for disprivilege). The persistent inequality of the serving classes is perhaps the latent but unarticulated bedrock of the river of fire, that place of recurring human labour which creates the very soil of temporal concurrence, that gives, ironically, a resilience to the 'civilization' (a term I will annotate later) that seldom dignified this labour.

The Spread of Time

Aag ka Darya lacks that tight 'organic' form to which the late nineteenth century bourgeois novel self–consciously aspired, and acquires its coherence as a narrative not in its episodes or content — the four stories are not of equal length, they can be contracted or enlarged, episodes can be dropped or replaced, as indeed they were in *River of Fire* — but in its structure: the spatializing of four moments. Even as it occupies the linear time of recorded history, the novel also unfolds it as spatial concurrence. This structure, shorn of some of the laboured elaborations of 1959, protrudes more in *River of Fire*; the sense of concurrence too is sharper, as if Hyder grasped her original conception and its significance with more precision.

The spatial concurrence of different temporal periods in *Aag ka Darya* is distinct from a simple cultural continuity; it involves continuities of transmission as well as retrievals of the past, and more broadly, an idea of history that is itself infused with forms of concurrence. The objective historical coordinates and semantic analogues for this metaphor spread across the late nineteenth and early twentieth centuries in historiography, theatre, early cinema, music, narrative and literary modernism. The modalities of transmission and retrieval were oral, aural, visual and written.

One form of concurrence was generated by the ideologically varied historical reconstructions that appeared not merely in historical writing but in high and popular literature — romances, poetry, plays, historical novels, school books, prescriptive pamphlets, political treatises, orientalist

204   Qurratulain Hyder and the River of Fire

tracts — throughout the colonial and nationalist period. This concurrence was distinct from revival, rather it was that pervasive phenomenon from which sectarian 'Hindu' or 'Muslim' revivals made their myopic recuperations of the past. Analogues for the millenial span and leaping time structure of *Aag ka Darya* can be found as much in the 'histories' of India by the British which compressed 'ancient', 'medieval' and colonial India into manageable maps, as in emergent anthological modes, such as the compendious canons of 'great women' assembled by the Indian *mofussil* intelligentsia which opened the past to a single and telescopic, if often tendentious, thematic gaze.[2]

If print culture had naturalized the synchronic spread of disparate historical moments within the covers of a book, shifting between historical periods had been naturalized in theatre and cinema. The languages of performance and theatricality, that re-enacted historically discrete affective grammars and reabsorbed them into contemporaneous modes, slid from print and performance into early cinema, which by the 1950s had reproduced and reinvented a vast historical repertoire. The concurrent times in *Aag ka Darya* not only replay these processes of retrieval, but are themselves unimaginable without them. Each historical moment unabashedly fades or 'cuts' into a new time on the same space in cinematic fashion, while each mutated character could be the same film 'star' in a new role, costume and time.

The other history of retrieval and concurrence, that was at once historical and stylistic, is that of oral and literary intertextuality. This is a history of the persistence and permutation of orality in music and narrative, the concurrence of narratives where originals and variants (ancient, medieval, colonial), flowed side by side into the twentieth century, the repetition of old oeuvres in many forms, the entry and absorption for centuries of new grammars, and finally with colonialism, an acceleration of the entry, the absorption and the reinvention, which found new stylistic coordinates in literary modernism for both concurrence and the transformations of time into space. If realism had instituted the law of omniscience, and modernism was read as 'spatial form' that liberated from realism's naturalization of linear temporality, then Hyder makes no exclusive choice. Authorial omniscience coexists with complex narration in shifting voices and registers, a modernist structure, and self-conscious modernist devices such as the flashback or the photograph as a visual mnemonic device. This unproblematic occupation of realism and modernism rolled both into a capacious secular imaginaire. The incorporation of other genres (discussed below) stretches the boundaries of realism, authorial irony destabilizes conventions of reproduction through imitation, while the palimpsest of forms evokes, with some verisimilitude, the modalities of layering, silting, and other cumulative processes that compose a cultural geography. Indeed Hyder's fulsome use of love stories is not surprising, since (at least in the north) these stories continued to live new lives and old lives, went from genre to genre, from orality and manuscript to print and performance, from print to orality, and were reframed by colonial and bourgeois ideologies in high and popular literature.

In literary-historical terms, not only did the uneven march of Indian literary forms display a degree of synchrony, but the several centuries of European and English literary forms which arrived *en bloc* (at least notionally, in practice in piecemeal, idiosyncratic and regional variations), also came to rest on the level plane of print with Indian literary forms. 'English' as a social, literary and ideological ensemble mediated the Urdu novel as much as any other. *Aag ka Darya* presented related, intersecting, and bifurcating histories of Indian and British culture long before they were theorized in critical discourse, and inaugurated a cosmopolitan gaze that could take in Britain with ease and authority. What the English version could more readily demonstrate were the concurrences produced by colonization and the imbrication of colonialism in systems of representation — as in the artifices of colonial history, Anglo-Indian fiction, travel or missionary accounts, Indological and anthropological evaluations of Indian religions or customs.[3] The language itself made available another layer of intertextuality, and certain cross-referential clusters. Some of the chapter titles introduced in *River of Fire* exhibit the pleasures and seductions of orientalism, travelogues, and English literature, as well as the absorption, translation and adaptation of literary English by Indian elites with a degree of irony: 'The Abominable Customs of the Gentoos and Mussalmans', 'The Forest of Arden', 'Miss Champa Ahmed (Graduation Portrait by C.Mull, Hazrat Ganj, Lucknow)'.

Some other valences of literary cross-referentiality change in *River of Fire*. *Aag ka Darya* carried a more intricate and text-derived exposition of ancient India (from the Rgveda and Arthashastra to the Natyashastra), a theory of religious change (the conflicts, unification and relocation of ancient and medieval sects), and an inventory of music (classical, devotional, popular and filmic); it had more memorative aspects (Walter Benjamin's phrase), and transmitted more orality : *shloka, doha*, song, poem, *shayri. River of Fire* connotes more the making of reflexive intertextualities, colonial and medieval, as in Kamaluddin's first-person travelogue, *The Marvels and Strange Tales of Hindustan*. It is not for this reason more 'anglicized' (surely a multilingual subcontinent permits the freedom to re-inflect!). In fact, the heavy mediation of T.S. Eliot in *Aag ka Darya* (the epigraph, the section on the Vedas in the first story, the descriptions of London, the consciousness, and conversation of characters in the fourth story), diminishes considerably. When I asked Qurratulain Hyder why the epigraph from *Four Quartets* had been dropped, she shrugged and said casually *'chut gaya hoga'* as if it were a minor and unimportant matter.[4]

Aag ka Darya also presents concurrence as a recurring experience of 'over-accumulation' or cultural compression that is not peculiar to or even restricted to modernity though it may be compounded by modernity. The cacophony of the dead sediments, layer upon layer, like the ancient Persian and new American coins that collect in the Saryu river. A contesting diversity assails each age, and this is too much for any single individual to carry or assimilate.

The weight of the past as embodied in literature, religion, philosophy, music, and popular culture mediates each present; it also fastens each character into a web of relationships and a grid of gendered textualities that compel him/her to move both backward and forward. The conflicting pressure of the Vedas and the Buddha's teachings, of sixty-two schools of philosophy, already burdens Gautam in the first story. (In *Aag ka Darya* he has a theatricalized mythological vision of Aryans travelling into the subcontinent along with Indra, Parvati, Saraswati and other gods). In the second story, Kamaluddin is beset in a dream by taunting spectres from fifteen centuries that include the emperors Chandragupta and Ashoka, Bharat Muni, Raja Bhoja, Gangu Teli, Kalidasa, Bhavabhuti, Bhartrhari, Harsha, Shudraka, Alha, Udal, sundry queens and Rajput clans who all remind him of his mortality. Significantly, many of these featured in print, theatric, cinematic and orientalist retrieval from the nineteenth century, and could just as well be spectres for the novels' colonial and contemporary protagonists. In the fourth story, the Lucknow gang conjure and converse with historical figures from Awadh. The experience of concurrence in moments of crisis for the characters comes encased as spectrality: as signs of a thickly-populated archive, spectres both literalize textuality and assert a grim performativity.

The authorial persona is also besieged by this multitudinous past. There is, however, a subtle distinction between what the characters read, their textual apprehension of India, and the authorial inscription of literary-cultural density through a combination of narrative excess and a selective 'placement' of character, emplotment and author, that together suggest a notion of elective affinity.

The author labours under the varying pressure of diverse configural narrative forms and temporalities. Many earlier notions of recurrence and concurrent time were circulating in the century that preceded *Aag ka Darya*, and these hover beneath the structure of the novels. They are variously acknowledged, incorporated or displaced, and each pushes towards the *longue duree*. There are traces of several structured notions of continuity, such as cyclicity and reincarnation, not only in the beliefs of characters in *yugas*, rebirth, and *karma* (especially in the first and second story), but in a larger rhythmic ebb and flow of characters, kingdoms, epochs. There is an insistent reminder of the *Jatakas* retrospective unfolding cycle of the rebirth of the Buddha as he accumulated good deeds and his 'placement' of himself through parable into numerous situations and identities. The *Jatakas* enumerate the Buddha's manifold previous existences as an animal (elephant, wise partridge, quail, antelope, lion), as prince, as Brahmin trader, dice-player, and his good deeds in every birth. These were often seemingly concurrent births (so very many took place 'when Brahmadatta ruled at Benaras'!), and all the stories were simultaneously, if retrospectively, recounted by the Buddha to his pupils. Other conserving genealogical forms such as the feudal pieties of the bardic *vanshavali*, the bourgeois longings of the Victorian dynastic novel and family saga also lurk in the structure of reference.

Hyder has insisted that her novel is not, as many readers believe, about reincarnation.[5] If both the claims and disclaimers of 'reincarnation' are bracketed, another meaning can be elicited: the novels evoke earlier modes of affiliation. For instance, when Champavati in the second story speaks to Kamaluddin of their bond established in previous births, this gently affines Kamal with Gautam of the first story, resituates the stranger as a familiar, the traveller as an insider. Karma and rebirth can be read as metaphors of the long civilizational time of belonging.[6]

The novels also re-enact the *longue duree* of the narrative

structures of curiosity that persisted till the nineteenth
century in the heroic quest cycles of the *dastaan*, with its
double access to fictional time and contemporary time, its
episodic structure, its syncretizing encounters with *pirs, jogis*,
Sufis, and mystics, its irrepressible desire to find the stories,
and the women, hidden behind the mysterious wonders that
filled the world. Though the desires of the protagonists of
Hyder's novels are seldom fulfilled, they are stirred by
similar, non-parochial, cognitive aspirations. The constant
repetition of seasons in nature and in song (*barahmasas* are
sung throughout) mark another sort of recurrence and
continuous transmission that is tied to structures of feeling
and desire.

Rather than cut, juxtapose, and paste earlier temporalities
in a collage, then, Hyder seems to travel through earlier
genres, or to borrow a term from music, 'shows' other forms
in the novels just as the *thumri* 'shows' one raga in another
(*ek raga mein doosre raga ko 'dikhana'*). Thus the Sufi genre of
malfuzat or the recorded conversations of spiritual masters
surfaces in *Aag ka Darya* when Kamaluddin becomes a
disciple of Kabir in the second story, and is submerged in
River of Fire where it lingers only as a strong 'quality' in
Kamal's dialogues with several people.

If all these notations of concurrent time 'speak' to each
other, they are also unsettled by each other or by an intense
if troubled historicity. The conservative potentials of some
of the genealogical forms that Hyder 'shows' are curtailed
by a conscious self-positioning in chosen 'lineages' that can
relegate feudal ties or class bonds, and loosen religious
identities. In one sense, earlier collations of 'tradition' in the
compendium, inventory, digest, Bhakti-Sufi hagiography or
romance narrative had not only built up a sense of textual
'weight', but also a precedent for non-family lineages. The
medieval *tazkira* or biographical compendium often traced
Sufi lineages, the lineage of *tariqas*, or the wider network of
allegiances. The spatial catholicity of compendious medieval
hagiologies implied being born into webs of narrative and

interlocution rather than being born into ascriptive primordiality, and so suggested modes of non-familial bonding or elective affinity.[7] The social production of *allegiance*, the activity of making a constellation by tracing the confluence of lines that intersect in an individual life (as biography), informs the emplotment and embedment of character in both novels. An 'elected' past (as opposed to a merely wilful or falsely constructed one), as expression of choice and affinity, is indispensable to a secular imaginaire. The cross-generic notations in the novels reproduce and ground this both formally and historically. At one level, even the epistemic difficulty of interpreting history is resolved on the plane of elective affinity. In *Aag ka Darya*, left and liberal South Asian students make a new elective community, an island of self-respect that defies partition; they reconsolidate their composite heritage in a moment of breakdown despite tensions on the borders between India and East and West Pakistan.

At another level, a sociology of mobility threatens to depreciate the transformative potential suggested by elective affinities. Though it is the subject of political discussion and affiliation in the fourth story, the novels do not bother overmuch with India's transition to capitalism, a dominant preoccupation of twentieth-century social realism. Perhaps shifts in the mode of production were too drastic to accommodate in a *longue duree* or into the reiterative narrative structure. The profoundest changes come with war, conquest, rebellion and partition: downward mobility and upward mobility seem to pivot on cataclysmic political events. There is an abiding fascination with the parvenu, the *declasse*, the reversal of fortune: Chandragupta Maurya, many Sultanate slave dynasties, the nabob Cyril Ashley, and Champa Ahmed are upstarts. If the downward class mobility and upward spiritual mobility of Kamaluddin in the second story is more marked in *Aag ka Darya* (as a *sharif* who becomes an *ashraf*, and who commingles low and high culture by writing Bengali *puthis* in Persian script), then the upward mobility of Champa

Ahmed is more emphatic in *River of Fire*. The related problematic of travel, the self-remaking it can enforce, and the parvenu, continues when Indians go to England.

If encyclopaedic narrative cycles (*Kathasaritsagar, Jatakas*) that could absorb, or even regroup around, new narrative forms and string diverse stories together lurk inside *Aag ka Darya*, it departs from the way in which they nested narratives within narratives, and suggests a deliberated outward narrative movement. This intertextuality pushes towards a socially inflected literary history, especially a history of the changing reception of texts. It is not self-referential but leads out into other contexts, evades the closures of religious or national identity. The implied reader (one who follows the cues), a reader of Indian and English, classic and popular literature, beseiged by a plethora of narratives from Sanskrit drama to French existentialism, is positioned to pursue the openness of this referential structure.

In both novels, narratives bind together the visual, literary, oral and performative—they are a form of concurrence, definitionally multiple, compulsively recycled, and synonymous with the spread of time, the *longue duree*. Narrative *saturation* becomes a *figure* for civilizational density while the narrative matrix corresponds to its mobile, migrant, and sedimenting history.

Secular Nationalism and Its Effects

The colonial period spawned many cyclic theories of decline. These ranged from Theosophy which propagated an attenuated set of reincarnations based on karmic law, to T.S. Eliot's conservative notion of the decay and fall of a monumentalized Europe and his vision of history as a debris that had to be spatially reassembled, to the imperious and eurocentric Spenglerian world view of cyclic decline. Though images from Eliot's circular past-animated present do float in *Aag ka Darya*, along with other conserving genealogical homologies, the end of a period is not synonymous with decay. These theories of 'decline' are noted and startlingly inverted in the novels in which becoming-modern is both old and new, heartbreaking but still promising.

Aag ka Darya belongs to, and *River of Fire* records, a particular moment when popular culture and popular-colonial-national retrievals were yet not-quite-archive, not-yet-retro or post-modern pastiche, but a sedimented, overflowing and paradoxically contemporaneous archive, which gave a sense of fullness, a fullness that was destroyed by partition but remembered and experienced as loss and as pressure. In *Aag ka Darya*, the fullness disrupted by partition is not that of culture but of its sharing: the rupture of individual, affective, and conjunctural webs of connection and reconnection. There is only one qualitative shift: after 1947, transmissibility is poised to become more the gesture of the scholar, the Indologist, the anthropologist, the state and its museums; and paradoxically, also that gesture of political protest against the artificial separation of 'national' heritages which indicts the new politics of recollection and recuperation (and the aporia of alienation that lies in between). The notations of concurrence in *River of Fire*, however, suggest a recollected constellation that remains the inalienable experience of the generations in transition but may well disappear with them.

Though concurrence had become a modernist device (as with T.S. Eliot), here concurrence is still affective, a historical sediment, that was secured, temporarily, by a secular nationalism. Both novels propose a secular nationalism imaged as a civilizational strength with still retrievable potentials, that is, nationalism in itself is a source of and a support for concurrence. This is borne out by the structure of the novels: a series of historical tableaux (as the *jhanki* of Parsi theatre and as filmic device) that position the characters and stretch across time through repetition, affinity and inflection; 'familial' lineages of disposition and vocation without, necessarily, blood descent; a dialogic arrangement of sections and characters in the river of fire that (as metapor) flows backwards and forwards; a topographic stability in which the same space is crossed and recrossed in different times by different persons. (The novels are circular only in that they begin and end in the monsoon, in the forest of Shravasti, on the banks of the Saryu.) The affinities across time, character, and religious belief make 'religious' divisions unsustainable: true nationalism (regardless of its origin) becomes a recession of parochial identities.

The narratives are dotted with polyglot and cosmopolitan cameos, for instance, the 'temporary' student formations sketched in the fourth story. The Hindu, Muslim and Christian students of Tattarwalla School in Lucknow (run by a Gandhian Congress-I *Kayasth*) sing bhajans and qawwalis. The Jewish, Buddhist, Hindu, Muslim, Sikh and Christian students of Isabella Thoburn College come from most regions in India, from America, Europe, Burma, and Sri Lanka; they learn Urdu, Persian, Hindi and Sanskrit; girls from different religions celebrate every festival and 'exchange' religious customs as much as clothes. A socialist internationalism grounded in a progressive nationalism (more detailed in *Aag ka Darya* but fading, with some historical veracity, in *River of Fire*), is lived out by Indian and Pakistani students who travel to eastern Europe and interact with the British left in post-war England.

Evidently this was a particular sort of nationalism, one that was closely linked in its images and affects to Jawaharlal Nehru's vision. Nehru described his 25,000 mile electoral tour in 1951-52 to Edwina Mountbatten thus:

> Vast multitudes gather at my meetings and I love to compare them, their faces, their dresses, their reactions to me and what I say. *Scenes from the past history of that very part of India rise up before me and my mind becomes a picture gallery of past events.* But more than the past, the present fills my mind and I try to probe into the minds and hearts of these multitudes....As I wander about, *the past and the present merge into one another* and this merger leads me to think of *the future. Time becomes like a flowing river in continuous motion with events connected with one another.*[8]

This spectrality, naturalized as a historiographic reflex, this concurrent past, the identification of this past with an irrevocably connected 'multitude,' and the river image are somewhat unilinear yet remarkably close to *Aag ka Darya*. Nehru too had seen India as an 'ancient palimpsest on which layer upon layer of thought and reverie had been inscribed.... All these existed together in our conscious or subconscious selves....and they had gone to build up the complex and mysterious personality of India'. The unity of India was more than 'an intellectual conception': 'it was an emotional experience' that 'overpowered' him.[9] Nehru's problematic, however, was that of binding a vast tract of event-filled time into a *moment*, a demarcating, eventful, transformative moment into which a modern and independant India could crystallize.

The Problematic of Civilization

Aag ka Darya marked a significant moment. For the first time a woman writer (as far as I can ascertain) annexed over twenty-five centuries of Indian history as subject matter. The grand nationalist vision of a pluralist civilization had till then been a male domain (Nehru was one among others), while women had been for almost two centuries the subjects of colonial, nationalist or sectarian histories, often invented and usually patriarchal. In the 1930s and 1940s, the discourse of antiquity and civilization (a now questionable term), also carried the ambivalent Hindu chauvinist or anticolonial and nationalist resonances of the 'already civilized': old civilizations like India did not not need to be civilized by new nations like England. However, the more significant meaning, that of a civilization having a greater binding force than a nation, carried the anguish of partition and emerged from the compulsion to defeat the two-nation/two-culture theory and defend a cultural space larger than a nation. Civilizations were not divisible into nations, national boundaries came and went, civilizations endured.

In Hyder's novels, civilization became a category extending beyond national, religious and state boundaries;

it included not just literature,[10] music, philosophy, myth or art but also affective structures, that in turn produced many of the coherences of that civilization. Ancient and medieval 'culture' for Hyder, whether Arab, European, or Indian was a cross-regional traffic, always conflict-riven, yet always familiar with, affected or influenced by, and aware of 'other' cultures, and at times almost cosmopolitan. Hyder's preface to the 1968 translation makes, on the lines of Nehru's *Discovery of India*, a creative relation between in-migration (Aryan, Arab, Turk) and cultural diversity, and also celebrates the civilizational capacity to synthesize and develop a varied and mixed culture. For her too the Indic civilization is unique: in the lability of its 'traditions' which were adapted, changed and invented, as a complex of linkages and differences that defines the entire subcontinent, and in its unity that encompasses but does not regiment diversity. Contemporary Indians are products of this Indic civilization rather than of its nations. As in Nehru's text, in *Aag ka Darya*, the syncretic is not just secular and multi-religious, it is also the dynamic of constant change, always poised on the new that surrenders neither to an insider's hegemonic assimilation nor to an outsider's imperious hegemony. For Hyder, as for Nehru, the modern adventure is not limited by national boundaries and it is neither a repetition nor a denial of the past. The first story displays the ancient commingling of Greek, Vedic, Buddhist, Persian; the second, the peak of religious syncretisms in which currents from many countries converged; while the third and fourth demonstrate the hybridization of both the British — from nabob to innkeeper, and the Indian — from feudal aristocracy to the colonial middle classes.

In each period there is an interplay of different epistemologies, languages and literatures. (Ancient and medieval 'India' was a part of a large Asian constellation stretching to the Middle East, parts of Europe and China, a geographical universe that persisted till the nineteenth century, as is evident in *dastaans* which encompassed central and south Asia and China). In such a continuously reconstellating view, 'India' is never an insular or ingrown entity, rather it becomes a point of convergence and reconvergence. The novels seem to bear out Irfan Habib's contention that the 'idea' of India as a cultural unity was not a modern secular invention but a much older one, one that was a product of conquest (Mauryan emperor Ashoka's inscriptions in circa 250 BC), and traveller's visions or a view from outside (Alberuni's *Kitab-ul-Hind* in the eleventh century), while the affect-laden idea of India as a distinctive composite culture emerged from immigrants and converts (such as Amir Khusrau's *Nuh Sipir* in 1318).[11] *Aag ka Darya* poignantly extends this view to South-Asian students in England who continue to represent a 'panoramic' and 'united India' in their cultural activities after partition, and to those, like Kamal Reza, who leave India for Pakistan. (Hyder herself was based in Pakistan when she wrote the novel.) 'India', then, has never existed in a settled and authoritative source culture, a culture of origin, but has 'lived' always in the form of encounters, surprises, conversations, transitions, translocations and reimagings.[12]

The History Lesson and the Sterotype

Indeed the basic problematic of the novel, in which much revolves around love, seems to be a classic secular one: how was the subcontinent to be defined as a historical community shaped by ancient, medieval, colonial and ongoing interactions and intertwining of languages, settlements and religions, and how was the line between diversity and systemic inequality, between religion and culture, to be drawn and navigated? How was historical evidence to be used to refute stereotypes, how was religious difference to be understood in ways that were at once historical and experiential, how could this complexity be narrated to reclothe the denuded stereotypes of communal propaganda and the stark evacuation of partition?

At one level of course, each character makes his or her

'India' — if civilization is a dynamic and changing entity, it is also an inevitably contested one. The most poignant is Kamal Reza'a newly-severed India. The so-called 'imperfection' of both novels — the uneven pace of narration, the occasional stilted or prolix passage, the awkwardnesses in translation — can perhaps be read in the same way. These rough edges are what make them subjective individual apprehensions of 'India': gestures governed by contingency, immediate concerns, and shifting preoccupations. The fluidity of the intersection between history, 'civilization' and individual lives may well be another name for such 'imperfection'.

However, the troubled problematic of history, especially sectarian and nationalist history mired in anachronism, cannot be resolved only through individual Indias, and here the novels make a quixotic, even paradoxical use of the history lesson and the stereotype.

The novels directly and unabashedly introject discrete chunks of textbook political history, freely mix schoolbook with romance, annotating the significance of historical narratives even as they display the quandaries of lovers. The one anchors the other, yet they are dissimilar in that the history lesson is too hard-edged to be recuperated into fiction, and the fiction too individuated to be absorbed into the 'representative' claims of history.

Unlike colonial historical novelists, Hyder did not need a chauvinist chronicle of self-respect to explain the subjection of Hindus by Muslims or Indians by the British. She needed a narrative to navigate the division and remaking of nations. *Aag ka Darya* relocated the late nineteenth century school textbook's characteristic interleaving of history, as well as the schoolbook's own imbrication in the history of novelization into a purposive secular politics.[13]

The history lessons are multi-accented. As cacophonous as the spectres, they are delivered, dialogically, in many voices other than that of the authorial persona: a Sufi, a peasant, a prince turned jogi, an old zamindar, a nawab, a coachman, a bhadro babu, a student. In *River of Fire*, Nawab Kamman, an aristocratic nationalist recounts the events of 1857 to his bhadro friend, Gautam, as a sign of Hindu-Muslim unity, a tale of British atrocity, and a proof of the valour of militant women — young and old, royal women and courtesans. Gautam cannot fully share the trauma of 1857 with Nawab Kamman because he is a loyalist who percieves the British as harbingers of modernity.

Hyder projects the persona of a scholar-novelist, and annexes what had largely been the provenance of male writers of the historical novel (few women wrote historical novels). The persona harks back to the tutelary woman of nineteenth-century popular writing (though here the novelist does not encash her gender in a female voice), and usurps the pedagogic authority that had been bestowed on dutiful women in the past century,[14] but with a new confidence that exploits the authority of history as the collective enterprise of a new nation, as well as the social, political, and nationalist legitimacy of the teacher in the 1940s and 50s. One may well ask, as I have done elsewhere, if the Indian novel itself began as a teaching text, then could women enter it save as teachers?[15] However, by the 1950s, social realism as well as women writers had acquired a stable narrative authority (for instance, Ismat Chughtai and Rashid Jahan). The pedagogy too enters a new register. The authorial persona suggests a learned woman, a *vidushi*, who displays her erudition and ability to read subcontinental history and world history as a mode of narrative authority, who puts herself in a lineage of ancient and medieval learned women, but who subverts the exlusive 'Vedic-Hindu' model of the learned woman. Indeed as a woman learned in *multiple* traditions, she puts this nineteenth-century stereotype to secular use.

Yet the four stories are dotted with learned women! Hyder holds up this and other textual and oral stereotypes — communal, regional, colonial, patriarchal, orientalist — with a bold frontality, allows them to be re-read. The stereotype is a 'preconstructed piece'[16] from which memories, narratives and history can be fashioned. It is also an end product of both the historical process and of historiogaphy, one that calcifies those wider typicalities which historians construct to represent period, class or region. The stereotype is too pervasive to displace entirely, too often transmitted, too much the *mise en scene*, the still, the stuff of the historical and mythological film, the colonial narrative, the romance; it lurks in stock images, formulaic themes, narrative conventions. Conducive to amnesia, the stereotype is, paradoxically, also a 'code' by which a period or genre is 'recognized' — it resists the complexity of history, but is also carried by it, and clings to any grand *recit* of a 'civilization'.

The novels show how inexorably typicality mediates a retrieval of the past, how heavily retrieval involves the construction and replication of stereotypes, how even thick historical contexts do not entirely displace them. Stereotypes are a part of the baggage that civilizations carry. 'History' and the 'stereotype' stand in relations of cooperation, friction and antagonism: if history as available through narratives comes replete with stereotypes, then the history lesson has to neutralize them.

The novels work through a narrative strategy of accumulation. Stereotypes are not disbanded, they are sometimes smudged by juxtaposition, or undermined by their sheer heterogeniety. This is partly because they are crucial to intertextuality, one of the ways in which it is made, as well as to the repeated textual apprehension of India. For instance, characters learn their world through them. In the third story, Gautam, is perceived as the stereotypical, provincial Bengali babu and bhadro reformer (ala Sarat Chandra) whose sympathy for women does not go beyond a passive ambivalence. He in turn, unable to understand the language of servile coquetry in an Awadh tawaif's salon, filters Champa Jan through the complementary lens of English literature and ancient Indian literature, mixes Shakespeare, Keats, Bhartrhari and Damodar Gupt. At least six nodes of intertextuality in the third story are also stereotypes: the nawab, the bhadro babu, the nabob, the tawaif, the bibi, the Eurasian vamp. The narrative unwinds them from common spools and lets them loose without 're-binding' them to a single ideological axis: it both absorbs and contends with the (stereo) typicality, the inter-changeability of character in popular representational modes.

In this sense, the novels work at once through a grid of familiarity and through the 'estrangement' of over-typification. The essentialization of stereotypes is frequently displaced by, paradoxically, intensifying an only-too-familiar descriptive grammar. The encounters with courtesans and bibis are distanced by a theatricalized stylization, and are almost typical enough to evoke the *mise en scenes* of legend, early theatre and cinema. In sum, they are almost typical enough to be a repertoire: maids who behave like 'stage *kutnis*' or go-betweens, sophisticated courtesans who fall in love with 'innocent' men, the 'good' prostitute who is a 'wife' at heart and desires marriage, a bibi-but-not-wife who uses *jadu-tona* to get rid of her rivals, gallant young men enlisted to detach courtesans or 'modern vamps' from unfaithful husbands, naive and forsaken 'native' girls.

This use of repetition and intertextuality begins to assemble a history of misogyny, begins to frame a question: why do the terms and tropes of misogyny change so little across time and cultural differences? Civilization, the novels suggest, may have come at a price.

Ex-centric Nationalism and the Traveller

The 'answers' in the novel move away from the Nehruvian problematic to arrive at what can only be called an 'ex-centric' or centrifugal nationalism, as opposed to an insular, inward-turning or sectarian nationalism, a plural culture constituted by travel, worked out through love troped as travel. In other words, a diffuse civilizational identity that is as much a matter of political modes of discovery and retrieval as of direct lines of inheritance, an ex-centric nationalism that can equally productively look backwards and turn outwards, and is

presented through an epic range that can anchor the diverse
'Indias' that have travelled in and out of the subcontinent.[17]
In this context, intertextuality becomes analogous to an ex-
centric nationalism: a narrative that directs attention
outwards to other narratives, genres and reading
communities, that does not assimilate or appropriate but
marks their space.

The novels are densely populated with travellers. They
travel because of the dislocation of war, famine, poverty,
economic need; travel for conquest, profit, pleasure,
education (Buddhist), proselytism, curiosity, spiritual quest.
The exigencies of wandering, settlement and uprooting
structure families and relationships, bonding and desertion.
Travel within India is as important as from without, in-
migration is as important as out-migration. No one is seen
as an insider everywhere: bhadro Gautam is perceived as an
outsider in Lucknow, the refugee Nawab Kamman as an
outsider in Calcutta, Champa Ahmed as an outsider in upper
class Lucknow and in England, the *muhajir* as an outsider in
West Pakistan. The stories are located in places that were
cultural crossroads — Magadhan Pataliputra, Jaunpur under
the Sharqi sultans, Awadh under princely rule, colonial
Calcutta, Lucknow and London. The characters travel to
several other cities; transitional or transnational spaces —
rivers, borders, ships, trains — recur in each story. Few
travellers can carry everything: what they leave behind is
transmuted into emotional structures and carried as
unarticulated 'depth'.

The proper history of the subcontinent seems to be a
history of travellers from time immemorial: the overlap of
'separate' historical periods, the way they shade into one
another, the way narratives, artefacts and ideas travel across
time and space, and come to be linked through life histories,
through the continuations of poverty, domestic service, the
caste order, social hierarchy, and instrumental modes of
legitimation. This entire complex is gained through
'repeating' a set of protagonists over twenty-five centuries.

The episteme of travel permits the traversal of two millenia and also suggests, as in the metaphor of the river, at once a sedimenting and a linear historicity.

Nehru wrote that 'some kind of dream of unity has occupied the mind of India since the dawn of civilization', and there is a 'distinctively Indian' 'national heritage'.[18] If Nehru looked for an essence, a unifying principle for modern India, then for Hyder the persistent preoccupation and anxiety about mortality and transience defined the distinctive character and heritage of the subcontinent. If travel notches into the individuality of cosmopolitanism and the collectivity of a Nehruvian nationalism on the one side, then on the other side it notches into transience: there are many travelling students of mortality in *Aag ka Darya*. The diagnosis of transience that lies at the heart of the impulse to believe in something permanent and unchangeable has more continuity than religious sects. Transience is the overarching trope that both defines and subsumes travel. The understanding that all things pass holds together all transient phenomena including love.

Love, too is a form of elective affinity, it insistently, even if casually or briefly, lifts the barriers of caste, class, religion, region and nation. Mediated by settled vocabularies of desire and alterity, it too produces a concurrent repertoire: generic repetition clings to love and the narrative enacts this in its structure. Love, cohabitation and marriage across borders are not only part of the episteme of travel but subject to the exigencies of travel — each story circles around desertion and separation. The way men love women they can not, will not, do not marry, the way they hover but never come up to scratch — these notations of male desire, male indifference and male self-division pluck out the similarity between the patriarchal assumptions of men from different religions: Brahmin, Buddhist, Muslim, Sufi, Brahmo, Christian. Common patriarchal ideologies and practices can hardly be hailed as signs of secular unity, but they do cut across religious identities with more tenacity than love.

The deserted and waiting women who dot each narrative also suggest that in the episteme of travel women may have signified 'home', women may have been deserted more often because they travelled less. Women who nativize male travellers are in this sense merely counterparts of the women who lose them. If the civilizational episteme is to be located in travel and transience, then waiting women are a harsh but inevitable corollary because beneath the varied trajectories of peripatetic men lies the continuity of patriarchies and the serving classes. The plot of female renunciation and/or sublimation is broken only when women travel, when they cease to wait for men (like Champa Ahmed), and more strongly, by the single working woman (like Talat) who rejects the bourgeois love plot altogether.

Aag ka Darya carries some traces of the concern with the low status of women that was common in male reformist and nationalist discourses. Apart from a critique of double standards, these tend to recede in *River of Fire*. Broadly speaking, the novels do not occupy the prescriptive space of the uplift and reform of women, or engage the progressive critique of tradition: the condition of widows, choice of marriage partner, enforced domestic labour, ill-treatment, issues related to property, divorce, *mehar* or dowry. Again, unlike Hindi and Urdu women's journals till the 1940s, they do not directly approach the issue of 'modernizing' women, whether in their domestic comportment, proper education or future professions. It may be this that led to Hyder being labelled bourgeois. However, it is likely that her civilizational problematic inhibited this discourse not only as a discourse of social transformation but also as a gendered discourse of communal prejudice. It may have been difficult to broach the condition of women without repeating the cliches of a civilizational rupture or a 'fall' from a golden past. Her narrative resolution is to instantiate and individuate the women characters as intensely as possible. The Champa women have lucid and complex agencies, and belong in the tradition of Tagore's and Chughtai's heroines. Hyder does not reserve punitive fates for transgressive or overweening women characters as did the reformist novel. Rather, the (usually) desolate denouements stem from the conjunction of stereotypicality, intertextuality, political events and patriarchies. For instance, the courtesan Champa Jan is not placed inside the 'social problem' tradition, her destitution results from the annexation of Awadh and the 1857 revolt. She is not a candidate for social reform. Though Hyder may not be a declared feminist, the novels show the centrality of textual, oral and visual representation in the construction of gender. Their discourse of civilization is not triumphal: it is visibly congealed with stereotypes, tempered with misogyny, disrupted by violence.

Configuring the Secular

The configural mode of 'grasping together' the diversity and dense affiliations of a multireligious subcontinent is more crucial to the secular imaginaire of *Aag ka Darya*, than the politically correct history lessons within it.[19] It stands as a full analogue of the secular in the sense that historical periods were held together concurrently (over and above the embedded pre-capitalist subject) in a vast temporal and spatial spread that asked now for a loyalty that was different from older loyalties of region, religion or language, loyalty to the idea of a civilization that was wider, deeper and more compelling than its division into separate nations.

River of Fire, by implicitly re-grasping the original moment of its own composition, completes a configural process, resituates the first moment of composition now as itself a part of a wider configuration, at the cost of some dis-identification, and with occasional irony. This original moment is separated by that gap of four decades in which communalism resurfaced and escalated, the self-aggrandizing discourse of Hindu civilization sharpened, altered the ideological location of Vedic India and created new vulnerabilities (which may well account for the abridgement of the first story).

If *Aag ka Darya* was a way of winning a certain poise and distance from 1947, a way of reclaiming the subcontinent from the violence that had torn it apart by pulling it into a consoling civilizational *longue duree* in which repeated destruction could be accommodated to the recurrent rise and fall of kingdoms (reminiscent of the fourteenth-century Ibn Khaldun's philosophy of history), then in the four decades which mediated *River of Fire*, the borders that had partitioned Bengal and Punjab began to crisscross India as expanding spaces of insecurity and communal violence. If in the relative calm of the Nehruvian period (now itself a past), Hyder had written briefly on pre-partition violence and essayed only a stark one-line chapter on partition in *Aag ka Darya*, in *River of Fire* she gives even less space to its atrocity and grief — perhaps because 'partition' lives within the nation, still needs to be distanced, and 'civilization' still has to be reclaimed.

Aag ka Darya marked a moment in Indian literary modernism. The nature of this modernism speaks of its own contingency. If in omniscient narration, sight can extend infinitely in a temporality that can be aligned into a single horizon (as in the modern notion of history) and string together a whole series of moments into one act of attention, then *Aag ka Darya's* modernism advances rather than fractures this realist 'consensus'.[20] If imagining a nation meant holding together the anonymous, simultaneous actions of all its members in a calendrical clocked time (as imaged in reading the daily newpaper or the omniscient narrator),[21] then imagining a civilization implied a simultaneity across differential and multiple temporalities, a holding together of past and present 'multitudes'. In *Aag ka Darya*, a modernism emerges not from the need to supersede realism, but from the pressure to exceed the nation and its formal limits.

European modernism, according to Perry Anderson, redeemed and released the classic stocks of high culture against the ravages of the market as the organizing principle of culture and society.[22] If I were to adapt his conjunctural explanation, then the modernism of *Aag ka Darya* set out to redeem the stock of a mixed culture, its complex affective-literary-historical resources, and released it, not against the market but against monolithic religious identities and political violence. The surrealist image brought differing commodity forms into collision, and as Frederic Jameson demonstrates, the objects in these images, as products of a not yet fully industrialized and systemized economy, still show the traces of an artisanal organization of labour, and a resonant depth that invites libidinal investment.[23] *Aag ka Darya* brought, not commodity forms, but the plenitude of a mixed culture into collision with the reduction of xenophobic ideologies. However, in this it too carries (like the objects in surrealist images), an uneffaced mark of artisanal labour: that resonant and affective depth of a not-yet-remote orality in which a storyteller could sign and transmit many given narratives, worked into, but not worked over or fully transformed by, literary modernism. In this respect, it remains bound to the 1950s, a decade in which it was still possible to circumvent the full ideological consequences and contradictions of the commodity forms which were to irrevocably change the very problematic of simultaneity and concurrence.

Author's note: I am deeply grateful to C.M. Naim for encouraging me to work on *Aag ka Darya*, to Shama Futehally for her generous help with the Urdu text, and to Ahmer Nadeem Anwer for his invaluable comments on the first draft of this essay.

This paper was published in A Wilderness of Possibilities: Urdu Studies in Transnational Perspective, *edited by Kathryn Hansen and David Lelyveld, Oxford University Press, 2005. It is reproduced here with the kind permission of the publisher.*

Bibliography

Anderson, Benedict, *Imagined Communities: Reflections on the Origin and Spread of Nationalism*, London, Verso, 1983.

Anderson, Perry, 'Modernity and Revolution', *New Left Review*, no. 44, 1984.

Bromley, Roger, *Lost Narratives*, London, Routledge, 1988.

Clifford, James, *Routes: Travel and Translation in the Late Twentieth Century*, Harvard, Harvard University Press, 1997.

Ermarth, Elizabeth, *Sequel to History*, Princeton, Princeton University Press, 1992.

Guha, Ram, 'The Biggest Gamble in History', *The Hindu*, 3 February 2002.

Habib, Irfan, 'The Envisioning of a Nation: A Defence of the Idea of India', *Social Scientist* 27:9-10, September-October 1999.

Hina, Zahida, 'Urdu Literature and the Patriarchal Family', in *Engendering the Nation State*, Vol. 2, eds. Neelam Hussain, Samiya Mumtaz, Rubina Saigol, Lahore, Simorgh, 1997.

Hyder, Qurrutulain, *Aag ka Darya* Delhi, Sahitya Akademi, 1968.

——— *Aag ka Darya*, Delhi, n.p., 1959.

——— *Aag ka Darya*, trans. N.K. Vikram, Delhi, Indraprastha Prakashan, 2000.

——— *River of Fire*, Delhi, Kali, 1998.

Jameson, Frederic, *Marxism and Form*, Princeton, Princeton University Press, 1971.

Nehru, Jawaharlal, *Discovery of India* (1945), New York, Doubleday, 1959.

Ricouer, Paul, *Time and Narrative*, Vol. 1, Chicago, University of Chicago Press, 1984.

Sangari, Kumkum, *Politics of the Possible: Essays on Gender, History, Narratives, Colonial English*, Delhi, Tulika, 1999.

Sangari, Kumkum, 'Tracing Akbar: Hagiographies, Popular Narrative Traditions and the Subject of Conversion' in *Mapping Histories: Essays Presented to Ravindar Kumar*, ed. N. Chandhoke, Delhi, Tulika, 2000.

Sangari, Kumkum, 'Feminist Criticism and Indian Literary History,' *Hindi: Language, Discourse, Writing* 2:4 January-March 2002.

Notes

1. Author's Preface, Hyder, 1968, p. 9 (Hindi). The other versions I have used are Hyder, 1959 (Urdu); Hyder, 1998 (English), and Hyder, 2000 (Hindi).
2. For one such late nineteenth century canon see Sangari, 1999, pp. 241-42.

3. For the concurrences and related histories produced by colonization, and the secular implications of cultural mixing in India see Sangari, 1999, pp. xxvi-xxviii, xxxvi-xlii.
4. Conversation with Qurratulain Hyder, 2002.
5. Author's preface, 1988, in Hyder, 2000, p. 7.
6. On karma as an ambivalent genealogizing device that gave souls a multi-religious trajectory in some medieval hagiologies, see Sangari, 2000, pp. 90-92.
7. On non-family or elective communities in medieval hagiographies that created synchronic and composite communities across historical time and space, see Sangari, 2000, pp. 79-80.
8. Quoted in Guha, 2002, p. 2. My emphasis.
9. Nehru, 1959, p. 272.
10. For a discussion of literature transcending the boundaries of India and Pakistan see Hina, 1997, p. 38.
11. See Habib, 1999.
12. I owe this formulation to Ahmer Nadeem Anwer.
13. On the relationship between school textbooks and early novelization, see Sangari, 1999, pp. xliv-xlv, 196-220.
14. On the pedagogic authority bestowed on dutiful and reformist women, through the use of female voices, in textbooks, tracts and other nineteenth-century narratives, see Sangari, 1999, pp.197-201, 238-39, 247, 341-43.
15. See Sangari, 2002, pp. 35-36.
16. Bromley's phrase, 1988, p. 101.
17. Though he discusses only contemporary travel, Clifford (1997) has been suggestive for my formulations here.
18. Nehru, 1959, pp. 61-62.
19. Paul Ricouer makes a useful but generalized distinction between the episodic and the configural dimensions of narrative that I have bent to my own purposes. He sees the configural act, the act of 'grasping together' as central to all narrative (1984, p. 67), whereas I have used it to indicate a conscious and modernist device.
20. On the realist consensus and the single perspective see Ermarth, 1992, pp. 27-28.
21. See Anderson, 1983, pp. 17-40.
22. Anderson, 1984, p. 105.
23. Jameson, 1971, pp. 96-105.

16

Transcreating History: A Reassessment of River of Fire

M. ASIM SIDDIQUI

There is an important episode in Qurratulain Hyder's *River of Fire* where Urdu-speaking Tehmina and Talat are talking about Urdu poetry (in this case the famous ghazal of Faiz Ahmad Faiz written about the independence achieved by the subcontinent in the aftermath of unparalleled violence) and trying to explain it to Malayalam-speaking Pothan Abraham. Talat attempts a translation of this ghazal with the comment: 'Translate Urdu poetry into English? How can you render *Jigar ki aag* as the liver's fire?'[1] Talat's comment raises the important issue of untranslatability of some aspects of language and culture. Her comment is also partly true about Qurratulain Hyder's *magnum opus Aag ka Darya* which the author has transcreated in English. Any number of readers who have read both the original Urdu version and its transcreation titled *River of Fire* may feel justified in feeling disappointed with the latter work.There is a view held by many that it would have been better if someone else (with probably better skills at translation and better command of English language) had translated *Aag ka Darya*. However, it can be said in the defence of Hyder that by writing in English she has chosen to reach out to a wider audience. Most of the works in world literature would not have the kind of appeal they have but for translations. Though it is also a fact that in a world driven by market forces readability rather than faithfulness or beauty of a text is an important factor in the success of a translated work. This is especially true about fiction it being a known fact that a Kafka in German is lot more difficult to read than in English translation. In the present case because Hyder has herself decided to transcreate, rather than simply translate her work, she has also taken the responsibility for any loss and gain in her work. The question can be asked as to the ownership of a work by a writer, whether the writer really owns the work once it is published or whether she can deliberately or inadvertently improve or mar the quality of that work through translation. Hyder seems to agree with Chinua Achebe who rightly pointed out that 'one can make even an imperfectly learnt second language do amazing things.'[2] In this novel though the formal beauty of the original is not quite accomplished, she has still managed to present aspects of a culture she intimately knows. Her world view, her vision of life and her idea of what can be called 'her imagined community' can be glimpsed in *River of Fire*.

The beauty of *River of Fire* lies in the fact that it defies easy classification. The author uses history in this work in good measure still it cannot be categorized simply as a historical novel in the sense in which we approach novels of, say, Sir Walter Scott. It has more to do with the subcontinent's fascination with history. Arguably more writers from India and Pakistan tend to use history in their writing than probably from other places. Not only does she present Indian history in essentially secular terms but she also probes the class angle in the classification of Indian history. Significantly she demonstrates her awareness of the power dynamics in each age.

The novel cannot be considered a historiographic metafiction either, a genre which has gained some popularity in recent decades, though it does share some features of historiographic fiction. But it certainly does not use metafictional techniques, something which marks the works of Hyder's contemporaries like John Fowles's *The French Lieutenant's Woman* or Milan Kundera's *The Unbearable Lightness of Being*, another important work of our time with which Indian readers are familiar through its English translation. However, it does have some similarities with these novels in the use of history though the treatment of history in these works is different from each other. Fowles looks at the Victorian period from the perspective of the twentieth century. He also touches on many grey areas in the nineteenth century about which history books are largely silent. Kundera's *The Unbearable Lightness of Being* is set against the background of Russian control of Czechoslovakia though Kundera has himself said that it is not important to know the history of his country in order to understand his work as 'Whatever needs to be known of it the novel itself tells.'[3] Probably knowledge of Indian history is not required in following *River of Fire* too as the novel does narrate and at times explain Indian history. Hyder largely dwells on known facts in Indian history but foregrounds certain essential aspects of a distinct culture and saves them from being forgotten. Post-colonial readings of history have reiterated the fact that the history of many marginalized people has simply been deleted. Hyder makes an effort to present the history of a cultural group in an immortal form. Unlike Kundera, Hyder is not simply interested in a certain period of history but rather in grasping the essential spirit of a syncretic culture which in her opinion defines Indian civilization.

The novel can also be approached as an epic of a people. In fact, in its canvas, scope and range it most certainly reads like an epic. Though it jumps centuries, it highlights three important phases of Indian history namely ancient, medieval and modern. The modern period can be further divided between the pre-independence and post-independence period. Hyder follows neither a nationalist nor an orientalist notion of historiography in the novel, still she partially borrows their classification of Indian history. The ancient period is dominated by Hindu and Buddhist ideas of religion and culture, the medieval by the Muslim contribution to this culture and the modern by the British intrusion in this culture. The large canvas of the novel with a plethora of characters and the circularity of situations remind readers of Gabriel Garcia Marquez's *One Hundred Years of Solitude*. In both the works the authors present characters whose names are repeated. In *One Hundred Years of Solitude* Aurelianos are imaginative and solitary figures, while Arcadios have a very strong physical side and a tragic fate. In *River of Fire* Gautam, Champa, Kamal and Cyril are born repeatedly in different periods of Indian history. Interestingly they also are born with almost similar characteristics. Hyder seems to conceive human beings in terms of types which, though conditioned by their time, display the same behaviour. The most interesting case is that of Champa who is born again and again as coquettish and flirtatious. Kamal, on the other hand, is a sensitive soul, an intellectual and somewhat of a loner. The *River of Fire* differs from *One Hundred Years of Solitude* in its treatment of historical incidents. Marquez draws on Columbian history but succeeds in fictionalizing most of the incidents. The Columbian Civil War is metaphorically presented through the many wars that Colonel Aureliano Buendia wages in the novel. Important incidents in Columbian history like massacre of workers is also presented though in an exaggerated form. In the same way is presented the Treaty of Neerlandia, an important event in Latin American history... But where Marquez treats these events using the technique of magic realism, Hyder presents Indian history using the persona of a chronicler of cultural events, if not an amateur historian of Indian culture. Although it must be mentioned that a fiction writer can never be as rigorous as a historian in the treatment of history. Even a writer like Amitav Ghosh who is well known for his treatment of history in a series of works is of the view that a writer cannot make any truth claims in his representation of historical facts.[4] Perhaps Kundera puts it aptly: 'The novelist is neither a historian nor prophet: he is an explorer of existence'.[5] As a novelist, Hyder also is not interested in the facts of history but rather in the essence of some historical periods.

In her treatment of history, Hyder is trying to grasp India's soul. The question is whether she conceives of it in terms of cultural essentialism or multicultural syncretism. In our time when there is a raging debate about cultural nationalism and India's plural traditions, Hyder's novel touches these subjects very sensitively. It cannot be denied that multiculturalism and pluralism are not merely theoretical constructs but real issues faced by a number of countries though one tends to think of only Britain, France and the United States of America when talking about these concepts. A number of countries are populated by diverse religious, ethnic and linguistic groups. India, a very ancient civilization, has also been inhabited by people from different linguistic and ethnic groups over the course of many centuries. Its culture has evolved over a period of several centuries drawing upon multiple traditions. In her treatment of the medieval and modern period, Hyder grapples with not only the issue of power but also the contribution of different traditions in constituting the identity of India. The real issue that pluralism addresses in our time is that if there is a genuine engagement with diversity. If there is no real understanding of the religious, cultural and linguistic differences between people then probably the country has not achieved the ideal of pluralism in the real sense of the term. Mere indifference to difference goes against the spirit of a real pluralist society. What is important is the real authentic relationship between different groups in society. If there is no real relationship, say, between Parsis, Christians and Muslims or for that matter between Brahmins and non-Brahmins then there is something lacking in that society. It then cannot take pride in its multicultural ethos. Also mere tolerance of the other group without an active effort on the part of the people to understand that group is not enough. Often people do not have a proper understanding of other people or the other point of view. Their opinions of others are based on stereotypes. Such thinking results from not only ignorance but also from an unwillingness to learn about others. The characters in *River of Fire* probably demonstrate this understanding of others. Gautams understand Kamals and Kamals understand Nirmalas.

Her *tour de force* of Indian history seems to suggest that she probably seeks the cultural essence of India in its plural traditions. And nowhere were India's plural traditions more alive than in Oudh, a region that Hyder fictionalizes in this novel. Representation of Oudh in Hyder's fiction reminds one of Benedict Anderson's thesis about nations being imaginative and cultural artefacts. 'They are imagined into coherence because 'the members of even the smallest nations never know most of their fellow members, meet them, or even hear of them, yet in the minds of each lives the image of their communion'.[6] It has been argued by critics that the genre of novel does the job of representing the diversity of a nation. 'In keeping with Anderson's assertions, critics like Fredric Jameson argue that the emergent third-world novel is especially committed to the rendition of nationalist realities.'[7] India's proverbial variety has been imagined by Hyder in terms of its cultural richness, communal harmony and a syncretic tradition. Oudh for her becomes a metaphor for all that is good and noble about Indian culture. With Lucknow its centre it was not merely a geographical place. After the decline of the Mughal empire it emerged as the centre of a unique composite culture known for its tolerance and sophistication and much celebrated in Urdu poetry. For people like Hyder it was also a state of mind. It was very painful for her to see the decline of this culture after the politics in India took a communal turn. Partition also dealt a severe blow to this culture with more and more refugees from across the border changing the culturescape of Oudh. Hyder experienced the pain of Partition first hand, as did many other writers like Manto and Khushwant Singh, and has tried to relive it in many of her works. To write is to simplify if not trivialize because the writing can never measure up to the real pain experienced by people. However, influential writers like Hyder succeed in at least reminding their readers of lessons that can be learnt from the cultural traditions of their country.

A related issue in our time is the reconciliation of diversity with national unity which again is a problem faced by many countries. Hyder also appears conscious of the idea of national unity though she tackles it in the later part of the novel where she pits this idea against the colonial ideology. In fact, a subtle post-colonial reading of history informs the whole narrative. While seeking some points of similarity between the Hindu India and the Muslim world she identifies the West with northern Europe. And at a time when Western civilization was at its peak, it assuaged the pride of the people of the East to believe that in some ways they have an old and possibly superior culture dating back to centuries. Thus as early as the fifteenth century, Abul Mansur Kamaluddin of Nishapur learns from an Andalusian 'that the Indians, Greeks, Romans, Arabs and Iranians had cultivated knowledge while the people of northern Europe were uncouth barbarians. (Unfortunately)A time may soon come when those barbarians will rule the world. (p. 58)' As if to show the nature of this cultivated knowledge, Hyder dwells on the advanced philosophical system that was developed by Hindus and Buddhists in ancient India. Dialogue and debate, an important part of civilization, was the order of the day in the ancient cities of Shravasti and Magadh. The argument between Gautam and Prince Hari Shankar on the relative merit of orthodox Brahmanism and Buddhism typifies the age when human thinking and learning had reached an advanced stage. Similarly their discussion on word and non-word anticipates pre and post-structuralist thinking about language. In saying that 'sound is everlasting', Gautam appears to support the Saussurean notion whereby permutation of phonemes is responsible for the creation of new words. However, Gautam's focus on meaning supports the representational theory of language. According to this view, language is a transparent medium and one can express meaning clearly. 'By concentrating on the word', says Gautam, 'you can reach the non-word' (p. 12).

In the same way, Hyder shows the cultivated knowledge of Indians in the medieval period when there was great development of music, poetry and dance. It was also the time when Sufis made the world a better place by their vision of the world which was based on love, understanding and tolerance of the other point of view. In a way their plural syncretism is the answer to all the discord which was common not only in the medieval period but also is a major problem in the modern period. The university town of Jaunpur was known for art and learning. His majesty Sultan Hussain Nayak was known for composing a number of melodies. Called Shiraz-i-Hind, the city of Jaunpur had several colleges, schools and many theologians.

Hyder's multicultural syncreticism makes her see a great affinity between Hindus and Muslims in different aspects of life. Thus Kamal wonders how Shaivite ascetics found a certain affinity with mystics of Islam. It is interesting to know that Hyder's sympathies lie with the mystic aspect of Islam and there is no place in her world for the Salafi version of Islam. In the same way, Pathans appear similar to Rajputs in their sense of honour and chivalry. She is especially interested in portraying the syncretic culture that developed in Oudh. Turning into a historian the narrator in *River of Fire* quotes many examples of the understanding that existed between Hindus and Muslims in Oudh. Thus the Nawab Vazirs of Oudh 'banned the killing of monkeys in deference to the Hindu monkey-god, Hanuman'. In the same way many Hindu festivals were officially celebrated in the courts of Mughal emperors and later in the period of Oudh rulers. When Wajid Ali Shah was asked to step down and was banished to Calcutta by the British, the Hindu populace which this loved its ruler immensely, was grief-stricken. During this period in Banaras, 'the shehnai players of the city were traditionally Muslim and were often employed by temple priests to play their wind instruments in the morning for the ritual of 'awakening' the deities. (p. 209)'At the individual level too there was great love between people. Tehmina, Kamal's sister, is shown to be a rakhi sister of Hari. Urdu poetry had an important place in this culture. In fact, Urdu was very much the symbol of the secular spirit of India. If Tehmina and Kamal find their moorings in Urdu, Hari Shankar is also perfectly at ease in explaining the intricacies of Ghalib's poetry to his students.

There is little doubt that *River of Fire* is an important post-colonial text. A major portion of the novel is set in the period beginning from the period of the revolt of 1857 to the decade after Partition. In our time the right wing parties often whip up communal frenzy by raking up the issue of the foreigner and the native. In their scheme of things, Muslims are considered invaders and are not accepted as sons of the soil. In a hard-hitting piece titled 'How Deep Shall We Dig?', Arundhati Roy takes to task the right wing version of history.[8] Many other commentators have voiced their concern about the danger of quoting history against Muslims and other minorities. Hyder takes the issue of foreigner and native in an earlier time when it was not discussed in religious terms. When Sher Shah Suri's soldiers called an eighty-five-year-old Abul Mansur Kamaluddin a traitor, he is badly hurt. At this time his predicament is similar to modern-day Indian Muslims: 'This was his country, his children had been born here, his dear wife lay buried here. He had put all his energy into making these fields bloom, spent years beautifying the language these men were speaking. He had written songs and collected stories and he was going to continue living right here. No one had any right to call him an outsider or a traitor (p. 102).' Perhaps this incident shows that Hyder indulges in an anachronistic reading of history in her bid to render the pain of being considered an outsider in one's own country.

The novel raises many questions which are often debated in the post-colonial discourse. Thus the question whether India would have made progress if the British had not come to India is raised by the novel. The novel seems to answer this question in the affirmative. Gautam realizes that if there had been 'lawlessness in India before the British came, commerce and industry would not have flourished to such an extent that it attracted the European powers (p. 144)'. Moreover the British themselves practised a certain kind of lawlessness. Gautam asks: 'True, we had no Roman Law, but did the English abide by the book when they broke their treaties with native rulers? (p. 144)' In fact, there is an honest acknowledgement of the efficiency of Indian institutions by Cyril Ashley. He remarks to Kamal: 'The East humbles a person...When I first came to this amazing subcontinent and stayed in out-of-the-way dak bungalows, I marvelled at John Company's efficiency. Then I learned...that there were dak chowkies every few miles in the Sultanate in India, complete with rest-houses and wells for couriers and travellers. The ICS is still governing India and Pakistan, but we merely superimposed our system over Akbar's administration... (p. 392)'

The colonial notion of India as an exotic land is also hinted at in the novel. India offers plenty of wonderful spectacles that can arouse the curiosity of Western filmmakers and anthropologists. The root-eating poor Santhals appear very dignified to a foreign cameraman. The Indian escort's ironic and bitter remark that 'we'll keep them hungry and dignified' and that the poor and dignified condition of Santhals is an 'excellent subject for *The National Geographic*' (p. 391) in fact sums up the attitude of the author.

At one place in the novel, Bill, a minor character, who is described as a trader in words, shows awareness of the fact that with the end of the Empire there would be 'a great demand for nostalgic novels about the Raj (p. 289).' In fact, there are quite a few remarkable works on this subject. Paul Scott sensitively handles this subject in his *Raj Quartet*. Before him E.M. Forster's *A Passage to India* had treated the issue of the interpersonal relationships between Indians and the British. Hyder treats this issue in a major portion of the novel with her creation of the character of Cyril Ashley. Cyril Ashley of Sidney Sussex College (later called Sir Cyril Ashley), Cambridge who knew his Voltaire and Rousseau is able to make a fortune in India. He 'approves' of Indian women, can have affairs with many of them, can take a mistress or two but can marry only a 'horsy aristocratic lady'. Even after the independence of India the marital alliances between the British and Indians are affected by the power dynamics of the ruler and the ruled. Champa Ahmed , who otherwise is a social climber, refuses to marry Cyril because she realizes that perhaps Cyril is interested in her because she is 'an exotic, interesting native woman' and also because she believes that British society would not accept her. She ironically reminds Cyril: 'You opted out as a young rebel, but eventually you'll go back to the Establishment, revert to type. People do, you know, when they grow old. Or you may divorce me as soon as your fascination for the East is over (p. 314).'

At the same time as the novel offers a post-colonial view about so many issues, the author also seems secretly conscious of the white gaze at what she has written. The Indian narrator is all too eager to 'explain' the strength, if not superiority, of Urdu literature, the wisdom of the East and the exclusive nature of Indian civilization. Tehmina's admonishing of Talat for bringing in the mention of Humpty Dumpty while talking about the great Urdu poet Faiz is possibly an example of explaining to the West the sophistication and refinement that characterizes Urdu poetry: 'From Faiz Ahmad Faiz you descend to Humpty Dumpty — grow up. (p. 275)' Champa and Kamal's discussion of Indian music, its being a performing art in India, and the mystic elements in the ghazals is also an example of explaining to the West the exclusivity of Indian culture. The untranslatability of this culture is not only a defence but also the strength of this culture. Thus Kamal referring to a song about Laila Majnu observes: 'The mystic import of such ghazals was readily understood by our common people — the West doesn't have an equivalent in its culture (p. 309).' In the same way when Gautam in his delirious state recites classical Urdu poetry, the white doctor, obviously unable to understand the import of those words, is made to think that it is the wisdom of the East (p. 359).

References

1. Hyder, Qurratulain, *River of Fire*. Women Unlimited: New Delhi (1998, 2003), p. 275. All further references to this book are indicated in the text of the paper by page numbers only.
2. Achebe, Chinua, *Morning Yet on Creation Day*. Heinemann: London, (1982), p. 62.
3. Kundera, Milan, *The Art of the Novel*. Rupa and Co., Calcutta (1986, 1992), p. 39.
4. Ghosh, Amitav in an interview with Barkha Dutt, 'We the People' NDTV 24X7, 22 June 2008.
5. *The Art of the Novel*, p. 44.
6. Quoted in Leela Gandhi, *Post-colonial Theory: A Critical Introduction*, Oxford University Press, New Delhi. (1998, 2006), p. 151.
7. Quoted in Leela Gandhi, pp. 151-152.
8. Arundhati Roy, 'How Deep Shall We Dig?' 1 May, 2004.http//www.panjab.orguk/English/howdeep.htm

Bibliography

English (Books and Articles)

Asaduddin, M. 2000. 'The Exile's Return: Qurratulain Hyder's Art of Fiction'. *Manushi*, 119, July-August, pp. 28-32.

Choudhury, Sonya D. 2005. 'Questions of Belonging'. *The Hindu*. New Delhi.

Dharmarajan, Geeta (ed.). 1998. *Separate Journeys*. New Delhi: Katha.

Hasan, Khalid. 2008. 'The Vision of Qurratulain Hyder'. *The Friday Times*. Lahore: Vanguard Publications.

Hyder, Qurratulain. 1979. *A Woman's Life* (another translation of *The Street Singers of Lucknow*) New Delhi: Chetna Publications.

Hyder, Qurratulain. 1994. *The Sound of Falling Leaves*. New Delhi: Sahitya Akademi.

Hyder, Qurratulain. 1998. *The River of Fire*. New Delhi: Women Unlimited.

Hyder, Qurratulain. 1999. *A Season of Betrayals*. Edited and Introduced by C. M. Naim. New Delhi: Kali for Women.

Hyder, Qurratulain. 1999. *The River of Fire*. New York: New Directions.

Hyder, Qurratulain. 2000. *Aag ka Darya*. Translated by N.K. Vikram. Delhi: Indraprastha Prakashan.

Hyder, Qurratulain. 2004. *My Temples, Too*. New Delhi: Women Unlimited.

Hyder, Qurratulain. 2004. *The Street Singers of Lucknow and Other Stories*. Introduction by Aamer Hussein. New Delhi: Sterling Publishers Pvt. Ltd.

Hyder, Qurratulain. 2008. *Fireflies in the Mist*. New Delhi: Women Unlimited.

Hyder, Qurratulain and Ali Sardar Jafri. 2002. *Ghalib: His Life and Poetry*. New Delhi: Sterling Publishers Pvt. Ltd.

Kabir, Ananya Jahanara. 2005. 'Gender, Memory, Trauma: Women's Novels on the Partition of India'. *Comparative Studies of South Asia, Africa and the Middle East*. 25.1, pp. 177-190.

Kidwai, A.R. (ed.). 2007. *Behind the Veil: Representation of Muslim Women in Indian Writings in English 1950–2000*. Delhi: APH Publishing Corporation.

Lal, Malashri and Kumar, Sukrita Paul (eds.). 2007. *Interpreting Homes in South Asian Literature*. Delhi: Pearson Longman.

Liyanage, Amarakeerthi. 2003. '*River of Fire*: Critiquing the Ideology of History'. *Annual of Urdu Studies*, Vol. 18, pp. 25-44.

Oesterheld, Christina. 2008. 'In Pursuit of Qurratulain Hyder – (Partly) a Detective Story'. *Annual of Urdu Studies*. Vol. 23, pp. 196-201.

Oldfield, Anna C. 2010. 'Confusion in the Universe: Conflict and Narrative in Qurratulain Hyder's River of Fire'. *Annual of Urdu Studies*. Vol. 25.

Raja, Masood Ashraf. 2006. 'Qurratulain Hyder's River of Fire: The Novel and the Politics of Writing beyond the Nation-State'. *Interactions*. Vol. 15, No. 2, pp. 49-60.

Shah, Hasan. 1992. *The Nautch Girl* (Translated by Qurratulain Hyder). New Delhi: Sterling Publishers Pvt. Ltd.

Sadiq, M. 1983. *Twentieth Century Urdu Literature*. Karachi: Royal Book Company.

Sangari, Kumkum. 2005. 'Joint Narratives, Separate Nations: Qurratulain Hyder's Aag ka Darya' in *Mushirul Hasan, and Asim Roy (eds.). Living Together Separately: Cultural India in History and Politics*. New Delhi: Oxford University Press.

Sangari, Kumkum. 2007. 'Qurratulain Hyder's Aag Ka Darya'. *Muse India*, Issue 14, Jul-Aug.

Spyra, Ania. 2006. 'Is Cosmopolitanism Not For Women?: Migration in Qurratulain Hyder's *Sita Betrayed* and Amitav Ghosh's *The Shadow Lines*'. *Frontiers: A Journal of Women Studies*. Vol. 27, No. 2, pp. 1-26.

Zaidi, Ali Jawad. 1993. *A History of Urdu Literature*. New Delhi: Sahitya Akademi.

Zaman, Niaz. 2001. *A Divided Legacy: The Partition in Selected Novels of India, Pakistan and Bangladesh*. New Delhi: Manohar.

Urdu (Books and Articles)

Akhtar, Jameel. 2005. *Andaaz-e-Bayaan Aur*. New Delhi: Farid Book Depot.

Akhtar, Jameel. 2001. *Navay-e Sarosh: Qurratulain Hyder Se Baat Cheet*. New Delhi: Anjuman-e-Tarraqui Urdu.

Akhtar, Jameel. 2007. 'Qurratulain Hyder—Savaeh-e Kavaif'. *Urdu Duniya*. Vol. 9, No. 10, pp. 18-21.

Ansari, Asloob Ahmad. 1960. *Fikr-o-Nazar*. (Urdu Quarterly) Aligarh.

Anwar, Khurshid. 1993. *Qurratulain Hyder ki Navelon Mein Tarikhi Shaoor*. New Delhi: Anjuman-e-Tarraqui Urdu.

Ayyub, Haroon. 1978. *Shaur ku u aur Qurratulain Hyder*. Lucknow.

Azad, Aslam. 2004. *Qurratulain Hyder: Bahaisiyat Novel Nigaar*. New Delhi.

Hyder, Qurratulain. 1952. *Safina-e-Gham-e-Dil*. Delhi: Khwaja Press.

Hyder, Qurratulain. 1952. *Mere Bhi Sanamkhane*. Delhi: New Taj Offset.

Hyder, Qurratulain. 1957 (2000). *Aag ka Darya*. Delhi: Educational Publishing House.

Hyder, Qurratulain. 1963. *Sheeshay ke Ghar*. Delhi: New Taj Offset.

Hyder, Qurratulain. 1966. *Man ki Kheti*. New Delhi: Maktaba Jamia.

Hyder, Qurratulain. 1968. *Aag ka Darya*. New Delhi: Sahitya Akademi.

Hyder, Qurratulain. 1970. *Patjhar ki Awaz*. New Delhi: Maktaba Jamia.

Hyder, Qurratulain. 1979. *Aakhir-e-Shab ke Humsafar*. Bombay: Alvi Book Depot.

Hyder, Qurratulain. 1990. *Jugnuon ki Duniya*. New Delhi: Anjuman-e-Tarraqui-e-Urdu.

Hyder, Qurratulain. 1990. *Yeh Daagh Daagh Ujala*. New Delhi: Bharatiya Jnanpith.

Hyder, Qurratulain. 1991. *Gardish-e Rang-e-Chaman*. Delhi: Educational Publishing House.

Hyder, Qurratulain. 1993. *Chandni Begum*. Delhi: Educational Publishing House.

Hyder, Qurraulain. 1998. *Chai ke Bagh*. Delhi: Indraprastha Publications.

Hyder, Qurratulain. 1998. *Chaar Novelette*. Aligarh: Educational Book House.

Hyder, Qurratulain. 1998. *Sheeshe ke Ghar*. Lahore: Sang-e-Meel.
Hyder, Qurratulain. 2000. *Roshni ki Raftar* (Short stories). Aligarh: Educational Publishing House.
Hyder, Qurraulain. 2000. *Koh-e-Damavand* (travelogues/essays). Delhi: Educational Publishing House.
Hyder, Qurratulain. 2001. *Daman-e Baghbaan* (Letters). Delhi: Educational Publishing House.
Hyder, Qurratulain. 2002. *Sitambar ka Chand*. Delhi: Educational Publishing House.
Hyder, Qurratulain. 2003. *Kaar-e Jahaan Daraaz Hai*. Vols. I & II. Delhi: Educational Publishing House.
Hyder, Qurraulain. 2007. *Aag Ka Darya*. Lahore: Sang-i-Meel Publications.
Hyder, Qurratulain. *Hum Hi Chiragh, Hum Hi Afsane* (Translation of Henry James).
Irtiza Karim (ed.) 1992. *Qurratulain Haider: Ek Mutalea*. New Delhi: Educational Publishing House.
Mughni, Abdul. 1994. *Qurratulain Hyder ka Fan*. New Delhi: Modern Book Company.
Salam, Abdul. 1985. *Qurratulain Hyder aur Novel ke Jadeed Fan*. Lucknow.
Sohail, Syed Aamir, et al. 2003. *Qurratulain Haider — Khasoosi Mutal'a*. Multan Arts Forum.
Tariq, Sayeed. 1992. *Aslubiyati Tanquid Tanazur: Wajhi se Qurratulain Hyder Tak*. Aligarh: Educational Book House.

Notes on Contributors

Huma Hyder Hasan was born in the illustrious Hyder family of Nehtaur, District Bijnor. After an initial education at Aligarh, she graduated from Allahabad. She learnt *Kathak* from Prayaag Sangeet Samiti, Allahabad. Her knowledge of Persian honed her flair for Urdu at which she had been adept. Qurratulain Hyder and Huma's mother, Zehra, were first cousins. In fact, Aini Khala dedicated her celebrated novel *Aag ka Darya* to her Apa Zehra. Huma died shortly after contributing this piece for this volume. Her essay was translated from the Urdu by her husband.

Noor Zaheer is a writer and social activist. For the last fifteen years she has been involved in researching the culture and oral traditions of the north-western Himalayan tribes. She has written more than fifty short stories, four full-length plays, twenty-four plays for children. *My God is a Woman, Barh Urraiye* both novels, *Mere Hisse ki Roshnai* memoirs of the Progressive Writers' Movement, *Surkh Karavan ke Hamsafar*, a travelogue of Pakistan are her major published works. A short story collection is under publication. She is at present working on another novel based in Kinnaur.

Khalid Hasan was a senior Pakistani journalist, translator and writer. He worked with several major newspapers including *The Pakistan Times, Daily Times, The Friday Times* as well as news agencies. He had published over 40 books, in Pakistan and abroad, on a host of subjects including Kashmir. He is well-known for his translations of Manto, Ghulam Abbas, and Faiz Ahmad Faiz. He had also published *Qurratulain Hyder ke Khat ek Dost ke Naam* (Urdu), Aaj Books, Karachi.

Gopichand Narang, Scholar, critic and linguist, writes in Urdu, English and Hindi; has more than 60 publications to his credit, the most important being *Hindustani Qisson se Makhuz Urdu Masnaviyan, Amir Khusro ka Hindavi Kavya* (research), and *Sakhtiyat, Pas-Sakhtiyat aur Mashriqi Sheriyat* (poetics), *Urdu par Khulta Dareecha* (essays); Professor Emeritus of Delhi University, recipient of D.Litt. (Honoris Causa) from three leading Central Universities: Aligarh Muslim University (Aligarh), Central University (Hyderabad), Maulana Azad National Urdu University (Hyderabad). Was President of the Sahitya Akademi; now its Fellow. Recipient of numerous national and international awards and honours including Ghalib Award, Amir Khusro Award, President of Pakistan Gold Medal, Mazini Award (Italy), Sahitya Akademi Award, Rajiv Gandhi Award, Padma Shri, Padma Bhushan; Visiting Fellow, Rockefeller Foundation, etc.

Raza Rumi is a Pakistani writer and an international development professional based in Lahore. He has worked for national and international organizations such as the United Nations and the Asian Development Bank. In addition to his day job as a development expert, he writes for the weekly *The Friday Times* and contributes to leading Pakistani national dailies and international publications. Raza blogs at Jahane Rumi (http://razarumi.com), edits a popular cyber-magazine Pak Tea House; and manages Lahore-Nama and Development Industry blogs. Raza has been trained in economics, social policy at the London School of Economics, UK. He may be contacted at razarumi@gmail.com

Fatima Rizvi teaches literature in the Department of English and Modern European Languages at Lucknow University. Her academic interests includes post-colonial literature, literature in translation and contemporary drama. She has worked on a UGC MRP to conduct a study on the fiction of Qurratulain Hyder. She is currently working on the Urdu *afsana*. Her doctoral thesis explores emotional patterns in the poetry of the Brontë sisters.

Asif Farrukhi is a fiction-writer, critic and translator. A public health physician by training, he was educated at the Dow Medical College, Karachi and Harvard University, USA. He has published seven collections of his short fiction and two collections of critical essays. He has also published translations of prose and poetry from modern and classical writers. He contributes regularly to the English- language press. Two of